THE LIGHT OF FAITH

AN OVERVIEW OF CATHOLICISM

Author
Janie Gustafson, Ph.D.

Theological Consultant
Rev. Robert J. Hater, Ph.D.

HARCOURT RELIGION HIGH SCHOOL

Nihil Obstat

Rev. Steven Olds, S.T.D.
Censor Deputatus

Imprimatur

✠ Most Rev. Norbert Dorsey
Bishop of Orlando
June 25th, 2003

The Ad Hoc Committee to Oversee the Use of the Catechism, United States Conference of Catholic Bishops, has found this catechetical text, © 2005, to be in conformity with the *Cathechism of the Catholic Church*.

The Nihil Obstat and Imprimatur are official declarations that a book or pamphlet is free of doctrinal or moral error. No implication is contained therein that those who granted the Nihil Obstat and Imprimatur agree with the contents, opinions, or statements expressed.

For permission to reprint copyrighted material, grateful acknowledgment is made to the following sources:

The Division of Christian Education of the National Council of the Churches of Christ in the U.S.A.: From *The Holy Bible: The New Revised Standard Version, Catholic Edition.* Text copyright © 1993, 1989 by the Division of Christian Education of the National Council of the Churches of Christ in the United States of America.

International Commission on English in the Liturgy, Inc.: From the English translation of the *Rite of Baptisim for Children.* Translation © 1969 by International Committee on English in the Liturgy, Inc. (ICEL). From the English translation of the *Rite of Penance.* Translation © 1974 by ICEL. From the English translation of the *Ordination of Deacons, Priests, and Bishops.* Translation © 1975 by ICEL. From the Order of Christian Funerals. Translation © 1985 by ICEL.

United States Catholic Conference: From the English translation of the *Catechism of the Catholic Church,* Second Edition. Translation copyright © 1994 by United States Catholic Conference, Inc.—Libreria Editrice Vaticana.

Additional acknowledgements appear on page 246.

Printed in the United States of America

0-15-901286-4

10   030   10 09 08

TABLE OF CONTENTS

1 Faith: A Moving Out of Darkness 2

Apostles' Creed:
I believe . . .
Nicene Creed:
We believe . . .

- Faith, Belief, and Religion
- The Meaning of Faith
- The Theological Virtues
- The Human Desire to Know God
- Revelation: God Is Making Himself Known

- Scripture, Tradition, and Creeds
- The Covenant and God's Plan of Loving Goodness
- Human Dignity: Made in God's Image
- Prayer and Relationship with God

A Person of Faith: Thomas Merton
Celebrating Faith: How majestic is your name in all the earth.

2 Let There Be Light 26

Apostles' Creed:
I believe in God, the Father almighty, creator of heaven and earth.
Nicene Creed:

We believe in one God, the Father, the Almighty, maker of heaven and earth, of all that is, seen and unseen.

- Faith and Science
- Attributes of God
- The Mystery of the Trinity
- Creation
- The Garden and the Fall

- The First Three Commandments
- Liturgy and the Sacraments
- Baptism and Matrimony
- Prayers of Adoration

A Person of Faith: César Chávez
Celebrating Faith: Let the light of your face shine on us, O Lord!

3 Light of the World...................... 56

Apostles' Creed:
I believe in Jesus Christ, his only Son, our Lord. He was conceived by the power of the Holy Spirit and born of the Virgin Mary.
Nicene Creed:

We believe in one Lord, Jesus Christ, the only Son of God eternally begotten of the Father, God from God, Light from Light, true God from true God . . .

- The Gospels
- Jesus, the Son of God
- The Incarnation
- Mary, Mother of God and Model of Faith

- Jesus' Miracles
- Jesus' Parables on the Kingdom of God
- Commandments Four–Ten
- The Beatitudes
- Scripture in Prayer and Liturgy

A Person of Faith: Katharine Drexel
Celebrating Faith: Create in me a clean heart, O God.

4 *Truth and Light* 86

Apostles' Creed:
He [Jesus] suffered under Pontius Pilate, was crucified, died, and was buried. He descended into hell. On the third day he rose again. He ascended into heaven and is seated at the right hand of the Father. He will come again to judge the living and the dead.

Nicene Creed:
For our sake he was crucified under Pontius Pilate; he suffered, died, and was buried. On the third day he rose again in fulfillment of the Scriptures; he ascended into heaven and is seated at the right hand of the Father. He will come again in glory to judge the living and the dead, and his kingdom will have no end.

- The Human Experience of Suffering
- The Paschal Mystery
- The Last Supper
- Jesus' Betrayal, Suffering, and Death
- Jesus' Resurrection and Ascension
- Sin, Virtue, and Conscience
- The Seasons of the Church Year and the Paschal Mystery
- Sacramentals Recall the Paschal Mystery

A Person of Faith: Elizabeth Ann Seton
Celebrating Faith: Litany of St. Elizabeth Seton

5 *Children of Light* 118

Apostles' Creed:
I believe in the Holy Spirit, . . .
Nicene Creed:
We believe in the Holy Spirit, the Lord, the giver of life, who proceeds from the Father and the Son. With the Father and the Son he is worshiped and glorified. He has spoken through the Prophets.

- The Holy Spirit: Advocate and Paraclete
- Jesus' Promise of the Holy Spirit
- Pentecost
- Symbols of the Holy Spirit
- Gifts of the Holy Spirit
- The Marks of the Church
- Images of the Church
- Confirmation and Holy Orders
- The Holy Spirit and Prayer

A Person of Faith: Pier Giorgio Frassati
Celebrating Faith: The Fountain of Life

6 *Your Light Must Shine* 146

Apostles' Creed:
I believe . . . in the holy catholic Church, the communion of saints , . . .
Nicene Creed:
We believe in one holy catholic and apostolic Church.

- The Church Community
- The New Covenant
- The Church's Mission
- Communion of Saints
- Laity, Clergy, and Religious
- Ecumenism and Respect for All Religions
- Catholic Social Teaching
- Mary, Mother of the Church and Model of Justice
- Eucharist: The Center of Church Life

A Person of Faith: Henriette Delille
Celebrating Faith: Hail Mary

7 *Walking in the Light* *178*

Apostles' Creed:
I believe . . . in the forgiveness of sins, . . .
Nicene Creed:
We acknowledge one baptism for the forgiveness of sins.

- The Meaning of Forgiveness
- Conscience
- Conversion and Contrition
- Forgiveness through the Sacraments
- Reconciliation and Anointing of the Sick
- Our Call to Forgiveness
- Peace and Love of Enemy
- Jesus' New Commandment
- War and Peace

A Person of Faith: Dorothy Day
Celebrating Faith: Have mercy on me, O God.

8 *Eternal Light* *206*

Apostles' Creed:
I believe . . . in the resurrection of the body, and the life everlasting.
Nicene Creed:
We look for the resurrection of the dead, and the life of the world to come.

- Looking Back, Going Forward
- Death and Eternal Life
- The Particular Judgment
- Heaven, Purgatory, and Hell
- The General, or Last, Judgment
- The Second Coming of Christ
- The Works of Mercy
- The Order of Christian Funerals
- Prayers for the Dead

A Person of Faith: Black Elk
Celebrating Faith: Praise the Lord, O my soul.

Catholic Source Book *234*

- Scripture
- Creed
- Liturgy and Sacraments
- Morality
- Prayer

Glossary *247*

Index *250*

Faith: A Moving Out of Darkness

"The unfolding of your words gives light;
it imparts understanding to the simple."

PSALM 119:130

In this chapter, you will:

- explore the meaning and importance of faith.

- see the different ways God reveals himself to us.

- realize the connection between faith, human dignity, and free will.

- appreciate how a community of faith nurtures and celebrates faith.

- understand personal prayer as a tool for growing in faith.

- learn how to put faith into action.

WORDS OF FAITH

Bible	faith	Messiah	Trinity
covenant	free will	revelation	vocation
creed	God	soul	
dignity	grace	Tradition	

LIVING LIFE FULLY

People today are accustomed to using artificial sources of light—flashlights, electric lights, fluorescent lights, neon lights, headlights, and so forth. In fact, we have so many ways to light up our world that it's easy to take ordinary sunlight for granted. We forget just how important the sun is, because we've developed the ability to go about our daily business whether the sun shines or not. But the basic truth remains: Without the sun, there would be no life.

Sad to say, we may not appreciate something until it's missing or gone. Sometimes it takes an extraordinary experience to "shock" us back to the truth. For example, we may take a friend for granted, until that friend moves away. Or perhaps we take our family for granted, until there is a divorce or a death. Maybe we don't appreciate the house we live in or all the possessions we have, until some disaster like fire takes it all away.

Sometimes we take our relationship with God for granted, too. When life is going along smoothly, it's easy to forget about the importance of faith, our response to God and all that he has made known to us. We may overlook him acting in our lives until something unexpected or bad happens. Only then may we remember the importance of a relationship with God. At these times we are reminded of who we are, where we are going, and what we need.

Activity

On a blank piece of paper in your notebook make three columns and label each column as *Faith, Belief,* and *Religion.* Under each heading define in your own words what each term means to you. Then, under the column marked *Faith,* write down at least two things or persons in whom you trust. Under *Belief* list at least two principles about which you have great conviction. Under *Religion* express at least two statements about your religion or religious beliefs. Be prepared to share your responses with the class. Make a class poster of everyone's responses.

A LIFE-CHANGING EVENT

The following is a true story about four high school students. A horrible event shook them in ways that nothing else had ever done before. It forced them to take a fresh look—not only at God's gift of life but also at his gift of faith.

Tony and Amy and Miguel and Angela had been friends since grade school. Tony and Amy were in the tenth grade and Miguel and Angela were just starting high school. All four of them were excited because it was Friday afternoon of Labor Day weekend—three long free days were ahead. It was a break to enjoy one last fling of the summer, since school had already begun on Monday of the past week.

Tony had just gotten his driver's license. Together the four of them were on their way home from school when Miguel dared Tony to do a little "hill-hopping," and Tony decided to meet the challenge. The teens yelled and screamed, hopping hill after hill; no one seemed to be afraid. It was, after all, true freedom—a long weekend, a beautiful day.

Suddenly, something went very wrong. Tony came off the top of one hill too fast, lost control of the car and landed in a ditch. When the smoke cleared, the sound of moaning, the smell of gasoline, and the feeling of blood and pain overcame the occupants of the car. A passing motorist, seeing it all happen, called in the emergency, and police and fire rescue responded. When the teens were pulled from the car and airlifted to the local hospital, one bystander said, "It will be a miracle if any of them survive."

Tony and Amy and Miguel and Angela lived to tell their tale. Tony hurt his back so badly the doctors told him he would never play football again. Six months later, Amy's face, so badly scarred, has only been slightly repaired with plastic surgery—more surgery remains to be done. Miguel and Angela, who were the backseat passengers, have been limited in mobility by multiple fractures and broken bones. Both of them continue physical therapy.

Through it all, the four teenagers agree, "We were lucky; what we did was foolish." As Tony put it, "God was looking out for us that day. I guess what everyone says about him is true—he does watch over us." Angela put it best, "It has actually increased my faith. Now I love God even more. I'm starting to live day to day instead of month to month and year to year, because you never know what might happen."

Since all of this happened, several similar accidents have occurred with other teenagers in the area. In every other case, someone has died. Tony and Amy and Miguel and Angela do know how lucky and blessed they are.

Reflection

Describe a dark time in your life. What happened? What were your feelings at the time? How did this experience affect your faith or your outlook on life?

Let's Talk!

1. How do you think you would have reacted if you were a survivor of such an accident?
2. Why do you think Miguel and Angela both say their faith was deepened as a result of the disaster?
3. What do you think Angela meant when she said, "I'm starting to live day to day instead of month to month and year to year"?
4. After hearing this story and participating in your group and class work, respond to these questions: What is faith to you at this point in your life? Do you think it is important to have faith? Why?

SEEING AND BELIEVING

Research

Using the library or the Internet, find out more about the Roman gods of light and darkness (Apollo and Pluto). In an oral report, tell a story about these gods and what the Romans believed about them. Discuss how these gods are similar to and different from Christian concepts about God and the devil.

We tend to form thoughts and beliefs based on the information we take in from our senses. We see a bird and hear it sing, so we assume that's how all birds of that species will look and sound. We smell cookies baking in the kitchen, so we assume that's what will be served at dinner for dessert. We taste something unpleasant, so we avoid eating such food in the future. We touch a hot oven or a cactus spine, and we learn not to touch that thing again.

Ancient peoples did not have the knowledge, technology, books, videos, or CDs we have today. They depended on their senses to teach them everything. Sometimes what they learned was correct. Other times what they learned was incomplete or incorrect. For example, many ancient peoples actually worshiped the sun. They thought the sun was a supreme god who shined down his blessings or withdrew in anger. They saw each twenty-four-hour period as a battle between the powers of darkness (evil and death) and the powers of light (goodness and life). People feared the darkness; they breathed a sigh of relief to see the dawn of each new day.

These primitive beliefs were still present in the days of Jesus, just two thousand years ago. The Romans—who governed Israel—saw the sun rise each morning and set each evening. So they worshiped Apollo, the sun god, who rode his chariot across the sky each day. They lived in fear of Pluto, the god of darkness and death, who ruled at night and during the dark days of winter. In order to keep these deities happy (and many other gods as well), the Romans built temples to them and offered them sacrifices.

These people saw with their eyes. But they did not see with correct understanding. Although they were sighted (had the physical ability to see), they were still in darkness concerning the truth. They were in a sense blind and in many ways; they were like the men in the story on the next page.

Activity

- After reading "The Blind Men and the Elephant" on the next page, take a few minutes to answer these questions in your notebook.

  1. Reflect on your present life, using the handout from your teacher. What do you worry about? What is your greatest worry? How does faith help you see the "bigger picture"?

  2. Describe a time when you made a judgment or came to a conclusion based on a partial truth. How did you come to know the "whole picture"? What did you think then?

  3. There is an old saying, "Ignorance is bliss." Do you think this saying is true when it comes to faith? Why? What do you think is the relationship between faith and knowledge and ignorance?

- In small groups share what you can of your answers. Prepare a diagram that shows how worry and ignorance, knowledge and faith, are related.

- Explain your group's diagram to the class, and hang it in the classroom for the next few days.

THE BLIND MEN AND THE ELEPHANT

There lived in India six friends who were all blind. Now India, of course, is a land of that greatest of land beasts, the elephant. But, naturally, since these friends were all blind, they did not know what an elephant looks like.

One day they were sitting together talking when they heard a great roar. "I believe that is an elephant in the street," one said.

"Now is our chance to find out what kind of creature the elephant is," said another. So they all went into the street.

The first blind man reached out and touched the elephant's ear. "Ah," he said to himself, "the elephant is a rough, wide thing. It is like a rug."

The second blind man felt the elephant's trunk. "Now I understand," he thought. "The elephant is a long round thing. It is like a giant snake."

The third blind man touched the elephant's leg. "Well, I wouldn't have guessed it," he said. "The elephant is tall and firm, just like a tree."

The fourth blind man felt the elephant's side. "Now I know," he thought. "The elephant is wide and smooth, like a wall."

The fifth blind man put his hands on the elephant's tusk. "The elephant is a hard, sharp animal, like a spear," he decided.

The sixth blind man touched the elephant's tail. "Well, well," he said. "It gives a mighty roar, but the elephant is just a thing like a long, thin rope."

Afterward the six blind friends sat down again to talk about the elephant. "It is rough and wide, like a rug," said the first.

"No, it is long and round, like a snake," said the second.

"Don't be silly," laughed the third. "It is tall and firm, like a tree."

"No, it is not," growled the fourth. "It is wide and smooth, like a wall."

"Hard and sharp, like a spear." shouted the fifth.

"Long and thin, like a rope." yelled the sixth.

And so a fight started. Each one insisted he was right. He had touched it with his own hands, hadn't he?

The owner of the elephant heard all the shouting and came to see what the fuss was about. "Each of you is right, and each of you is wrong," he told them. "One man may not be able to find the whole truth by himself—just a small part of it. But if we work together, each adding our own piece to the whole, we can find wisdom."

William Bennett, The Moral compass
(William J. Simon and Schuster, 1995), 192-193.

Learning to See

Have you ever imagined what it would be like to be born blind? We are all blind in some sense. We all need to learn how to see the world around us and interpret it correctly.

That's where faith comes in. And that's why the physical experience of seeing is often used as a metaphor for faith. Jesus spent three years teaching his followers how to see the truth about God and his great love. But they still didn't "get it." They still needed to be "enlightened." They still needed to be filled with the light of faith.

Faith is not the same as *belief* or *religion*. Beliefs are intellectual concepts—things we regard as true. "The sky is blue," "Stealing is wrong," "The earth is round," are examples of beliefs. Religion, on the other hand, is the particular way we choose to express our beliefs. Faith, however, is the deepest kind of seeing. It not only helps us interpret what we see, hear, taste, touch, and smell, it also tells us who we are and where we are going. It affects how we see everything—ourselves, others, life itself, the past, and the future. In short, faith is our light, or, as the *Catechism of the Catholic Church* says, our "superabundant light." If we truly have faith, we cannot live in darkness.

Reflection

Make a list of the questions you have right now about faith. In what ways do you wish to grow in faith?

WHAT IS FAITH?

There are many different ways to describe *faith*. Here are just a few of the ways the *Catechism of the Catholic Church* describes it:

- Faith is a gift of God.
- Faith is an authentically human act, by which we trust in God and his love.
- Faith is the beginning of eternal life, the experience of friendship with God.

All of these descriptions are true. A more formal definition tells us that **faith** —like hope and charity—is a theological virtue, a gift from God. Of course, this definition will not be very helpful if we don't know the meaning of *theological* or *virtue*. Basically, the word *theological* means "concerning God." The word *virtue* means "a good habit or response." In simple terms, we might explain faith as our freely chosen habit of responding positively to God. Notice that this explanation does not say that faith begins with us. Rather, faith begins with God. God's gift to us, faith, is our positive response to God, who *first reveals himself* to us.

To understand faith, then, we need to consider who God is. There is only one **God:** the almighty Father, his only Son, and the Holy Spirit. The **Trinity** always existed and will always continue to exist. "The mystery of the Most Holy Trinity is the central mystery of the Christian faith and of Christian life" (CCC, #261).

God is good and truthful. He is all-powerful. But even more importantly, he is relational. God is love itself—unselfish, unconditional love. As the First Letter of John explains, "God is light and in him there is no darkness at all" (1 John 1:5). As the Book of Daniel in the Bible says, "He reveals deep and hidden things; he knows what is in the darkness, and light dwells with him" (Daniel 2:22).

We might take a look at today's world and think that religious faith is old-fashioned or not very important. But we'd be wrong. Many modern-day people are turning to religious faith in the course of living their lives. Faith gives meaning to human life. Faith gives us a dimension and ability to see as nothing else can give us. Faith helps us to become more fully who we are, the best we are capable of being.

According to a recent survey, 95 percent of people in the United States believe in God. Eighty percent prayed to God in the previous week, and 83 percent believe religion has helped them change their behavior.

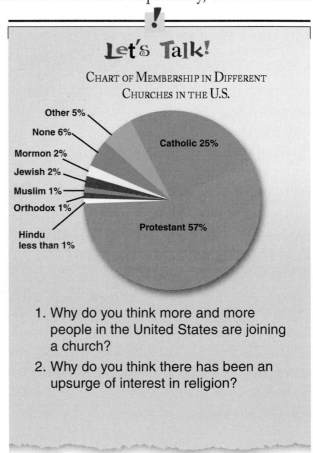

Let's Talk!

CHART OF MEMBERSHIP IN DIFFERENT CHURCHES IN THE U.S.

Other 5%
None 6%
Mormon 2%
Jewish 2%
Muslim 1%
Orthodox 1%
Hindu less than 1%
Catholic 25%
Protestant 57%

1. Why do you think more and more people in the United States are joining a church?
2. Why do you think there has been an upsurge of interest in religion?

We Are Religious

The Catholic faith teaches that God created everything in the world out of love. God has loved into existence each person throughout history. He created each of us! That means God wanted us to be here.

God made humans in such a way that human life is different from all other forms of life on earth. Let's examine this idea more closely. The human body consists of the same physical elements found elsewhere on the planet. Sixty percent of the human body consists of water. Other components are proteins, carbohydrates, calcium, phosphorous, and small amounts of minerals such as copper, iodine, and zinc. But humans are much more than these physical components. Humans are made in the image and likeness of God. They possess a spiritual principle that is a reflection of God. Thus, humans are body and **soul.**

Our minds have the ability to imagine God. Our hearts seek to have a relationship with our Creator. Humans are not only made *by* God. We are created *for* him, to have communion with him. In short, we are "religious" by our human nature. We can't be fully human (or happy) without faith. Each of us has a built-in yearning for the transcendent—a higher power, a divine Creator, a God who loves us. It is in our innermost spiritual being—the soul—where this yearning rests.

Humans desire to know and love God because he first calls each of us to grow close to him. God continually sustains our lives and invites us into relationship with him. Thus we can say that we are "religious" by **vocation.** The word *vocation* means one's calling, purpose, or destiny in life. God calls us beyond ourselves to friendship with him. All humans share this vocation.

Different people live out this common vocation in different ways, as priests, married or single people, religious brothers or sisters. An important way people live out their vocation is by working with and sharing the gifts and talents God has given them. Our ultimate vocation, our destiny, is union with him. Our purpose here on earth is to know, love, and serve God.

Saint Augustine, an early bishop in Africa, wrote extensively about our religious nature and vocation. He wrote, "Our hearts are restless, O Lord, until they rest in you." What Augustine means is that we can never be completely satisfied, or happy, without God's friendship. On our own, something will always be missing; we will always feel empty.

Having a friendship with God means finding God, being one with him. It means living in communion with the Blessed Trinity in mutual love. It also means developing a relationship with God the Father, God the Son, and God the Holy Spirit. Finding God helps us find our purpose, or meaning, in life. We achieve complete happiness because we finally "see" the whole picture of what human life is about. As Pope John Paul II once explained,

❝ God has placed in the human heart a desire to know the truth—in a word, to know himself—so that, by knowing and loving God, men and women may also come to the fullness of truth about themselves. ❞

FAITH AND REASON (1998), PROLOGUE.

Research

Using the library or the Internet, find out more about Saint Augustine of Hippo. In an oral or written report, tell how faith changed his life.

Activity

Interview at least three other people to get their reactions to the following questions. Write up your findings and then answer the questions *yourself*.

1. Who is God?
2. How do you experience God in your life?
3. Would you say God is important in your life or just out there somewhere on the margin of your life?

— HOW CAN WE FIND GOD? —

Creation shouts God's existence and love.

Many people ask this question, but it is not really the correct question to ask. Do you remember the definition of faith? Faith is our positive response to God, who *first reveals himself* to us. To reveal means *to make known*. **Revelation,** then, is God's communication of himself and his plan of loving goodness throughout history. In doing so, God reveals himself as a Trinity of Persons. We do not really find God; rather, he finds us. God takes the first step to let us know that he is there and that he cares. How does he take the initiative?

One way God manifests himself is through the physical world of nature. When we look carefully at the physical world, we can appreciate that he exists and is "the cause and end of everything" (CCC, #46). Just think of the immense diversity of life forms on earth. There are vast oceans teeming with life as big as whales and smaller than sea horses. There are flowers and plants galore. And if you've ever looked into a microscope, you know that nature includes another whole world beyond ordinary vision. Again, the variety and complexity of things is astounding. Everywhere you look, there is some type of beauty or color or marvel that cries out, "Look at me. God is here."

A second way that God comes to us is through the human person, our very selves. We can find God through "the natural light" of human reason. The human brain is indeed a miracle, far more advanced than that of other animals. In addition to responding to the physical reality of the world, our brain can sense that there is purpose and meaning to human existence. We don't act simply on instinct or habit as animals do. We can think. We can reason.

Furthermore, humans have a conscience, an inner sense that certain actions are morally right and others are morally wrong. We feel guilty when we choose the wrong actions. We feel content when we choose what is right. When we listen to the voice of conscience, we have yet another way to know of God's existence.

As humans, we can grasp concepts of things we cannot see—ideas, the past, the future, goodness, truth, principles of law, and so forth. We can add, subtract, multiply, and divide. We can imagine. We can appreciate beauty simply for itself. We can realize there are mysteries in life—things we will never understand completely. In short, we can sense there is something or someone bigger than we are, someone more powerful and all-knowing.

A third way to find God is through other people, especially our family and Church community. Remember, God is unselfish, unconditional love. Wherever we find people who love us or help us, we experience him. Just think about all the people who enrich our lives. These people may be parents, teachers, coaches, scout leaders, friends, neighbors, or even strangers who smile at us on the street. Good people give us a glimpse of what God must be like.

But what about teens who have had mainly negative experiences with others? Even then—when the relationships have been mainly negative or abusive—the teens can still experience him. Reflect for a moment on the goodness you find within yourself. This goodness is coming from God and God is indeed present within you. Seeing the goodness within yourself will help you be more aware of all the goodness around you, even when you are confronted with negative experiences.

We can be "the other person" who brings God into the lives of others. Through our kind words, helping hands, positive attitudes, and willingness to be a friend, we can make him real for others. And we can do this without ever talking about God, faith, or religion.

A fourth way God comes to us is through history. As faith tells us, throughout historical events, he makes himself known to humans. When we look at history with the eyes of faith, it becomes apparent that he is continually at work for our good. Everything good that happens can be a manifestation of God to us. When bad things happen, he can somehow use them for good. God cares about humans and acts for their good through events and words. He wishes to share with us his own life and eternal love.

Let's Talk!

Gather in small groups. Take a few moments to think about these questions; then share your answers. Make four columns on a sheet of paper and title each column with one of the four ways God can be met. Place each answer under the appropriate column. When you are finished, hang your poster in the classroom.

1. Explain a specific way that you have been aware of God's presence because of an experience of the natural world.

2. Talk about someone who has loved you or helped you. Tell how this person has manifested or disclosed God to you without necessarily talking about God, faith, or religion.

3. What are some ways we can manifest or disclose God to other people (other than directly talking about God)?

4. Relate an event from your past in which you really felt the presence of God. How did his presence become real to you?

5. Describe the times when you prayed to each person of the Trinity.

WHAT IS THE BIBLE?

Christians learn about God's revelation through the **Bible,** which is his word recorded by humans, and through **Tradition,** which is the living and authentic transmission of the teachings of Jesus in the Church. Another name for the Bible is *Sacred Scripture.* Scripture and Tradition together make up the one source of God's revelation. Scripture forms the basis of Tradition, and Tradition helps the Church correctly interpret Scripture.

The Bible is a collection of seventy-three books, arranged in two major parts. The Old Testament contains forty-six books that deal with the time from the beginning of creation to shortly before the coming of Jesus (approximately two thousand years ago). The New Testament contains twenty-seven books. These books deal with the life, death, and Resurrection of Jesus and the beginnings of the Church. The New Testament together with the Old Testament makes up the Bible.

The Bible is God's word. The Holy Spirit inspired the Bible's human authors to write down the Scriptures. God worked through the talents and abilities of the human writers to reveal the truth about himself. We must be careful, however, of the way we interpret the Bible. If we concentrate only on certain passages, or only on the literal meanings of certain sentences, we can become like the blind men with the elephant. We can get caught up in minor details and lose perspective of the overall message—how much God loves us and wishes to share with us his life of love, peace, and joy.

God speaks to his people in Scripture.

Activity

Divide into four groups. The groups should consult the chart on the next page. Be prepared to share your findings with the class.

GROUP 1: Find four psalms or portions of a psalm that express thanks to God, praise of God, sadness, and anger.

GROUP 2: Choose one of the Old Testament prophets. Discuss what the prophet tells about hope and why it is important to have it.

GROUP 3: Search through one of the Gospels. Compile a list of ten things the Gospel tells about Jesus.

GROUP 4: Search through the Letters of the New Testament. Compile a list of ten ways the Letters tell how to live as Christians in today's world.

BOOKS OF THE BIBLE

Old Testament

Torah (Pentateuch)
Genesis
Exodus
Leviticus
Numbers
Deuteronomy

Historical Books
Joshua
Judges
Ruth
1 Samuel
2 Samuel
1 Kings
2 Kings
1 Chronicles
2 Chronicles
Ezra
Nehemiah
Tobit
Judith
Esther
1 Maccabees
2 Maccabees

Wisdom Books
Job
Psalms
Proverbs
Ecclesiastes
Song of Songs
  (Song of Solomon)
Wisdom
Sirach
  (Ecclesiasticus)

The Prophets
Isaiah
Jeremiah
Lamentations
Baruch
Ezekiel
Daniel
Hosea
Joel
Amos
Obadiah
Jonah
Micah
Nahum
Habakkuk
Zephaniah
Haggai
Zechariah
Malachi

New Testament

Gospels
Matthew
Mark
Luke
John

Historical Book
Acts

Apocalyptic
Revelation

Letters (Epistles)
Romans
1 Corinthians
2 Corinthians
Galatians
Ephesians
Philippians
Colossians
1 Thessalonians
2 Thessalonians
1 Timothy
2 Timothy
Titus
Philemon
Hebrews
James
1 Peter
2 Peter
1 John
2 John
3 John
Jude

Research

In the Bible, read the Book of Tobit. Write an essay that answers these questions: What is Tobit "blind" about in his life? By the end of the story, what does Tobit learn? What does Tobias learn on his journey? Why do you think Tobias is able to "cure" his father?

Every book in the Bible reveals some truth about God. All seventy-three books of the Bible are inspired, or written with the help of the Holy Spirit. For this reason, the Old Testament and the New Testament are both important. As it is recorded in Paul's Second Letter to Timothy:

> " All scripture is inspired by God and is useful for teaching, for reproof, for correction, and for training in righteousness, so that everyone who belongs to God may be proficient, equipped for every good work. "
>
> 2 TIMOTHY 3:16-17

Both the Old Testament and the New Testament contain God's word. They tell us of God's ongoing commitment of love to his people. That is why we believe what is said in Psalm 119: "Your word is a lamp to my feet and a light to my path" (Psalm 119:105).

"Moses with the Tablets of the Law" by Rembrandt.

As followers of Jesus, we realize the value of the Old Testament. God chose the Israelites, the descendents of Jacob (also called Israel), to be his chosen people. He made a covenant with the Israelites. In the **covenant,** he promised the Israelites to be their God, and they promised to be his people. The Old Testament deals with this covenant God made with the Israelites through Moses. The Israelites were not always faithful to this covenant. At times they turned away from his way of love. But he did not turn away from the people. In the fullness of time, he sent a Savior or **Messiah,** to save people from the power of sin and everlasting death.

The New Testament tells about the coming of this Messiah, Jesus, who was the Father's own Son. The New Testament deals with the *new* covenant God made through Jesus. The four Gospels occupy a central place in the New Testament and in the entire Bible because they tell about the life, teachings, and saving death and Resurrection of Jesus. Through Jesus, God extended the covenant to all humanity. This new covenant began with Jesus and continues today in his Church. Jesus himself is the fullest revelation of who God is. Jesus is the Word of God who invites everyone to return to God and his plan of loving goodness.

God's Loving Goodness

What exactly is God's plan of loving goodness? The bishops of the Second Vatican Council explained that his plan is this: "through Christ, the Word made flesh, man has access to the Father in the Holy Spirit and comes to share in the divine nature" (*Dogmatic Constitution on Divine Revelation*, #2). It is important to know that, while God's plan is the best possible reality for us, he never forces himself on us. Instead, he *invites* us into a relationship with him. He reveals himself slowly, a little bit at a time.

The Bible records the events associated with the revelation of God's plan for humans. Here is a brief look at those events.

- After God created everything in the world, humans chose to turn away from him. Instead of abandoning them, he promised to be with the people, slowly bringing them back to himself. *(See Genesis 3:15.)*

- The story of Noah shows us how God made his covenant of love with humans, even though those humans were not always faithful to him. He saved Noah and his family from a great flood. He promised to be with the descendants of Noah forever and gave them a sign of his eternal love. *(See Genesis 9:12–15.)*

- Centuries later, God chose a Middle Eastern nomad named Abram to explain his covenant more fully. He promised to make Abram and his wife Sarah the parents of a great nation, God's own chosen people. *(See Genesis 12:2–3.)*

- God further revealed his intentions to humans by entering into a covenant with Moses and the Israelites at Mount Sinai. He promised to save them if they, in turn, would keep his commandments. *(See Deuteronomy 30:15–20.)*

- The prophets continually reminded the people to be faithful to their covenant with God. They told of his great love that would come to the people in the form of a Messiah who would free them forever from the chains of sin and death. In the fullness of time, he revealed himself in his own Son, Jesus Christ. Through Jesus we know what God is like. *(See John 3:16 and John 14:5–14.)*

- During his lifetime, Jesus chose twelve Apostles and entrusted them with the task of continuing his teaching. With the guidance of the Holy Spirit, they were to form his Church, to preach the gospel—the good news about God's saving love—to people in all nations. *(See Matthew 28:16–20.)*

The Church's Creeds

In its Tradition the Church continues the task of the Apostles—to preach the gospel to every generation. One way the Church does this is in a summary of faith known as a **creed.** The Church has two main creeds that are very similar—the **Apostles' Creed** and the **Nicene Creed.**

The Apostles' Creed dates from the first decades of the Church, perhaps coming from an earlier creed known as the *Old Roman Creed* (which existed in the second century). We believe that the Apostles' Creed conveys the "mind" or "intention" of the Twelve Apostles. A version of this creed is professed at the Sacrament of Baptism.

The Nicene Creed is a statement that was formulated by Church leaders at the Council of Nicaea in A.D. 325. The Council of Constantinople later added to this creed in A.D. 381. Today Catholics say the Nicene Creed at Mass on most Sundays.

Let's Talk!

1. Using the Scripture passages cited with the events on this page, how can faith help you "see" the big picture of God's loving plan?

2. Some people think that God's "plan" means that the future is all mapped out. This implies that humans have no choice but to live according to his plan. How does God's plan still leave you free? In what ways does his plan depend on humans?

Activity

Turn to the Catholic Source Book, page 238. Compare the Apostles' Creed and the Nicene Creed. In your group, make a list of how the creeds are similar and different.

HUMAN DIGNITY

All humans are made in God's image. All people—young, old, rich, poor, black, white, and so forth—have God-given **dignity.** The word *dignity* means "worthwhile and deserving of respect." Every person on earth is deserving of respect. Christians have a responsibility to treat all people with respect. Furthermore, all people have rights, simply because they are human. Among these rights are the right to earn a living, the right to marry, the right to travel, the right to own possessions, and the right to medical care.

In addition to giving them rights, God calls all people to be responsible for one another. We must care for each other and be sure that the rights of others are protected as well. The more we care for and about others, the closer we move toward God and the happier we become.

It is important to remember that humans are not robots or slaves of God. God made each of us free. He gave us the gift of faith, and it is our choice to use it. He gave us a conscience—the ability to know right from wrong. He also gave us **free will.** *Free will* is the ability to make decisions without being forced to choose or act in a certain way. We can make our own choices. We can decide to respond in positive or negative ways to God's invitation of love and friendship. God never forces himself on us. We can, however, abuse this God-given freedom by assuming that we have the right to say and do anything we wish. We use our freedom correctly when we freely give ourselves over to God and become the persons he wants us to be.

Faith encompasses our intellect and our will—our whole being. Its purpose is a personal relationship of love with God. Central to the Catholic faith is the belief that there is only one God in three Persons: God the Father, God the Son, and God the Holy Spirit. Throughout life, we do not see God face to face, but we can see evidence of his loving presence if we are open to faith. We act as responsible and moral people whenever we translate our faith into real-life actions.

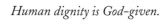
Human dignity is God-given.

Let's Talk!

In your notebook, write a response to each of the following uses of freedom and the importance of faith in the use of free will. Be prepared to discuss your responses in class.

1. A student who had to serve detention after school because he broke a classroom regulation says, "Rules take away our freedom."

2. A girl who has developed a drinking problem says, "It's my life and I can do whatever I want with it."

3. A woman who has been unkind to her aging mother says, "I couldn't have acted differently; I am under so much pressure."

4. A teacher who tells his class, "It is very naïve to waste time dreaming dreams about the future."

Human Life

Human life is sacred because every human being is created in God's image and has God-given dignity.

- Murder. Taking the life of a person is gravely contrary to human dignity and God's holiness.

- Abortion. From the moment of its conception, an embryo is to be safeguarded, treated as a person with human dignity, cherished, and given medical care like every human person. "Direct abortion, that is, abortion willed as an end or as a means, is a 'criminal' practice, gravely contrary to the moral law" (CCC, #2322). Excommunication is the penalty for this crime against life.

- Euthanasia. "An act or omission which, of itself or by intention, causes death to eliminate suffering constitutes a murder gravely contrary to the dignity of the human person and to the respect due to the living God, his Creator" (CCC, #2277). Handicapped, sick, and dying individuals deserve to be respected and to have the opportunity to lead lives characterized by dignity.

- Suicide. Our lives have dignity. We are guardians, not owners, of our God-given life. Therefore, suicide is forbidden by the fifth commandment as an offense against hope, justice, and love.

God Is at Work in Us

God assists us in many ways to lead lives worthy of our dignity and freedom as his adopted children. He reveals to us his Law, plants within us his wisdom, and gives us his grace to accomplish what he commands.

We find God's Law in Scripture. This Law is his fatherly instruction teaching us the rules of behavior that reflect our love for him and others and that condemns the paths of evil that reject his love. In the Old Testament we find the Old Law or Law of Moses; its moral rules are summarized in the Ten Commandments. The Old Law prepared the way for the New Law or Law of the Gospel, which Christ revealed and embodied. Basically, the New Law is the law of charity, energized by our belief in Jesus and the grace of the Holy Spirit. We get a clear expression of the New Law in Jesus' Sermon on the Mount (Matthew 5–7).

God's Law is also written on our souls and as such is called *natural law*.

- Natural law is an internal moral sense that enables us to tell the difference between good acts and evil acts, between truth and lies. This natural law within us is like having a built-in compass, pointing us toward good moral decisions.

- Natural law helps us to live as God's children. It is both a participation in his wisdom and loving kindness and an expression of our human dignity. As such, natural law helps us to lead lives worthy of sons and daughters created in God's image.

- Natural law is a permanent, unchanging feature within all humans. Thus, it is the foundation of moral rules and civil law. If we look across the globe and throughout history, we will find societies and nations observing the same rights and duties and enacting similar civil laws. This phenomenon demonstrates natural law at work.

In addition to God's revealed Law in Scripture and his natural law implanted within us, he provides us another way to help us act as his adopted children. He gives his **grace**, and by doing so introduces us into the life of the Trinity.

God "has placed in man a longing for truth and goodness that only he can satisfy. The promises of 'eternal life' respond, beyond all hope, to this desire" (CCC #2002). God does not force us to respond to this longing. His grace, however, prepares us to *receive* the grace to respond freely to this deep-seeded longing for truth and goodness. Nothing that we do makes us worthy of this initial grace; rather, the grace of the Holy Spirit is the way that God takes the initiative to help us to respond to our longing for him. However, once we have cooperated with God's initial grace and are moved by the Holy Spirit, we can merit for ourselves and for others the graces necessary to attain eternal life as well as many things we need in this life.

The Communal Aspect of Faith

Humans do not live in a vacuum. We are social beings; we need to communicate with others in order to survive. The same is true of faith. We cannot believe in a vacuum. "Faith is not an isolated act. No one can believe alone, just as no one can live alone."

We learn about faith from the faith and example of other people. Our faith development begins in our family life. With our family members and among our friends and acquaintances our faith grows. It is in a community of faith that our faith is nurtured. We call this community of faith the *Catholic Church*.

The Catholic Church's faith supports and nourishes our faith. Our faith grows as our relationship with God and with the Church community grows. Faith is necessary for salvation, our eternal life with God.

Reflection

1. Write the story of your faith development, from the time you were a child until now.
   - How have you grown in religious faith?
   - Who were the people who "taught" you about faith?
   - How did these people teach you?
   - How has the Catholic Church nourished your faith?

Faith grows in community.

WHAT IS PRAYER?

Prayer is the tool for making our relationship with God "real." Prayer can be between a person and God (private prayer) or it can involve a community of persons and God (communal prayer). Basically, prayer is a conversation, or dialogue, with God. We can talk to him aloud or in our hearts. He talks to us through the events of daily life, our relationships with others, the Church sacraments, or moments of quiet. Prayer is a gift from God, who strengthens and guides us in our prayer. Ongoing prayer keeps us in touch with him and helps faith grow.

There are many different times to pray. Some include:

- In the morning, soon after waking
- While watching a beautiful sunrise or sunset
- While listening to the ocean waves
- In the car during the morning or evening, driving to and from school or work
- While taking a walk
- In church
- At Mass
- At night, before bed

The Lord's Prayer

Jesus' disciples made this request of him, "Lord, teach us to pray" (Luke 11:1). This is the prayer that Jesus taught them:

> Our Father who art in heaven,
> hallowed be thy name.
> Thy kingdom come. Thy will be done on earth,
> as it is in heaven.
> Give us this day our daily bread,
> and forgive us our trespasses,
> as we forgive those who trespass against us,
> and lead us not into temptation,
> but deliver us from evil.
>
> *Luke 11:2–4*

If we spent a lifetime studying and praying the Our Father, we would come to realize that it is, in truth, a wonderful summary of the whole gospel of Jesus. With knowledge that God is the most loving and trustworthy Father imaginable, we turn to him in humble trust and childlike love. And then following Jesus' instruction, we call God "our Father." We do this because Jesus, the Son of God made man, has made it possible for us, through Baptism, to become God's children. This simple yet profound prayer joins us with the Father and with his Son. It also makes our true selves more known to us.

Reflection

1. What is your favorite way and time to pray? Why?

2. Describe a time when praying to God was particularly meaningful to you. What did you talk to God about? Why do you think your prayer was so important to you?

3. When do you find it especially helpful to engage in communal prayer?

Activity

Based on the sheet your teacher will provide, conduct an anonymous survey of students in your school. Tally the results and discuss them in your small group. Prepare a report for the class.

Open to God's Gift of Faith

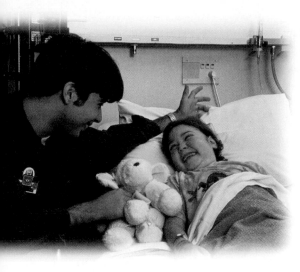

Spiritual and physical well-being are closely connected.

It seems that faith is not just good for your *spiritual* well-being. More than 300 recent studies have found that having a strong spiritual faith is also good for your *physical* health. People of faith are healthier than nonbelievers and are less likely to die prematurely from any cause. Having faith can also speed recovery from physical and mental illness, surgery, and addiction.

It's good to know that God always offers us faith—there's no cutoff time or expiration date. We simply have to respond to his gift. Many people who are new to faith (or who are thinking seriously about their faith for the first time) often have questions about how they can let God find them. There is no one right way to let faith into your heart. But here are some ideas that can help you become more open to faith:

1. Think about and appreciate the beauty around you—in yourself, in your family and friends, in your world.

2. Listen to your thoughts and reactions throughout the day. Recognize these thoughts and reactions, but do not judge them. Relax with them and let them take you deeper into your spiritual core.

3. Take time each day to pause and slow down. Take some deep breaths to slow down your thoughts and to focus on what God may be trying to say to you.

4. Find good friends. Participate in a faith-based community. Don't be afraid to ask questions about faith or to share your own insights.

5. Do good deeds. Be kind to others. Be sincerely interested in helping others. Start small, but believe that you really can make a difference in the lives of others.

6. Develop the habit of prayer. Sometimes pray for the strength you need to be true to yourself. Other times, pray for the needs of others.

7. Develop a group of peers with whom you can pray.

Activity

Do an electronic presentation, or, on a blank sheet of paper, draw a large circle and divide it as a pie into six equal sections (such a paper with a circle already divided on it may be provided by your teacher). Using an artistic format, show the importance of faith in your life. (Title your piece: **My Circle of Faith.** Use mainly drawing and sketching; try to limit the number of words to only a few.) Fill each section as follows:

1. Section one: the people who help your faith
2. Section two: the places that help your faith
3. Section three: the things that help your faith
4. Section four: the deeds that help your faith
5. Section five: the events (past or present) that help your faith
6. Section six: the way you best celebrate your faith

A PERSON OF FAITH

Thomas Merton

Thomas Merton was born January 31, 1915, in Predes, France. Soon thereafter, in an effort to escape World War I, Merton's family moved to Long Island, NY. His mother died of stomach cancer when he was six years old. Thomas and his father traveled to France. His father soon became involved with the writer Evelyn Scott, thus neglecting Thomas. Two years later Thomas returned to New York to be raised by his grandparents. He traveled back to Europe off and on with his father, who died when Thomas was 16.

Although he won a scholarship to Clare College, Cambridge, Thomas rarely attended classes. He preferred to party and became very irresponsible.

By 1935, Merton grew more and more concerned with the existence of God and what God might mean in his life. He returned to the United States and attended Columbia University. This time he was more serious about studying. He edited the yearbook and college literary magazine. After graduation, he stayed on for a master's degree in English literature. Merton converted to Catholicism in 1938 and did volunteer work at Friendship House in Harlem. Here he worked to provide shelter and help to homeless people. His behavior—although better—remained chaotic and without discipline.

In 1941 Merton made a radical choice to change his life. He entered the Trappist monastery, Our Lady of Gethsemani Abbey, near Bardstown, Kentucky. The Trappists are a Catholic religious community known for their simple and strict lifestyle.

In the monastery, Merton's faith grew. He wrote about his religious conversion in *The Seven Storey Mountain,* a book that became a bestseller. He was ordained in 1949.

In 1951, Merton became a naturalized U.S. citizen. He was appointed master of scholastics, assuming the responsibility for teaching the priests- and monks-to-be. During this time, Merton wrote *The Living Bread, No Man Is an Island,* and *The Silent Life,* three books that expanded his classroom notes. From 1955 to 1965, Merton served the monastery as master of novices. He continued writing two to three books a year.

From 1965 to 1968, Merton received permission to live as a hermit apart from the monastery. He concentrated on contemplative prayer and writing. He also corresponded extensively with spiritual authors and thinkers throughout the world, regardless of their religion.

Merton wrote clearly and courageously about issues such as racial integration in the South, the Holocaust, the Vietnam War, world peace, nonviolence, and the merits of eastern religions, especially Zen Buddhism.

> **"**At the height of the escalation of the Vietnam War, he welcomed a Vietnamese Buddhist monk to speak at the abbey, met with peace activist Joan Baez, corresponded with Daniel Berrigan (a Catholic priest arrested for burning draft cards), and planned a retreat for Dr. Martin Luther King Jr., a plan thwarted by King's assassination.**"**
>
> "THOMAS MERTON,"
> CONTEMPORARY AUTHORS
> ONLINE

Throughout his life, Merton wrote at least ten books of poetry and more than forty books on the spiritual life. He died of accidental electrocution in Bangkok, Thailand, on December 10, 1968, and is buried in the cemetery at Gethsemani Abbey.

Research

In the library or on the Internet, research one of the following topics, and prepare an oral or written report.

- Friendship House and its founder, Catherine de Hueck Doherty
- The Trappists or Trappistines in general, or one of their monasteries

Celebrating Faith

Opening Song:	"Follow the Light"
Leader:	Lord, we thank you for bringing us together today. We have many unanswered questions about who we are and what our purpose in life is to be. Open us to your gift of faith. Change our darkness into light, through your Son Jesus Christ and your Holy Spirit.
All:	**Amen.**
Reading:	The Healing of the Blind Beggar (Luke 18:35–43)
All:	**LORD, please let me see.**
Side 1:	O Lord, our Sovereign, how majestic is your name in all the earth. You have set your glory above the heavens.
Side 2:	Out of the mouths of babes and infants you have founded a bulwark because of your foes, to silence the enemy and the avenger.
All:	**Lord, please let me see.**
Side 1:	When I look at your heavens, the work of your fingers, the moon and the stars that you have established;
Side 2:	what are human beings that you are mindful of them, mortals that you care for them?
All:	**Lord, please let me see.**
Side 1:	Yet you have made them a little lower than God, and crowned them with glory and honor.
Side 2:	You have given them dominion over the works of your hands; you have put all things under their feet,
Side 1:	all sheep and oxen, and also the beasts of the field,
Side 2:	the birds of the air, and the fish of the sea, whatever passes along the paths of the seas.
All:	**O LORD, our Sovereign, how majestic is your name in all the earth.**

Psalm 8

Leader:	Let us take turns sharing one or more questions we would like to ask God. After each question, respond: Lord, please let me see.
	Let us pray.
All:	**Father of light, in you is found no shadow of change but only the fullness of life and limitless truth. Open our hearts to the voice of your Word and free us from the original darkness that shadows our vision. Restore our sight and enlighten us, that we may find the way to your glory. Amen.**

Based on the Opening Prayer for the Second Sunday of Lent

Review

1. What are four descriptions of faith? Explain what the term *theological virtue* means.

2. What are four ways that God takes the first step to let us know that he is there and that he cares?

3. What is revelation?

4. What is the Bible? How many books does it contain? How are these books arranged?

5. Which books occupy a central place in the New Testament? Why?

6. What do we mean when we say that God is the author of Scripture?

7. Why must we be careful about the way we interpret the Bible?

8. What task of the Apostles does the Church continue? What is one way the Church does this?

9. What are the names of two Christian creeds? How are they the same and different?

10. What is the relationship between faith and human dignity?

11. What is prayer?

12. What are five different types of prayer?

WORDS OF FAITH

Bible—God's written word, composed by human authors and inspired by the Holy Spirit

covenant—a solemn promise, or agreement, made between two parties; the word means testament

creed—a summary of the true beliefs held by a group

dignity—the respect owed to all humans because they are made in God's image

faith—a theological virtue, a gift from God; the habit of responding positively to God

free will—the human ability to make decisions without being forced to choose or act in one specific way

God—the one and only Supreme Being who always existed and who will always continue to exist; there are three Persons in one God, the Father, the Son, and the Holy Spirit (CCC, #249)

grace—our sharing in the Life of God. "Grace is *favor*, the *free and undeserved help* that God gives us to respond to his call to become children of God, adoptive sons, partakers of the divine nature and of eternal life" (CCC, #1996).

Messiah—a savior sent by God to redeem people from the power of sin and everlasting death and to restore them to God's friendship

revelation—God's communication of himself and his plan of loving goodness throughout history; Scripture and Tradition together make up the one source of his revelation.

soul—the spiritual principle of humans

Tradition—the living and authentic transmission of the teachings of Jesus in the Church

Trinity—the mystery of one God in three Persons: Father, Son, and Holy Spirit

vocation—one's calling or destiny in life

Enrichment

Choose one of the following to present to the class.

1. Do a role-play with another student taking the part of an atheist (one who says there is no God). Try to convince him or her that there is a God. How do the "atheist" and you respond to such topics as human life, goodness, beauty, justice?

2. Do an oral or written presentation that addresses the following points: How do the following kinds of expressions of faith differ? How are they the same?

   • I believe in God.

   • I believe God.

   • I believe my sick grandfather will get well.

   • I believe I will get a car for my sixteenth birthday.

   • I believe in you.

   • I believe that no matter how bleak things look now, things will work out for the better.

   Explain if and how belief and hope are related.

3. Write your own prayer of thanksgiving to God for his creation and the other gifts he has granted you. You might want to put the prayer to music and sing it for the class if you are musically inclined.

4. Take a nature walk and listen for God—did you hear him? How can God be found in the noise and busyness of the city?

5. After watching some television shows or videos, set up an interview show in which you converse with a movie producer and a television producer about the television shows or movies they produce. Use the following questions as a guide to formulating your own questions. How do these shows or movies deny or ignore God? How do they support a belief in God and the importance of faith? How do they sell an antireligious attitude or message or how are they positive toward religion? Explain.

6. Visit a grandparent, an elderly neighbor, or a person at a care center. Take some time to talk with the person and read the newspaper or a magazine to him or her. Relate how this makes a difference in that person's life and yours.

Let There Be Light

> "Then God said, "Let there be light"; and there was light. And God saw that the light was good; . . ."
>
> GENESIS 1:3–4

In this chapter, you will:

- consider the relationship between science and faith.

- explore belief in God as Trinity and as Creator.

- recognize that the first three commandments call people to put God first in their lives.

- appreciate how the Church celebrates its Trinitarian belief in God through its liturgy and sacraments.

- explore the value of prayers of adoration in developing a relationship with God.

- assess how to respond to the Creator's love and how belief in God affects one's attitude and behavior.

WORDS OF FAITH

adoration	idolatry	sacrament
angels	liturgy	salvation
atheism	Matrimony	stewardship
Baptism	monotheism	Ten Commandments
creationism	original sin	
evolution	polytheism	

FAITH AND SCIENCE

In the last chapter, you learned that humans can come to know God by using their human abilities, such as reason, to recognize God's presence in the created world and to respond to God's manifestation of himself. It is important to realize that the world in which we live does not always lead others to believe in God's existence. Unfortunately, it can sometimes lead people to disbelief.

For centuries, there has been an ongoing tension between scientific findings, based on rationality and provable facts, and religious teaching, based on faith. Both science and faith are supposed to point to "the truth." When they disagree or seem to disagree, the conflict can become emotional and disturbing.

For example, the Polish astronomer Nicolaus Copernicus (1473-1543) published his findings that the earth revolved around the sun. The Church deemed these findings contrary to the Bible. The Ptolemaic view of the universe, that the sun revolved around the earth, influenced Catholic teaching at that time. The controversy continued well after the Italian explorer Christopher Columbus established that the earth was round instead of flat. In 1632 Italian astronomer Galileo Galilei published his findings supporting the Copernican theory. The Church condemned Galileo as a dissenter from Church doctrine and sentenced him to house arrest for the last years of his life. However, centuries of research and a greater understanding of how to read and interpret Scripture led the Church in 1992 to retract its condemnation of Galileo and acknowledge that his viewpoints were neither contrary nor threatening to the Christian faith.

Another figure in the debate between science and religion was English naturalist Charles Darwin. In 1859 in *On the Origin of Species,* Darwin presented his theory of **evolution** by natural selection—that all living things evolved from a single organism by natural means. Early advocates of this theory believed it called into question the theory of **creationism** based on a literal interpretation of the Genesis story. In this story God created the universe in six days and created all things—including humans—mostly as they are today. Hence, many people thought that belief in evolution was in opposition to belief in God's existence. Some equated the term *evolution* with **atheism,** the belief that there is no God.

As time went on, numerous people began to write about a "middle way," a theory that reflected both the Judeo-Christian belief in God's creative power and the theory of evolution. One proponent of this theistic, or God-centered, view of evolution was the English theologian William Paley. His theory was known as *intelligent design*—the idea that the development over time of an organism's complexity is evidence for the existence of a cosmic designer.

Let's Talk!

1. What do you believe about the origin of the universe?
2. Is there really any conflict between a faith-filled way of saying something and a scientific way of saying it? Give reasons for your answer.

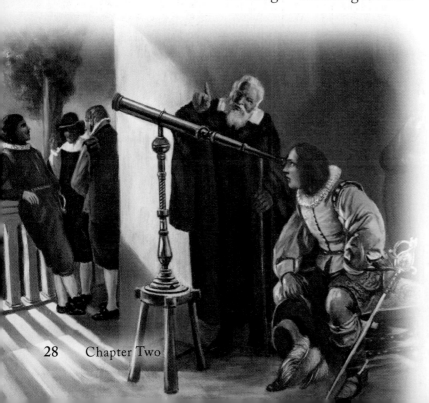

Galileo's use of the telescope opened the door to a new way of looking at the world.

It is very important to understand that there is no conflict between the scientific view of evolution (science) and the Bible (faith). For example, the creation story in the first chapter of Genesis was written thousands of years ago, before the time of scientific thinking. It was intended to convey religious truths, not to give scientific explanations for the origin of the world. The Book of Genesis stresses that the one true God is the power behind all of life. He continues to be present in the midst of creation, guiding and sustaining it.

Further Thinking

In the twentieth century, a Jesuit priest named Pierre Teilhard de Chardin devoted his life to working in the area of science and religion. As a paleontologist and geologist, Teilhard spent over twenty years working on scientific expeditions in Africa and China. His work with human fossils resulted in important scientific publications. Teilhard's view was based on both his faith and his scientific perspective of the world.

Pierre Teilhard de Chardin was both a priest and a paleontologist.

Basically Teilhard viewed Christian belief from an evolutionary perspective. For example, Teilhard believed that all living things—including humans—evolve from simple forms to complex forms with higher levels of consciousness. God is behind this evolution, moving it forward toward a future time when all creatures will live in harmony and peace, in union with God.

According to Teilhard, the existence of the soul is one "proof" of the existence of God. Christian love constantly challenges the human soul to further growth, toward eventual communion with God. According to Teilhard, as he wrote in *The Divine Milieu*, the goal of each individual is "to become a life in common with the life of Christ." This view does not set the physical world (science) and the spiritual world (faith) at odds with one another. Rather, this God-driven evolutionary process eventually weds science and faith into one.

> " We are sometimes inclined to think that the same things are monotonously repeated over and over again in the history of creation. That is because . . . the transformation is too vast and too inward by comparison with our superficial and restricted outlook, for us to see the progress of what is tirelessly taking place in and through all matter and all spirit. Let us believe. . . . Under the commonplace envelope of things, . . . new earth is being slowly engendered. "
>
> PIERRE TEILHARD DE CHARDIN, *THE DIVINE MILIEU.*

For Teilhard, "everything forms a single whole." There is no further conflict between the physical and the spiritual. We, at last, are truly one in Christ Jesus. *(See Galatians 3:28.)*

In addition to the ideas explained here—which are consistent with Church teachings—Teilhard also proposed certain theories that were problematic. The Church was not comfortable with all of his teachings. Since many of the objectionable views were interspersed with theories that were in line with Church teaching, the Church did not allow Teilhard's works to be published during his lifetime. Many subsequent Catholic theologians were influenced by some of Teilhard's insights, most of which were published by friends after his death. His insights helped theologians see the connection between scientific theory and Catholic belief.

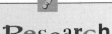

Research

Using the library or Internet, find out more about the life and theories of Nicolaus Copernicus, Galileo Galilei, and Charles Darwin. Why did their theories trouble people of faith? In what ways can we reconcile these scientific findings with belief in God? Prepare a brief report of your findings. Be prepared to discuss what effect these three scientists have had on understanding what faith really is.

In the late nineteenth and early twentieth centuries, many people felt that the theory of evolution challenged their belief about creation and God as Creator. Where do people stand on the issue of God and evolution today? Here are the results of a 2001 Gallup poll:

- 45 percent of people in the United States believe that God at some time in the last ten thousand years or so, created humans pretty much in their present form. In other words, these people believe in creationism—God created everything, as it is, in six days.

- 12 percent believe in the theory of evolution—that humans evolved gradually over millions of years from less advanced forms of life—without God having any part of it.

- 37 percent believe in the theory of evolution *with* God's guidance.

- 6 percent had no opinion on the question.

The first cloned sheep, Dolly, lived only six years, half the normal lifetime of sheep.

In 2002 Channel One asked young people which theory they thought should be taught in school: creationism, evolution, or both.

- 31 percent said creationism.

- 17 percent said evolution.

- 52 percent said both.

Thanks to many people of faith, Catholic theologians now see that evolution is not inconsistent with Christian faith. The creation stories found in Genesis are not meant to be taken literally as science. Evolution does not necessarily negate God; rather, it can be seen as one possible way that he might have chosen to create.

Activity

After reading Genesis 1:1—2:4 and the handout your teacher will provide, choose sides for a class debate. In the debate, present the pros and cons of each position: atheistic evolution, creationism, and intelligent design (theistic evolution). Discuss how a person of faith could or could not hold each position. Then decide which position you hold and explain why.

Scientific Discovery and Religion

Today, new scientific developments, such as genetic research and medical techniques for artificial reproduction, challenge us to think about what we believe. Although these modern issues are different from the issue of evolution, they do deal with the beginnings, or creation, of human life.

For centuries, people have thought of God as an all-powerful deity. People believed in him because there was so much in the universe they could not explain. They reasoned that God must exist because he was the only one capable of making the planets and stars, trees and flowers, animals and humans. But now that science is enabling humans to acquire some of these powers for themselves, the religious questions present themselves: Is God really so powerful? Could the universe have been made without God's intervention? Do we need God? Does he really exist?

God created humans in his own image; humans have an immortal soul that cannot be created by human means. Furthermore, all human life—from the moment of conception—is sacred and should not be manipulated or destroyed for scientific experimentation. It is only within the sanctity of marriage that sexual activity and procreation should occur.

We need to appreciate the life-giving discoveries of science in medicine, healthcare, environmental life, and communications. The issue is not that science or religion alone can provide the right answers. The issue is *how we use* what we know, and whether it is "scientific knowledge" or "spiritual knowledge." We need to use what we know in the right way. And the right way respects all of life, including the earth itself. We are caretakers of God's creation and caregivers to one another—and to all life. The right way leads to peace and harmony among all people.

Does God Exist?

You have already learned that atheism is the belief that God does not exist. Belief in many gods (as with the ancient Romans and Greeks) is called **polytheism.** Belief in one God is called **monotheism.** The faith of Jews and Christians alike is monotheistic. This belief is centuries old, coming from the ancient Israelites. "Hear, O Israel: The LORD is our God, the LORD alone" (Deuteronomy 6:4). "I am God, and there is no other" (Isaiah 45:22).

The percent of believers in the United States population has not changed much in the last sixty years. Depending on the poll, those who believe in God have consistently accounted for 94 to 98 percent of the population, while the percentage of those who don't believe in God has varied between 1 and 5. Over this time, when people were asked to rate how strongly they believed in God's existence, the percentage of people who were "absolutely certain" that God exists ranged from 72 percent to 87 percent. Despite the recent developments in science, a Gallup poll in 2000 found that 96 percent of U.S. citizens continued to say they believed in God or a universal spirit. According to the same poll, nine out of ten U.S. citizens believed that God loves them. Eighty-four percent thought God was actively involved in their lives.

Let's Talk!

1. Suppose scientific experimentation were someday able to produce every living thing. Would that mean that God does not exist? Explain.

2. Humanity has acquired a great deal of knowledge. How do humans use this acquired knowledge?

3. What is the difference between knowledge and wisdom? When might they be the same and under what circumstances?

Reflection

1. How strongly do you believe in God's existence? Why?

2. Do you believe that God loves you and is actively involved in your life? Why?

WHAT IS GOD LIKE?

Specifically, the creed says the following about God the Father:

- **Apostles' Creed:** I believe in God, the Father almighty, creator of heaven and earth.

- **Nicene Creed:** We believe in one God, the Father, the Almighty, maker of heaven and earth, of all that is, seen and unseen.

Have you ever tried to describe your best friend to someone else? Chances are, there was a lot about your friend that you weren't able to put into words. The same is true of God. Words don't begin to encompass all that God is. Nevertheless we can begin to talk about God by using descriptive images. These images compare God to things we know, by saying that he is *like* some things and *not like* other things. "God is light and in him there is no darkness at all" (1 John 1:5). "God is not a human being, that he should lie, or a mortal, that he should change his mind" (Numbers 23:19).

You have already seen that you can learn about God through nature and the human ability to reason. In addition, you can learn a lot about God through personal and communal prayer. A very important way you learn about him is through the Bible. Likewise you can learn about God through your family and the Church.

Research

1. Read the story of Moses' encounter with God in the burning bush: Exodus 3:1–8, 11–14. Note: The words "I AM WHO I AM" are an English translation of the Hebrew YHWH (Yahweh). For the Israelites this was the most holy, not to be spoken, name of God—a special name for God not used in everyday conversation.

2. This Scripture passage tells us that God is the God of all times. Find the verse that addresses each of the following.
   - God is the God of the past.
   - God is the God of the present.
   - God is the God of the future.

Reflection

1. What thoughts or feelings do you think Moses had when he saw the burning bush? (At this time in his life, he was running away from the pharaoh to escape punishment for killing an Egyptian.)

2. How do you think you would react if you "saw" God or heard his voice after school today? Why?

A Teen's Experience of God

As Moses learned, God is "from everlasting to everlasting." He never stops loving us nor does he stop inviting us to friendship with him. Many ordinary people experience God's presence in unexpected ways. Here is the account of one high school senior:

It was a dreary Saturday afternoon, and I'd decided I had nothing better to do than clean my room. But when I leaned over to pick up the stack of dusty yearbooks from my closet, I realized I was holding a record of my life from elementary through high school.

Cleaning can wait, I thought, as I carried the stack to my bed. Picking up a yearbook from my early school years, I came across a photo of my third-grade class. Suddenly I remembered "The Great Mail Race." For this activity, our teacher had us writing other third graders all over the United States. The guy I wrote turned out to be a Christian. We continued to keep in touch over the years and I even got to meet him last summer.

For most of the afternoon, I traveled through the years and years of memories. There were the field trips, the tests, and those horrible pop quizzes. And there was the wintry day when school was cancelled. My friends and I spent the afternoon making snowmen, sledding, throwing snowballs, and just having a great time.

Then there was Ms. Boyd, my math teacher. She not only taught me math; she showed me what it meant to be passionate about something you believe in. And she was passionate about teaching! I could see it in her eyes and hear it in her voice. She also loved students. She went that extra mile to help me understand difficult assignments.

As I looked at those yearbooks scattered about my bed, I realized something about God. He was there, that invisible presence in each and every memory. He was there during all the difficult tests and quizzes. He was there when I just "happened" to pick a pen pal who was a Christian. He was there on that winter day when I had so much fun with my friends. And he was the one who placed a wonderful teacher like Ms. Boyd in my life.

In recent weeks, I'd worried a lot about going to college this fall. Would I be able to get all my assignments done? Would I make new friends? Would I get homesick?

But as I sat there surrounded by all my memories, I felt like God was saying, "Rachel, I've been with you over the past twelve years of school. Why wouldn't I stick with you over the next four?"

"Thank you, God," I whispered. "Thanks for being with me—in the past, in the present, and, yes, even into the future."

Rachel Schlabach, "No Reason to Worry," Campus Life *(July 2001).*

Let's Talk!

1. How do you think people of faith experience God's presence even, and perhaps especially, in difficult times? Explain.

2. How do you think people of faith can experience the presence of God in everyday situations like cleaning their rooms, taking out the garbage, sharing with a younger sibling, studying for a test, and so forth?

Reflection

Describe ways you have experienced the presence of God in your life.

Attributes of God

What else do the Scriptures tell about God? The Bible presents many attributes (characteristics) for him, including power, majesty, wisdom, love, mercy, and justice. He has many other wonderful attributes as well—for example, patience, truth, faithfulness, and goodness.

- **Power.** We believe that God is omnipotent; this means all-powerful. "[F]or God all things are possible" (Matthew 19:26). God created everything. He also rules everything.

- **Majesty.** We believe that God is the Lord of the universe, infinitely more mighty than earthly kings and presidents. "The LORD is king, he is robed in majesty" (Psalm 93:1). God is almighty "in heaven and on earth" (Psalm 135:6).

- **Wisdom.** We believe that God knows all things and has perfect judgment. He never makes a mistake. "For God's foolishness is wiser than human wisdom" (1 Corinthians 1:25).

- **Love.** We believe that God is perfect, unselfish, abounding, steadfast love. "I have loved you with an everlasting love" (Jeremiah 31:3). God's very being is Love.

- **Mercy.** We believe that God is compassionate and forgiving. He does not punish us as our sins deserve. Instead, he is "rich in mercy, out of the great love with which he loved us," even when we do wrong (Ephesians 2:4).

- **Justice.** We believe that God respects the true dignity of humans and treats all people fairly. "I am the LORD; I act with steadfast love, justice, and righteousness in the earth" (Jeremiah 9:24). He deals equally with those who are rich and those who are poor.

- **Patience.** We believe that God is long suffering and "slow to anger" (see Exodus 34:5–6). "[Y]ou are a God ready to forgive, gracious and merciful, slow to anger and abounding in steadfast love" (Nehemiah 9:17).

- **Truth.** We believe that God is Truth. His word can always be trusted. "O Lord GOD, you are God, and your words are true" (2 Samuel 7:28). Indeed, God is Truth itself.

- **Faithfulness.** We believe that God abounds in fidelity, or faithfulness. "The LORD . . . abounding in steadfast love and faithfulness, keeping steadfast love for the thousandth generation" (Exodus 34:6–7).

- **Goodness.** We believe that God is perfect goodness. Indeed, God is infinitely good. His works are good, too. For this reason, we "give thanks to the LORD, for he is good" (Psalm 107:1).

It is important to remember that although these attributes are an attempt to describe God, they are not completely adequate. He is always more than humans can describe. That is why the Church sometimes calls God, "the inexpressible, the incomprehensible, the invisible, the ungraspable" (The Divine Liturgy of Saint John Chrysostom). Whenever we try to reduce God into human categories and definitions, we fall into a type of **idolatry,** or worship of a false god. We fail to worship the real God, who is always a transcendent mystery.

Activity

God is a transcendent mystery, and yet God chooses to communicate himself to us in a personal relationship. Choose a medium, such as song, dance, or art, to express your feelings and thoughts about the mystery of God. Be prepared to share your work in class.

THREE IN ONE

We believe in one God, but we also believe that there are three divine Persons in the one God: the Father, the Son, and the Holy Spirit. We call this mystery of three Persons in one God the **Trinity**. Whenever we make the Sign of the Cross, we profess our belief in God as Father, Son, and Holy Spirit.

The Catechism states, "the mystery of the Most Holy Trinity is the central mystery of Christian faith and life" (#234). Remember the definition of *faith*—a free and positive response to God's initiative. Also remember the purpose of faith—to praise God with whom we have a loving relationship. The Trinity is the bedrock of Christian faith. It is important to look more closely at what we mean by *Father, Son,* and *Holy Spirit.* Understanding what we mean will help us get a better appreciation of how the Persons of the Trinity relate to us.

The Mystery of the Trinity

Throughout the centuries, the Church has recognized God's role in creation, redemption, and sanctification. God is Creator, Redeemer, and Sanctifier. Christians sometimes identify each of these aspects with a different Person of the Holy Trinity. Sometimes, they relate the Father to the work of creation, although the three Persons are involved in the work of creation. Sometimes they relate the Son of God to the work of redemption, although all three Persons are involved in the work of redemption. Sometimes they relate the Holy Spirit to the work of sanctification, although all three Persons are involved in the work of making holy.

Each divine Person in the Trinity shows forth what is proper to that divine Person as Father, Son, or Spirit. At the same time, we believe the divine Persons are inseparable in who they are and what they do. As it is written in the Catechism, "God himself is an eternal exchange of love, Father, Son, and Holy Spirit, and he has destined us to share in that exchange" (#221). Jesus taught, "Those who love me will keep my word, and my Father will love them, and we will make our home with them" (John 14:23).

Reflection

1. Write about some of the ways that you experience God as a Father.
2. Write about your experience of Jesus. Who is Jesus to you? How can you be like Jesus for others? How have you experienced being a child of God through Jesus? As God's child, list three ways you can imitate Jesus.
3. Describe a time you felt God's Spirit working in you. In what ways did you feel inspired or empowered by the Holy Spirit?

Let's Talk!

1. Define your concept of a good father.
2. How do you think the image of God as Father affects how you are supposed to act toward others, especially children?

God the Father

God our loving Father is a continuing presence in our lives. He truly cares about us and is with us every step of the way throughout life, as described in the following Scripture passage.

" When Israel was a child, I loved him,
   and out of Egypt I called my son.

The more I called them,
   the more they went from me;
they kept sacrificing to the Baals,
   and offering incense to idols.

Yet it was I who taught Ephraim to walk,
   I took them up in my arms;
   but they did not know that I healed them.

I led them with cords of human kindness,
   with bands of love.

I was to them like those
   who lift infants to their cheeks.
   I bent down to them and fed them. "

HOSEA 11:1–4

By calling God "Father," we express many things about our faith. Firstly, we proclaim that God is the origin of everything and that he has authority over everything he has created. Secondly, we express our faith in God's fatherly care for all his children. And thirdly, we witness to the fact that he is the Father of his only begotten Son, who in turn is the Son only in relation to his Father. Jesus himself said, "All things have been handed over to me by my Father: and no one knows the Son except the Father, and no one knows the Father except the Son and anyone to whom the Son chooses to reveal him" (Matthew 11:27).

God's loving kindness and tenderness can also be described by the image of motherhood. The image "emphasizes God's immanence, the intimacy between Creator and creature. The language of faith thus draws on the human experience of parents, who are in a way the first representatives of God for man" (CCC, #239).

Activities

1. Reread Isaiah 66:13 in the text, and read Psalm 131:2. In a small group, discuss how comfortable or uncomfortable you are in relating to God with the qualities of a Mother. Discuss reasons for your reactions.

2. Using the handout your teacher will provide, read and summarize the Scripture passages referring to God as Father. Then write a poem or use another medium to describe God as Father.

God the Son

God the Son is the second Person of the Trinity who took on human nature. The Gospels twice record the voice of God the Father calling Jesus "beloved Son"—at Jesus' baptism and at the Transfiguration. Here is Matthew's account of Jesus' baptism.

" Then Jesus came from Galilee to John [the Baptist] at the Jordan [River], to be baptized by him. . . . And when Jesus had been baptized, just as he came up from the water, suddenly the heavens were opened to him and he saw the Spirit of God descending like a dove and alighting on him. And a voice from heaven said, 'This is my Son, the Beloved, with whom I am well pleased.' "

MATTHEW 3:13, 16–17

The baptism of Jesus is recorded also in the Gospels according to Luke and John. John the Baptist, after baptizing Jesus, declares, "I myself have seen and have testified that this is the Son of God" (John 1:34).

At his Transfiguration, Jesus takes Peter, James, and John up the mountain away from the crowds; there God the Father refers to Jesus as his Son. While they are there, Jesus is transfigured—changed in appearance. A bright cloud comes over them, shining on Jesus, and a voice from the cloud says, "This is my Son, the Beloved; with him I am well pleased; listen to him." (Matthew 17:5). Jesus calls himself the "only Son of God" (John 3:18). And at the crucifixion of Jesus, even the Roman soldier declares, "Truly this man was God's Son." (Mark 15:39).

From his Resurrection on, the followers of Jesus believe in him as the Son of God, and early in its councils, the Church declared its faith in "the only Son of God, eternally begotten of the Father, God from God, Light from Light, true God from true God, begotten, not made, one in Being with the Father" (Nicene Creed).

The second divine Person of the Trinity, who became a man, took on human nature. He became one like us in all things except sin. Jesus was here, is still here, and will always be here. Listen to Jesus' words:

" All authority in heaven and on earth has been given to me. Go therefore and make disciples of all nations, baptizing them in the name of the Father and of the Son and of the Holy Spirit, and teaching them to obey everything that I have commanded you. And remember, I am with you always, to the end of the age. "

MATTHEW 28:18–20

Activities

1. The New Testament applies the title *Son of God* to Jesus 97 times. Using the handout your teacher will provide, read and summarize the Scripture passages referring to God the Son.

2. To reflect on God the Son, research the Luminous Mysteries of the Rosary and pray with them to enhance your biblical appreciation of Jesus' life and ministry.

God the Holy Spirit

There are different ways God relates to us.

- God is transcendent, that is, beyond all possible experience and knowledge. He is greater than us; he is *outside* us.

- He is personal, that is, united through love with all of creation. This is the God we find in loving relationships with *others*.

- He is immanent, in other words, embedded within creation. God is *within* us.

Although all three Persons of the Holy Trinity relate to us in all of these ways, we sometimes identify the Holy Spirit (Sanctifier, Helper) as the God within. For example, the Church teaches that he dwells in the entire Church and in each baptized person. Paul tells the Christians in Rome, "the Spirit of God dwells in you" (Romans 8:9). Thus, the Holy Spirit is a personal being; he knows and loves the Father and the Son. He also loves the human race whom he created. He stands in sharp contrast to a society that often represents divinity as impersonal power or force.

We cannot see the Holy Spirit, just as we cannot see air or breath. And yet we all know what happens to a balloon or a tire when the air has been let out. The balloon or tire is deflated or flat. In a similar way, the Holy Spirit fills us with God's own life. Through Scripture we come to know who he is. In the Old Testament the word *rûaḥ*, which means "breath or principle of life," is used over and over. The Holy Spirit is the breath—life—of God. The opening lines of Genesis tell of the creation of the world: "In the beginning when God created the heavens and the earth, the earth was a formless void and darkness covered the face of the deep, while a wind from God swept over the face of the waters" (Genesis 1:1–2).

The Holy Spirit breathes God's life within us. As it says in the Book of Numbers about Moses and the elders, "Then the LORD came down in the cloud and spoke to him, and took some of the spirit that was on him and put it on the seventy elders; and when the spirit rested upon them, they prophesied . . ." (Numbers 11:25). The Holy Spirit is at work in us, giving us hope and courage. He changes us by creating in us a new spirit and a caring heart, "a heart of flesh" (see Ezekiel 11:19).

Activity

Using the handout your teacher will provide, read and summarize the Scripture passages referring to the Holy Spirit. Then draw a picture or create a collage representing what the passages tell you about him.

The Holy Spirit opens us to the gift of faith, freeing us to respond fully to God's invitation of love. For example, in the New Testament, Mary agrees to become the mother of Jesus: "The angel said to her, 'The Holy Spirit will come upon you, and the power of the Most High will overshadow you; therefore the child to be born will be holy; he will be called Son of God'.... Then Mary said, '...let it be with me according to your word'" (Luke 1:35, 38).

And at the first Pentecost:

" And suddenly from heaven there came a sound like the rush of a violent wind, and it filled the entire house where they were sitting. Divided tongues, as of fire, appeared among them, and a tongue rested on each of them. All of them were filled with the Holy Spirit and began to speak in other languages, as the Spirit gave them ability. "

ACTS 2:2–4

We learn from Scripture that Jesus is God and man from the moment of his conception. The Holy Spirit is in the Apostles and in the Church. He fills Church members with wisdom, faith, encouragement, truth, joy, love, and hope. He is an agent of holiness. As people of faith, we are temples of the Holy Spirit; he makes his home in us (1 Corinthians 3:16) and helps us pray.

Sometimes, people worry because they cannot see God directly. They ask: How can we really be sure that God is there, loving and caring for us? Because, in times of quiet attention, of quiet awareness, we look at our lives and we *know* that the Holy Spirit was there—and *is* there, and *will be* there.

Let's Talk!

1. What are five attitudes and behaviors we should have toward ourselves if we truly believe we are temples of the Holy Spirit?

2. What are some practical ways young people can act as a channel of the Holy Spirit for others?

Activity

Without God's Spirit, we are lifeless—much like the dry bones in the vision of the Old Testament prophet Ezekiel. Read Ezekiel 37:1–14. What message is there for you in this passage?

IT IS GOOD

In the first part of the creed, we state not only our belief in God's existence but also our belief in God as Creator. This belief conjures questions humans have asked for centuries: Where do we come from? What is our origin? Is the universe governed by blind fate or by a transcendent, intelligent Being? If the world does come from God who is good, why is there so much that is *not* good? Why are there tragedies? Why are there disasters in nature—like devastating hurricanes and earthquakes and tornadoes and floods? Why is there sickness? Why is there suffering? Why is there death?

To attempt to answer these questions, we must start at the beginning. At one time nothing existed. Then, God, in his infinite wisdom and power, created the universe, the world, and man. Here, the word *creation* doesn't just mean to make something. It means to make something *ex nihilo*, which means "out of nothing." Only God can create out of nothing. To make new things, humans have to use previously existing elements. For example, an artist makes a picture by using paints, canvas, and a paintbrush. A contractor makes a new building by using concrete, steel beams, wood, nails, screws, bricks, and other materials. We don't know how God created the world. Even the Bible doesn't present one definitive answer to this mystery. In fact, there are two accounts of creation in the Book of Genesis, and these accounts differ in their details.

The first story of creation is found in Genesis 1:1—2:4. God creates the world in six days and rests on the seventh. The author of this story did not intend to write historical or scientific facts. Rather, they were trying to convey truths of faith about God, creation, and his plan for his creation. While we cannot know precisely the authors' purpose for writing, we have a sense of what the authors wanted to affirm and what God wanted to make known to us through their words.

Through the first creation account, the authors:

- explained their belief that the one God is the Creator of all things in the universe. "God alone created the universe freely, directly, and without any help" (Catechism, #317). He created everything out of nothing.

- showed the unique presence of God in the creation of humans. Humans are special among God's creation. They have dignity because they are made in his image (Genesis 1:27). Humans are not the same as animals, nor are they the same as **angels.** Both angels and humans have intellect and free will. Angels, however, are pure spirits, whereas humans have both a body and an eternal soul. Angels continually behold the face of God in heaven; they act as his servants and messengers.

- illustrated that the created world is good: ". . . indeed, it was very good" (Genesis 1:31). God created the world according to his wisdom and love. All creatures are called to share in his truth, goodness, and beauty.

- showed that humankind is to take care of the earth and all that is upon it. This we call **stewardship.**

Activity

Working in a small group, come up with five ways that young people today can act as good stewards of the earth. Then formulate a stewardship creed by which you will live and abide. Decorate and post the creed as a reminder of your responsibilities.

The Origin of Evil

The second story of creation is found in Genesis 2:4—3:24 and includes the story of the Fall. The author of this story seem to have had a purpose different from the author of the first story. He tells of a lost paradise in the Garden of Eden, and he attempts to answer the question: Why does evil exist in the world?

This second story of creation is about the first humans, called Adam and Eve, and their disobedience of God. The author explains that the created world is not perfect or complete. There is sin; there is evil. But God is not the source of evil; humans are. He created humans with free will, the ability to choose. Because humans are created with free will, they can also choose to sin by not following God's will.

According to the author of this creation account, God created Adam and Eve, in a state of holiness and friendship with him. The first humans lived in a lush garden where they did not want for anything. When tempted by the serpent (Satan, the devil, a powerful person of evil), they freely chose to disobey God, thus bringing sin and death into the world. In this story, Adam and Eve give in to temptation. They choose to sin by preferring themselves over God. We call their sin the **original sin.** Furthermore, we believe that this first, original sin has been passed down to all humans (except Jesus and Mary) ever since. Because of original sin, human nature is weakened. For that reason, we are often tempted to sin, to turn away from God, and to be less than he intended (CCC, #s 388, 399, 402-05).

To understand what God is revealing through the second creation story in the Bible, a look at the conclusion will help. He promises to be with the human race and save people from their own tendency to sin. Within the second creation story, we find evidence of the existence of Satan. We also find hints of God's promise of future **salvation,** which is God's forgiveness of sins and the complete reconciliation of humans with him through Jesus.

> " I will put enmity between you [the serpent, the devil, evil] and the woman,
>   and between your offspring and hers;
> he will strike your head,
>   and you will strike his heel. "

GENESIS 3:15

Regardless of what scientific discoveries are made in the future, the message in Scripture will always remain true: Humans, although basically good, are capable of committing terrible acts of evil against God and one another. But we believe that God sent his Son to free us from evil. He is infinitely creative and loving. He knows how to derive good from any situation of evil or suffering.

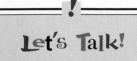

Let's Talk!

Discuss this statement: The devil is a powerful person who sometimes tempts us to sin.

Reflection

Write about a time when good came from a situation of evil or suffering in your own life or the life of your family.

PUTTING GOD FIRST

Belief in God's existence and role as the supreme Creator of all things leads us to a further belief—that we have certain responsibilities, or obligations, toward him. Essentially, "our duty toward God is to believe in him and to bear witness to him" (Catechism, #2087). This duty was originally expressed in the **Ten Commandments,** the ten fundamental moral laws given by God to his people and recorded in the Old Testament. The commandments relate to loving God and others. The first three commandments read as follows.

1. I, the Lord, am your God: you shall not have strange gods before me. *(See Exodus 20:2, 3.)*

2. You shall not take the name of the Lord your God in vain. *(See Exodus 20:7.)*

3. Remember to keep holy the Lord's day. *(See Exodus 20:8.)*

The first commandment teaches us to put God first in our lives, to place our hope and trust in him, to believe in him and all that he has revealed. We have a duty to nourish and protect our faith, as well as help it develop and grow. The second commandment says that we should be careful about how we use the name of God, Jesus Christ, his mother Mary, and the saints. It is not right to swear, using God's name to condemn someone else. The third commandment tells us to worship and praise God on Sunday, to avoid unnecessary work on the Lord's Day, and to "avoid making unnecessary demands on others that would hinder them from observing the Lord's Day" (CCC, #2195).

In short, these commandments remind us that we owe respect and reverence to God. We are to adore, or worship, him alone. He is to be first in our lives—in our priorities, in our thoughts, in our words, in our actions, and in our hearts. Jesus summarized these three commandments in the Great Commandment: "You shall love the Lord your God with all your heart, and with all your soul, and with all your mind" (Matthew 22:37). Love of God is to be the motive behind everything we do.

Perhaps you are thinking that these commandments were meant only for ancient peoples who worshiped many gods. Actually, they are quite relevant to people today. Our "false gods" are not necessarily the many gods of the Romans and Greeks, gods like Apollo or Pluto. Instead, they can be any of the things we consider more important than God.

Let's Talk!

Who are some of your idols? How do you want to be like them? Who or what are some of the false gods of today? Why?

The third commandment is a call to worship and praise God on the Lord's day.

Activity

Put together a list of questions that teens could use to examine their conscience in terms of the first three commandments.

Modern-day Idols

Many young people today idolize movie stars, musicians, and sports heroes. They have posters of these people in their bedrooms; they have all their DVDs, CDs, or trading cards. They may even talk and dress like their idols. Having a favorite movie star or sports hero is not wrong in itself. However, it becomes sinful when it becomes more important than loving God or loving other people.

Some young people today pursue the "false gods" of popularity and money. In order to "fit in" and be liked, they focus on having the most possessions, driving the hottest cars, and spending a lot of money. Some teens think nothing of stealing, cheating, committing sinful sexual acts, or selling drugs in order to live the lifestyle they idolize.

Other young people may "worship" the latest fashion fad. They spend hours on their make-up, clothes, or hair, and are overly worried that others will judge them on these externals.

Reflection

What is most important in your life (popularity, money, possessions, pleasure . . .)? Do you think your priorities are in line with your faith, or do you think they need some altering? Explain.

Superstition as an Idol

For many people, the false god is superstition. They may ascribe magical, godlike powers to certain actions or charms. For example, some teens may believe that no harm will happen to them as long as they wear a special necklace. Others may carry around a rabbit's foot or four-leafed clover, believing that it will bring them good luck. Or they may place their faith in numerology, palm reading, New Age auras, or the horoscope.

The truth is: Whenever we try to control or limit God, we are sinning against the first three commandments. Whenever we neglect our relationship with him—by not taking time for personal prayer, participating in the Holy Sacrifice of the Mass, or acting as Christians—we are placing something else ahead of God. Whenever we place so much emphasis on one part of life and neglect loving him and others, we are practicing idolatry.

Let's Talk!

1. What are some superstitions with which you are familiar? How do you think people can be less superstitious and grow more in real faith?

2. When do you think praying before a sports event is a form of superstition? When is it a healthy expression of faith?

3. In a recent movie or video that you have seen, what examples are there of people who are guilty of idolatry or superstitions?

Superstitious practices are not always as harmless as they may seem.

WORSHIP OF THE TRINITY

Catholics gather to praise and worship God in **liturgy,** the official public prayer of the Church. The original meaning of the word *liturgy* was a public work, or a service in the name of or on behalf of the people. In Christian terms, the word *liturgy* describes the participation of the whole People of God in the work of God.

The majority of Catholics today are baptized as infants.

Liturgy consists of the celebration of the sacraments, first and foremost the Eucharist, and the Liturgy of the Hours. A **sacrament** is an effective sign that conveys grace. Sacraments were established by Jesus and given to the Church through which God shares his life by the work of the Holy Spirit. In the sacraments Jesus continues his saving work. During his life, Jesus welcomed, fed, healed, and forgave people. Through the sacraments he continues to share God's life and love with his followers.

The Catholic Church celebrates seven sacraments: Baptism, Confirmation, Eucharist, Reconciliation, Anointing of the Sick, Holy Orders, and Matrimony. In addition to the sacraments, the Liturgy of the Hours is a prayer that includes psalms and readings and is prayed several times a day as a way to mark time as holy and recall God's saving work in creation.

In its liturgy, the Church uses prayers, symbols, and ritual gestures to celebrate the Holy Trinity. The Trinity acts in and through those gathered.

- God the Father is blessed and adored for the many blessings of his creation and for the salvation and new life that he shares through his Son, Jesus.

- God the Son is present among the people gathered, and the saving work of Christ is made present by the power of the Holy Spirit.

- God the Holy Spirit readies the hearts and minds of those present to encounter Christ. The Holy Spirit helps those gathered to recall their faith and unites them as Church.

Reflection

Imagine that God is speaking to you and saying to you the words he said of his own Son: "You are my beloved son (or daughter), with whom I am well pleased." Think about these words. Then write your response to them.

In the Sacrament of **Baptism,** the first sacrament celebrated, the Church continues the mission of the Apostles to "Go therefore and make disciples of all nations, baptizing them in the name of the Father and of the Son and of the Holy Spirit, and teaching them to obey everything that I have commanded you" (Matthew 28:19-20). Baptism is the first of three Sacraments of Christian Initiation. Through the waters of Baptism, there is a new birth, a new identity, if you will. The baptized are no longer just the children of biological parents, but they become the adopted sons and daughters of God through Baptism. God forgives both original sin and any actual (personal) sins committed prior to Baptism. The Holy Spirit is received at Baptism (Acts 19:2, 6; 2:38), and those baptized become brothers and sisters of Jesus; they are incorporated into the Body of Christ as members of his Church. "For in the one Spirit we were all baptized into one body—Jews or Greeks, slaves or free—and we were all made to drink of one Spirit" (1 Corinthians 12:13). In essence, those who are baptized become members of the Christian family of God.

In the Sacrament of Baptism, the Church uses important words and symbols to help celebrate and remind people of their new relationship with God as Trinity.

- The person being baptized is immersed in water, or water is poured over the person's head; the water used is called the "matter" of the Sacrament. While the water is poured, the words of Baptism are pronounced: "N., I baptize you in the name of the Father, and of the Son, and of the Holy Spirit." These words are called the "Form of the Sacrament."

- **Water** is a reminder of the waters God created at the beginning of the world, the waters that eventually gave birth to all material forms of life. The baptismal water washes away original sin. Through water it is recalled how God helped the ancient Israelites escape from Egypt, cross the waters of the Red Sea, and later cross the Jordan River to enter the promised land.

- Holy **oil,** called *chrism,* is a reminder that God has chosen and called each one to be his own. The baptized person is anointed with the Holy Spirit and given a mission to live as a follower of Jesus.

- The **candle** is a reminder that Jesus is the light of the world and that all those who are baptized are called to bring his light to others.

- The **white garment** is a reminder of purification and being clothed in Christ, to live in imitation of him.

Let's Talk!

Discuss how people, particularly young people, can be made to feel welcomed to the Church, the Body of Christ, God's family.

Activity

Make or decorate a candle whose shape, symbols, and color express what Baptism means to you.

Celebrating God as Creator

One way that Catholics gather to celebrate God as Creator is in the sacrament of **Matrimony,** or Marriage. This Sacrament at the Service of Communion celebrates the commitment of a man and a woman, both being baptized Christians, to love each other in imitation of the faithfulness that God has shown to humanity throughout history. The man and woman affirm God's image in one another and pray that he will bless their union as a new family in the Church. They also pray that they will be good parents if he wishes them to have children.

Marriage is a holy and equal partnership between a man and a woman. It finds its origins in the Genesis creation stories, as God created man and woman for a sacred partnership—a covenant relationship reflecting his covenant relationship with humankind and reflecting the union between Christ and his Church.

> " 'This at last is bone of my bones
> and flesh of my flesh;
>
> this one shall be called Woman,
> for out of Man this one was taken.'
>
> Therefore a man leaves his father and his mother
> and clings to his wife, and they become one flesh. "
>
> GENESIS 2:23–24

Through marriage, the couple embarks upon a life of commitment to each other and to God to love one another with self-giving love and faithfulness. The grace of the sacrament of Matrimony strengthens the couple to be true and to love each other as Christ loves the Church. The Catholic Church supports them in their promise of fidelity.

Likewise through marriage, the bride and groom share in God's own creativity. Each person of the Trinity helps them carry out their responsibilities. The bishops state: "By its very nature the institution of marriage and married love are ordered to the procreation and education of the offspring and it is in them that it finds its crowning glory" (*Documents of Vatican II*, "The Church in the Modern World," #48). Parents have the duty to pass on their faith to their children. They also have the obligation to provide for the health, safety, and education of their children.

Married couples are a great gift to the Catholic Church, serving it in many ways. Their mutual love and self-giving inspire other Church members to grow in unselfishness and faithfulness. "[B]elieving families are of primary importance as centers of living, radiant faith" (Catechism, #1656). For this reason, the Catholic family is a *domestic church.* It is the place where a new generation receives life, expresses its faith, and grows in holiness.

Rings are often exchanged in marriage. Just as there is no beginning or end to the ring's circle, so there is no beginning or end to God's love for us. Thus there can be no end to a sacramental marriage, a union formed by God.

Let's Talk!

1. What are some ways that married couples can serve the Church?

2. What are the characteristics of a truly sacramental marriage, a union formed by God? (See CCC, #1638)

Activity

Draw a design for a wedding ring that expresses what the Sacrament of Marriage means to you.

PRAYERS OF ADORATION

One kind of prayer is **adoration,** or worship and honor given to God. Recall that the first three commandments deal with worship of and respect for him as the Creator and Sustainer of all that is. When prayers of adoration are prayed, there is affirmation of God as Creator of all. There is an acknowldgement of respect, honor, and reverence of him who is the Creator from the one who is created.

In the earliest prayers of the Bible, the psalms, or *song-prayers,* are examples of prayers of adoration:

> " The LORD is my light and my salvation;
> whom shall I fear? "
>
> PSALM 27:1

> " For with you is the fountain of life;
> in your light we see light. "
>
> PSALM 36:9

> " Bless the LORD, O my soul.
> O LORD my God, you are very great.
> You are clothed with honor and majesty,
> wrapped in light as with a garment. "
>
> PSALM 104:1–2

Other examples of prayers of adoration can be found in the Mass. During the first part of Mass, the Glory to God is prayed. Just before the Great Amen, which is prayed before the Lord's Prayer, the priest prays in adoration: "Through him [Jesus Christ], with him, and in him, in the unity of the Holy Spirit, all glory and honor is yours, Almighty Father, forever and ever." The Doxology, or *Glory to the Father,* and the Lord's Prayer are also prayers of glory and adoration.

God as Father is acknowledged and adored in community but also in the silence of one's heart. Jesus has this to say about private, silent prayer:

> " . . . whenever you pray, go into your room and shut the door and pray to
> your Father who is in secret; and your Father who sees in secret will reward
> you. . . . your Father knows what you need before you ask him. "
>
> MATTHEW 6:6, 8

Growing in trust of God as a good Father and Provider, Creator and Sustainer is an important aspect of the prayer of adoration.

Activity

In the Bible, adoration psalms tend to follow a specific literary structure. Choose one of the adoration psalms listed on the handout your teacher will provide. Show how the psalm follows, or does not follow, the typical literary structure.

1. Read Matthew 6:25–34. What do you think this story is telling us about prayer?

2. Do you think God would be acting as a good Parent and Provider if he allowed us to be lazy and do nothing to better the world? Explain.

Surrender to God

Learning how to trust God—to let him take charge of one's life—requires deep faith. It also requires prayer. On the one hand, we need to realize that God loves us and always wants what is best for us. His will is what is most important—not necessarily something we think we want at the moment. We need to "let go and let God." Instead of worrying or living in fear of the future, we need to surrender ourselves to God's loving plan for us.

Yet, we need to remember that he gave us the duty of stewardship, that is, to do our part in taking care of creation and in helping to build his kingdom. To put it simply, when we pray, we cannot expect God to do all the work for us. There's still work we have to do for ourselves. Prayer doesn't allow us to be lazy.

For example, suppose there is a big test coming up on Friday. Student A prays to God, asking that she will pass the test. But she never studies ahead of time. Student B prays to God, asking that he will pass the same test. And he studies every day that week so he is prepared to take the test. Which person will likely receive a good grade on the test? You guessed it: student B.

Wise people tell us that prayer doesn't change God. He, after all, always knows and wants what is best for us. Instead, prayer changes *us*. Prayer makes us more open to the grace of God the Father, God the Son, and God the Holy Spirit. It opens us up to his will. It helps us do our part, to shoulder our own responsibility in making good things happen.

Activity

After reading the story on page 52, use the handout your teacher will provide to read more about the legacy of César Chávez, especially on Mexican American immigrants. Then, using the Internet or library, do additional research on one of the following topics and present your findings to the class.

- The situation of migrant farm workers in your state
- The number and involvement of Mexican American Catholics in your diocese
- Why it is important that Catholics of all ethnic groups feel that they belong to the Church, and what we can do to help people of all ethnic groups feel welcome?

Faith must be lived!

Your Relationship with God

It is important to act on your prayers—to translate your faith into everyday actions. God calls you to do this in your own way, in the situations in which you find yourself today. If you really believe in him, here is how your life will likely be affected.

1. You will be humble because you will never forget your place before God. You remember that you are the created and that he is the Creator. Your purpose is to serve him, and not the other way around.

2. You will live every day with a sense of thanksgiving for the gift of life, in imitation of Jesus, who always thanked his Father. You are ever mindful that everything you have comes from God, not just from your own efforts.

3. You recognize the human dignity of all people—regardless of age, race, gender, or nationality—that comes to everyone through the power of the Holy Spirit. You believe every person is made in the image and likeness of God and is therefore worthy of respect.

4. You accept your responsibility to take care of the world. You try to make good use of created things, not wasting them. You have a certain detachment from created things because you know they are not God and cannot make you completely happy. You don't worship created things; instead, you worship him alone.

5. You trust God in every circumstance. You truly believe that "all things work together for good for those who love God" (Romans 8:28). He not only created you; he also sustains you through Jesus, his Son, and the gift of the Holy Spirit and helps you reach him—your destiny.

Activity

Using a Bible and your journal, complete the handout your teacher will provide. Bring your journal to the closing prayer.

A PERSON OF FAITH

César Chávez

This Mexican American was born on March 31, 1927, near Yuma, Arizona. The Chávez family lived in unrelenting poverty on a small farm. In 1939 when the Great Depression and unpaid taxes forced them off their land, the family became migrant workers. Migrant fieldwork results in a short, poor, and unhealthy life. The rate of hypertension, diabetes, and infectious disease is higher than in the general population. The per capita income is 50 percent lower than the national average.

The Chávez family traveled through Arizona and California to harvest crops by hand. During this time the family lived in tents or shacks in migrant labor camps. César attended sixty-five different elementary schools because of this nomadic existence, and he dropped out of school after the seventh grade so that he could work in the fields himself.

In 1946 Chávez married another migrant worker, Helen Fabela. Together they raised eight children. In 1952 Chávez met Father Donald McDonnell, who taught him about the Church's social teachings and explained the right of workers to organize. From that time on, Chávez worked day and night to improve the lot of migrant workers by organizing them.

In 1962 with the assistance of Dolores Huerta, Chávez formed the National Farm Workers Association. By 1965 the union had 1,200 members. That same year the National Farm Workers joined the Agricultural Workers Organizing Committee to stage a strike and a boycott against the grape growers in Delano, California. The strike lasted five long years and became the largest agricultural strike in California history.

At the basis of the strike was Chávez's firm belief in the dignity of all people, including the migrant farm workers. The farm workers, he taught, were entitled to decent wages, safe and sanitary working conditions, health insurance, and humane hours. In addition, he worried about the long-term human and environmental impact of the pesticides, herbicides, fungicides, and insecticides used in farming. These beliefs formed "The Cause" ("*La Causa*") to which Chávez dedicated the rest of his life.

During the strike, Chávez worked tirelessly to advocate nonviolence based on the teachings of Jesus and Saint Francis of Assisi. The only weapons Chávez used were public marches, economic boycotts, and volunteer fasting, in addition to daily Mass. In *The Confessions of the Tortilla Priest* (*National Catholic Reporter,* 7 May 1993), Father Victor Salandini quotes Chávez himself: "It is my deepest belief that only by giving our lives do we find life. I am convinced that the truest act of courage . . . is to sacrifice ourselves for others in a totally nonviolent struggle for justice." In fact, in 1967 Chávez led a twenty-five-day march that spanned three hundred miles from Delano, California, to Sacramento. Starting with sixty-five farm workers, the march swelled to ten thousand supporters and made newspaper headlines.

After the strike ended, Chávez's union grew rapidly; it also changed its name to the United Farm Workers Association (UFWA). On April 23, 1993, Chávez died of a heart attack. Over 35,000 mourners were part of the funeral procession.

In the funeral eulogy, Cardinal Roger Mahony said, "Deeply rooted in his Catholic faith and its social teachings, everything César did was underpinned by the strength of the gospel of Jesus Christ. . . . César really believed that God was with him and his band of pioneering organizers. His message to the workers was simple but powerful: God did not intend for them and their families to live and work as human robots, devoid of dignity, decent wages, and benefits most United States workers take for granted. . . . His vision always saw far beyond the immediate obstacles and crosses that he and his workers so often encountered. His faith was deeply grounded in God's words and promises, and like the prophets of old, he spoke truth and justice with penetrating words and images" (*National Catholic Reporter,* 7 May 1993).

Celebrating Faith

Opening Song: "Holy Ground"

Leader: Let the light of your face shine on us, O LORD! (Psalm 4:6)

All: **Let the light of your face shine on us, O LORD!**

Reading:

In the beginning was the Word,
  and the Word was with God,
  and the Word was God.

He was in the beginning with God.

All things came into being through him,
  and without him not one thing came into being.

What has come into being in him was life,
  and the life was the light of all people.

The light shines in the darkness,
  and the darkness did not overcome it.

John 1:1–5

In silence, reread the journal entry you made.

Leader: Those who wish may now share their own spontaneous prayer of adoration to God. *(Allow time for sharing.)*

Leader: Let us conclude our prayer with the prayer our Lord taught us: Our Father...

Review

1. How can the Catholic faith be best described: polytheistic, monotheistic, or atheistic? Why?

2. What are the six traditional attributes of God? What are additional attributes of God? Do these attributes adequately describe God? Why?

3. What does it mean to say that God is Father?

4. What does it mean to say that God is Son?

5. What does it mean to say that God is Spirit?

6. What are the first three commandments? What do they tell about humans' relationship and obligations toward God?

7. How does Baptism celebrate God as Trinity?

8. How does Marriage celebrate God as Creator?

9. What is a prayer of adoration?

10. How does belief in God affect a person's life?

WORDS OF FAITH

adoration—worship and honor given to God as Creator and Sustainer of all that is

angels—created beings who are pure spirits with intelligence and free will, but without bodies, who act as God's messengers

atheism—the belief that there is no God

Baptism—the sacrament of new life in God and of incorporation into the Church performed with water and the words, "I baptize you in the name of the Father, and of the Son, and of the Holy Spirit"; the first Sacrament of Initiation

creationism—the theory that the Genesis story in the Bible is literally true, that God created the universe and everything in it in six days and out of nothing

evolution—a process of continuous change from a simple form to a more complex form. As a theory of the development of life forms, evolution includes the idea, for example, that apes and humans have a common ancestor.

idolatry—worship of a false god

liturgy—the official public prayer of the Church through which Christ continues the work of redemption through the Church's celebration of the Paschal mystery

Matrimony—a Sacrament at Service of Communion, the sacrament that celebrates the sacred covenant between a baptized man and woman who promise to be faithful to one another until death. Marriage is ordered to the mutual love of the spouses and to the procreation and education of children.

Enrichment

Choose one of the following to present to the class.

1. Saint Patrick used the shamrock or three-leaf clover to explain the Trinity. Create your own symbol for the Trinity by using a model as Saint Patrick did or by drawing a picture. Write a brief explanation of your symbol.

2. Interview your parents about your Baptism. Find out when and where (church, place) you were baptized, who your godparents were, who baptized you, and why you were baptized.

3. Select three of your favorite songs. Write out some of the words from each song, along with the song titles and artists or groups. Explain how each song either represents the values behind the first three commandments or goes against these values.

monotheism—the belief in one God only

original sin—the first decision by humans to disobey God. All people (except Jesus and Mary) are born with original sin, a wounded human nature that is tempted to choose wrong over right.

polytheism—the belief in many gods

sacrament—an effective sign, established by Jesus and given to his Church, by which God shares his life through the work of the Holy Spirit

salvation—God's action accomplished through Jesus of freeing people from sin and restoring them to friendship with God

stewardship—the responsibility God gave humans to take care of the earth and everything in it

Ten Commandments—the ten fundamental moral laws given by God to his people and recorded in the Old Testament

CHAPTER THREE

Light of the World

> "Again Jesus spoke to them, saying, 'I am the light of the world. Whoever follows me will never walk in darkness but will have the light of life.'"
>
> JOHN 8:12

In this chapter you will:

- recognize Jesus as the Son of God, fully divine and fully human.

- discover what Scripture records about the childhood and public life of Jesus.

- describe true obedience to God's commandments as involving a sincere attitude as well as actions.

- see how the Church incorporates the New Testament letters and Gospels in the Mass.

- learn how to pray using Scripture, in particular the Gospels.

- discuss the meaning of the Beatitudes.

WORDS OF FAITH

Annunciation	gospel	kingdom of God
Assumption	holiness	Mary
Beatitudes	Immaculate Conception	reconcile
Christ	Incarnation	Transfiguration
Epiphany	Jesus	

MEETING GOD IN JESUS

Christian faith differs from the faith of Muslims, Jews, Buddhists, Hindus, and other non-Christians in that it centers on a person—Jesus Christ of Nazareth, the Son of God and the second Person of the Trinity.

Jesus is the Son of God. Jesus is true God and true man. His divinity does not take away from his humanity, and his humanity does not take away any of his divine nature. As the Catechism says, "He became truly man while remaining truly God" (CCC, #464). Scripture reveals that God the Father and God the Son have a unique relationship. The Son is the only begotten of the Father. The voice of God the Father calls Jesus his "beloved son" at the transfiguration (Matthew 3:17, 17:5). In John, Jesus refers to himself as the "only son of God" (John 3:16, 10:36).

Historical records indicate that Jesus really walked the earth. He was born an Israelite, a descendant of King David of the tribe of Judah. His mother was Mary; his foster father was Joseph. He was born in the town of Bethlehem around 4 B.C.—while Herod the Great was king of Judea and Caesar Augustus was emperor of the Roman Empire. Jesus died in Jerusalem around A.D. 30 when Pontius Pilate was procurator (a Roman governor) in Judea.

Research

Using the list of suggested Internet or library resources provided by your teacher, find out more about the time of Jesus by researching one of the following topics. Be prepared to present your findings in class.

- Herod the Great
- Caesar Augustus
- Pontius Pilate
- Life in first-century Palestine
- Bethlehem, Nazareth, the sea of Galilee, and Jerusalem

Jerusalem today.

ONE SOLITARY LIFE

By most human standards, Jesus could be considered a failure. And yet in today's world, over two billion people place their faith in him. Think about the improbability of that happening! As James Allen Francis, a Baptist minister, once noted:

Here is a man who was born in an obscure village, the child of a peasant woman. He grew up in another obscure village. He worked in a carpenter shop until He was thirty, and then for three years was an itinerant preacher.

He never wrote a book. He never held an office. He never owned a home. He never had a family. He never went to college. He never put his foot inside a big city. He never traveled two hundred miles from the place where He was born. He never did one of the things that usually accompany greatness. He had no credentials but himself. . . .

While [He was] still a young man, the tide of popular opinion turned against Him. His friends ran away. One of them denied Him. Another betrayed Him. He was turned over to His enemies. He went through the mockery of a trial. He was nailed upon the cross between two thieves. While He was dying, His executioners gambled for the only piece of property He had on earth—His coat. When He was dead, He was taken down and laid in a borrowed grave through the pity of a friend.

. . . wide centuries have come and gone, and today He is the center of the human race and the leader of the column of progress.

I am far within the mark when I say that all the armies that ever marched, all the navies that were ever built, all the parliaments that ever sat, and all the kings that ever reigned—put together—have not affected the life of [humans] upon the earth as powerfully as has this one solitary life.

Dr. James Allen Francis, "Jesus—A Brief Life." A sermon first delivered at the First Baptist Church of Los Angeles on July 11, 1926. Reprinted in Dr. James Allen Francis, The Real Jesus and Other Sermons (Philadelphia, PA: Judson Press, 1926).

Let's Talk!

1. What is your description of a successful adult in today's society? What is your description of a successful teen in today's society? What do you think Jesus would say about your idea of success?

2. In view of the essay on this page, how should someone's success or failure be determined? Why?

Winner of the "Jesus 2000" art contest: "Jesus of the People" by Janet McKenzie.

Reflection

1. How can you find Jesus in a person who is homeless? Explain.

2. How can you find Jesus in a criminal on death row? Explain.

3. Who is the one person who has made the most difference in your life—for good or for bad? Why?

Making a Difference

There are various reasons why Jesus—a relatively obscure person who lived in an era without rapid transportation or communication—became so influential. One reason is that his followers witnessed his being truly raised from the dead by God the Father. Even though Jesus died, he was seen by his disciples after his Resurrection. They knew that he had really risen from the dead. Jesus' Resurrection drew them, as well as many other people, to a deepened faith life. Another reason is the actual message Jesus taught. His message was not just something people needed to hear; it changed them in revolutionary ways. It made a real, positive difference in people's lives. That is why Jesus' message of the kingdom of God and salvation is called the **gospel,** or "good news." Jesus taught that each person is important and loved by God. Still another reason for Jesus' influence is the miracles he performed, which are a sign that he is the Son of God.

To appreciate the overwhelming significance of Jesus' teaching about the value of every person, we have to reflect a bit further. Consider this: According to the 2000 census, there were approximately 281.4 million people in the United States, these among billions of other people make up the world population. With all these people, one individual might seem very unimportant and insignificant. And yet Jesus tells us that God knows and loves each of us individually. Each person truly matters in God's eyes.

Jesus' life, death, and Resurrection indicate what a difference one person can make in the course of human history—and his story doesn't end there. As the Son of God, Jesus assures us that if we have faith in him, we too can make a lasting difference in the world. "For truly I tell you, if you have faith the size of a mustard seed, you will say to this mountain, 'Move from here to there,' and it will move; and nothing will be impossible for you" (Matthew 17:20–21). "Very truly, I tell you, the one who believes in me will also do the works that I do and, in fact, will do greater works than these" (John 14:12).

Believing in Jesus is a lot more than just believing in ideas about him. Believing in Jesus means having a personal relationship with him. It is about responding to the gift of his divine love. Responding to Jesus' love for us leads to a greater appreciation for our own worth. Believing in Jesus means understanding and believing in ourselves—and that, in turn, means acting like Jesus—letting ourselves become instruments of God the Father's love in the world. It means growing to appreciate the Holy Spirit, who is the love between the Father and the Son. Instead of being paralyzed with fear or feelings of inferiority, we are emboldened by faith to act without hesitation. We are able to love others in new ways because we are first able to *love ourselves.* We can become an example of faith, hope, and love, as Jesus is. We can make a difference.

WHO IS JESUS?

In order to follow Jesus' example and to become more like him, we need to get to know him. The New Testament is our primary source for information about Jesus. The first books in the New Testament to be written were the epistles, or letters, all written between A.D. 50 and A.D. 100. Paul, the author of many of the letters, does not include facts about the historical Jesus. For example, Paul does not tell us how tall Jesus was, what he looked like, or what he liked to eat. Instead, Paul writes about Jesus from the point of view of faith.

First, Paul says that Jesus is the Savior whom, from the beginning of time, God promised to send. The name *Jesus* (*Yesuah* in Jesus' language, Aramaic) means "God saves." Jesus is the full revelation of God's saving love. The title *Christ* (from the Greek *Christos*) means "Anointed One" (Messiah).

Jesus is the Messiah whom, from the time of the Fall, God promised to send. Jesus renews God's covenant of love with humanity; he saves people from the power of sin and eternal death. Through his life, suffering, death, and Resurrection, he restores mankind to friendship and communion with the Trinity. As we read in the Letter to the Ephesians:

What are the symbols for Christ in this illustration?

“ In him [Christ] we have redemption through his blood, the forgiveness of our trespasses, according to the riches of his [God's] grace that he lavished on us. With all wisdom and insight he [God] has made known to us the mystery of his will, according to his good pleasure that he set forth in Christ, as a plan for the fullness of time, to gather up all things in him, things in heaven and things on earth. ”

EPHESIANS 1:7–10

Second, Paul states that Jesus is *Lord*. Along with being truly man, he is truly God. Jesus is the only Son of God. Jesus is the second Person of the Holy Trinity. He is God himself.

“ . . . God . . . gave him the name
that is above every name,
so that at the name of Jesus
every knee should bend,
in heaven and on earth and under the earth,

and every tongue should confess
that Jesus Christ is Lord,
to the glory of God the Father. ”

PHILIPPIANS 2:9–11

When you say that Jesus is *Lord,* you are professing your faith in his divinity.

The Four Gospels

The four Gospels were written after the majority of the letters, about forty to sixty years after the death of Jesus. The purpose of the four Gospels was not to record every detail of Jesus' life. Rather, the Gospel writers tried to give people a better idea of who Jesus was and how he embodied the loving God of the covenant. Like the letters, the Gospels are testaments of faith. They teach that, "Christ did not live his life for himself but *for us*" (Catechism, #519). Each Gospel writer had his own purpose and audience in mind.

To understand how the Gospels differ from one another and yet still record the truth about Jesus, consider the passages in the following chart. The Gospel according to Matthew answers the question of Jesus' identity with a story. The Gospel according to Mark presents the same story a bit differently. The Gospel according to Luke is slightly different still.

The Synoptic Gospels

Matthew 16:13–17	Mark 8:27–30	Luke 9:18–21
Now when Jesus came into the district of Caesarea Philippi, he asked his disciples, "Who do people say that the Son of Man is?" And they said, "Some say John the Baptist, but others Elijah, and still others Jeremiah or one of the prophets." He said to them, "But who do you say that I am?" Simon Peter answered, "You are the Messiah, the Son of the living God." And Jesus answered him, "Blessed are you, Simon son of Jonah! For flesh and blood has not revealed this to you, but my Father in heaven."	*Jesus went on with his disciples to the villages of Caesarea Philippi; and on the way he asked his disciples, "Who do people say that I am?" And they answered him, "John the Baptist; and others Elijah; and still others, one of the prophets." He asked them, "But who do you say that I am?" Peter answered him, "You are the Messiah." And he [Jesus] sternly ordered them not to tell anyone about him.*	*Once when Jesus was praying alone, with only the disciples near him, he asked them, "Who do the crowds say that I am?" They answered, "John the Baptist; but others, Elijah; and still others, that one of the ancient prophets has arisen." He said to them, "But who do you say that I am?" Peter answered, "The Messiah of God." He [Jesus] sternly ordered and commanded them not to tell anyone,. . .*

The Gospel according to John does not include this story. John answers the question, "Who do you say I am?" by various "I AM" statements of Jesus. "I am the bread of life" (John 6:35). "I am the light of the world" (John 8:12).

The details in these Scripture passages vary. In Matthew and Mark, Jesus is on his way to Caesarea Philippi; in Luke, he is praying in solitude with his disciples. In Matthew, Peter calls Jesus "the Messiah, the Son of the living God." In Mark, he calls Jesus "the Messiah." In Luke, he calls Jesus "The Messiah of God." In John, Peter is not even present when Jesus explains who he is.

These differences occur because each Gospel writer is writing to different people and wishes to emphasize something in particular. The Gospels according to Matthew, Mark, and Luke are called *synoptic* Gospels. Matthew and Luke seem to rely on Mark and on another common source. All three reflect definite similarities in presenting Jesus' life and teaching. About 80 percent of Mark is used in some form in Matthew and about 65 percent of Mark in Luke. Scripture scholars believe that there was a common source, or were common sources, for these Gospels. The Gospel according to John, on the other hand, seems to have been written independently. Its focus is on the divinity of Jesus rather than on a synopsis of his life.

It is essential to remember that the details are not as important as the overall revealed message: Jesus is the Messiah, the Son of God.

Research

1. Using the introduction to the Gospels in the Bible, research the background of each of the Gospels. Make a chart of the following information. Who wrote it? When was it written? For whom was it written? How does this Gospel present Jesus, that is, what does this Gospel seem to emphasize about Jesus? Why might that be the emphasis? Be prepared to present your findings in class.

2. Using a Bible, compare the Gospel accounts of the baptism of Jesus (Matthew 3:13–17, Mark 1:9–11, Luke 3:21–22, John 1:29–34). How are the accounts the same? How are they different? What do you think is their overall message regarding the identity of Jesus?

3. Using a Bible, compare the Gospel accounts of the temptations of Jesus in the desert (Matthew 4:1–11, Mark 1:12–13, Luke 4:1–13). How are they the same? How are they different? What do you think is their overall message regarding the human and divine nature of Jesus?

Activity

Write about or visually present your depiction of who Jesus is for you.

TRUE GOD, TRUE MAN

Let's Talk!

1. Cite an example of someone in today's world whom you consider holy. Why do you think this?

2. How can teens today be holy—living a life of loving kindness—without seeming weird or overly devout?

We call the mystery whereby the Son of God, while remaining God, became man through the **Incarnation.** This word means, "to become flesh, to take on a human body." The Incarnation is a great and awesome mystery. God's plan of salvation reached its fulfillment in Jesus. Jesus remained true God while becoming true man. Jesus becomes "the light of the world" (John 8:12).

As it is written in the Gospel according to John: "For God so loved the world that he gave his only Son, so that everyone who believes in him may not perish but may have eternal life. Indeed, God did not send the Son into the world to condemn the world, but in order that the world might be saved through him" (John 3:16–17).

So, why did the divine Son of God choose to become human? The Catechism in #s 457–460 lists four major reasons:

1. The Son of God (also called the Word of God) became man in order to *"save us by reconciling us with God."* The word *reconcile* means "to bring together again in harmony." Ever since original sin entered the world, humans have tended to sin and have not "been right" with God. Jesus is our mediator, restoring us to friendship with God.

2. "The Word became flesh *so that thus we might know God's love."* Through the life and teachings of Jesus, we learn the meaning and magnitude of God's unconditional love. He *always* loves us and is always ready to forgive us when we sin.

3. Jesus became incarnate *"to be our model of holiness."* The word *holiness* implies a state of becoming more like God, living in his presence or with his love. By the example of his life, Jesus taught us what it means to have a loving relationship with God and other people.

4. The Son of God became man in order to make us *"partakers of the divine nature"* (see 2 Peter 1:4). In other words, Jesus enables us to become sharers in his divinity—the life and love of the Holy Trinity. We share in his divinity when we live in God's grace, participate in the Church's sacraments, and experience moments of oneness with God.

The bishops of Vatican II wrote, "… it is only in the mystery of the Word made flesh that the mystery of humanity truly becomes clear" (*Documents of Vatican II,* "The Church in the Modern World," #22). Because of Jesus, we know how "to be right" with God, with other people, and with ourselves.

The Announcement of the Incarnation

Have you ever really liked someone? If so, you probably found yourself becoming curious about this person's life history. Where was he or she born? Where did the family live? What schools did he or she attend? What experiences did the person have? People in the early Church had the same curiosity about Jesus. They knew about his teachings and actions as an adult. But what was he like as a child?

The writer of the Gospel according to Luke was writing for non-Jewish people who had never met Jesus. They were especially curious about who Jesus was and how he lived. So this writer started at the beginning—not with the birth of Jesus, but with Jesus' conception. The writer began by describing the **Annunciation** —the announcement by the angel Gabriel that, through the power of the Holy Spirit, **Mary,** though a virgin, was to be the Mother of the Son of God, who would be called Jesus.

In the Gospel according to Luke, Mary does not understand why God has chosen her for this honor or how the events will take place, since she is not yet married and is a virgin. As Gabriel explains to her, "nothing will be impossible with God" (Luke 1:37). Despite her fears, Mary responds with heartfelt faith to God's invitation. "Here am I, the servant of the Lord; let it be with me according to your word" (Luke 1:38). And at that moment, Mary conceived Jesus in her womb!

The writer of the Gospel according to Luke was not present at the Annunciation. When writing about the conception of Jesus, the Holy Spirit inspired the author of Luke to explore the event in a way that would help people understand how Jesus could be both true God and true man.

The account of the Annunciation in the Gospel according to Luke also lays the foundation for many of the Church's teachings about Mary herself.

- Mary is truly the Mother of God, since Jesus is God himself who became man.
- God favored Mary in a special way by preserving her from all stain of original sin from the first moment of her conception. We call this belief the **Immaculate Conception.**
- Mary remained sinless throughout her life.
- At the end of her life, sometime after the death and Resurrection of Jesus, Mary was "taken up into heaven" in body and soul. We call this the **Assumption** of Mary.

Christian faith is to be like the faith of Mary. Christians are to follow Jesus wholeheartedly throughout life, as Mary did. Mary is a model of faithfulness.

Activities

1. Read the Annunciation story in the Bible (Luke 1:26–38). Rewrite the story using modern-day language or draw or paint a modern version of the story. Be prepared to share your Annunciation story with the class.

2. Make a chart comparing the Annunciation story (Luke 1:26–38) with the birth of Abraham and Sarah (Genesis 16 and 18), Elkanah and Hannah (1 Samuel 1–2), Zechariah and Elizabeth (Luke 1:5–25). What is special about the birth of Jesus that sets it apart (and above) the other births?

JESUS' BIRTH AND CHILDHOOD

The Church celebrates the Nativity, or birth, of Jesus each year on December 25, although this date is most likely not his actual birth date. In the early Church, this date was selected for Christmas when Christianity was spreading throughout the Roman Empire and becoming more accepted. Christmas replaced an ancient Roman feast of the Sun celebrated on December 25 to honor the "triumph" of light over darkness at the winter solstice. At Christmas, Christians celebrate the birth of Jesus, the true Light that overcame the world's darkness.

Of the four Gospels, only those according to Matthew and Luke give a glimpse into the birth and childhood of Jesus. Remember, the purpose of these accounts was to answer people's questions about Jesus' identity rather than to present a factual day-by-day account of historical events. Here is a brief outline of what can be found in the Gospel according to Luke concerning Jesus' birth and childhood:

- Jesus was born in a humble stable. His birth was announced to ordinary shepherds. Although he descended from the royal family of King David, Jesus was born into a simple family—demonstrating God's special love for those who are poor and oppressed *(see Luke 2:1–20)*.

- According to Jewish law, Mary and Joseph had Jesus circumcised on the eighth day after his birth *(see Luke 2:21)*. Since the time of Abraham, the circumcision of males had been a sign of membership in God's people. Circumcision was a reminder of God's covenant with his people *(see Genesis 17:9–14)*.

- After the birth of Jesus, God revealed to people other than the Jews, represented by the magi who were wise men from the East, that Jesus was the long-promised Messiah, Son of God, and Savior of the World. This revelation is called the **Epiphany.** The Church in the East celebrates the feast of the Epiphany on January 6. In the West, Catholics celebrate the Epiphany on the first Sunday after New Year's Day. Matthew tells the story of how wise men from the East followed a star to Bethlehem and found the baby Jesus *(see Matthew 2:1–12).* This story links back to ancient prophecies regarding the Messiah:

> " The people who walked in darkness
>   have seen a great light;
>   those who lived in a land of deep darkness—
>   on them light has shined. "
>
> ISAIAH 9:2; SEE MATTHEW 4:16.

- Mary and Joseph were faithful Jews. They fulfilled the Jewish requirements of purification. Forty days after Jesus' birth, they presented him at the temple in Jerusalem and offered sacrifices for the purification. There, as seen in the Gospel according to Luke, they met a man named Simeon *(see Luke 2:22–38).*

- The Holy Family fled to Egypt to escape persecution. In the Gospel according to Matthew, the story of the flight into Egypt connects Jesus with the ancient Israelites who were persecuted in Egypt *(see Matthew 2:13–23).* Just as God chose Moses to liberate the ancient Israelites, so God chose his Son to liberate all God's people from the slavery of sin.

Research

1. Make two columns on a piece of paper, and title one column *Matthew* and the other one *Luke*. Compare the accounts of the birth of Jesus in Matthew and in Luke (Matthew 1:18–25 and Luke 2:1–20) by listing the important points in each account. How are the accounts the same? How are the accounts different?

2. Read the account of the Epiphany to the magi in the Gospel according to Matthew (Matthew 2:1–12). Using a Bible and the Internet or library, explain the symbols found in the story (star of Bethlehem, the wise men, Bethlehem, gold, frankincense, myrrh). Be prepared to discuss in class what you think to be the overall message of the story.

FINDING JESUS IN THE TEMPLE

Mary, Joseph, and Jesus returned from Egypt to live in Nazareth. We do not know much about those years of Jesus' life, sometimes called the hidden years. We do learn from the Gospel according to Luke that they traveled to Jerusalem each year for the feast of Passover. When Jesus was twelve, he followed the custom of traveling with relatives and friends to Jerusalem. When it was time to return to Nazareth, the boy Jesus stayed behind without Mary and Joseph knowing this. Upon discovering that Jesus was not in the caravan, Mary and Joseph returned to find him in the temple talking with the teachers.

"Finding Jesus in the Temple" by William Holman Hunt (Birmingham City Gallery and Museum, England).

" And all who heard him were amazed at his understanding and his answers. When his parents saw him they were astonished; and his mother said to him, "Child, why have you treated us like this? Look, your father and I have been searching for you in great anxiety." He said to them, "Why were you searching for me? Did you not know that I must be in my Father's house?" But they did not understand what he said to them. Then he went down with them and came to Nazareth, and was obedient to them. His mother treasured all these things in her heart. And Jesus increased in wisdom and in years, and in divine and human favor. "

LUKE 2:47–52

This story shows a continued love and obedience to Mary and Joseph. By loving and obeying Mary and Joseph, Jesus illustrates how to observe the fourth commandment to honor one's father and mother. By loving and obeying Mary and Joseph, Jesus began at a very early age to show us the way to live with respect and dignity. Begin today to follow in the footsteps of Jesus by showing that same kind of love and obedience to your parents and guardians.

Jesus taught his disciples the importance of observing and following the Ten Commandments, the first three of which focus on loving God above all other persons and things. The fourth through the tenth commandments call us to love other people. The fourth commandment requires that we begin first with those closest to us—our parents and guardians.

Let's Talk!

1. What does the story of Jesus in the temple at age twelve say to teens today?

2. How can teens imitate Jesus in their attitudes and actions, especially toward their parents?

3. What can you do to show obedience to your parents or guardians? Give specific examples.

THE PUBLIC LIFE OF JESUS

All four Gospels recount events in the public life of Jesus, but not every event is recorded in all four Gospels. Although Jesus' public life did not begin until he was about thirty, his whole life was a continual teaching about God's existence, his plan for humanity, and his unconditional love. Jesus was a teacher and preacher, bringing the good news of God's love and salvation to all. Jesus was an advocate for those who were poor or marginalized in society. He was a healer and reconciler, curing people of their sicknesses and forgiving their sins. He did miraculous deeds that only God can do.

Jesus' public ministry began with his baptism with water by John the Baptist in the Jordan River. This baptism is not the same as the Sacrament of Baptism, but it was a sign of a person's willingness to turn from sin and toward God. Even though Jesus was without sin, he desired to be baptized, for in the baptism of Jesus the Holy Spirit reveals Jesus as God's Son.

"There was a man sent from God, whose name was John. He came as a witness to testify to the light, so that all might believe through him. He himself was not the light, but he came to testify to the light. The true light, which enlightens everyone, was coming into the world. "

JOHN 1:6–9

After his baptism, Jesus was tempted in the desert. The temptation in the desert demonstrates the way Jesus truly is the Messiah, in opposition to Satan's proposals. In the temptation, the vanquishing of the tempter for us is already taking place in the person of Jesus Christ. Unlike Adam, however, who gave in to temptation, Christ is totally obedient to his Father's will. Unlike all other humans, Jesus remains sinless throughout life.

Activity

Do a dramatization or electronic slide presentation depicting the temptations of Jesus. Give examples of the meaning of the temptations for modern-day Christians.

Jesus' Saving Actions

Jesus worked miracles to show God's love. To understand the significance of Jesus' actions, we first need to understand what a miracle is. A miracle is "a sign or wonder, such as a healing or the control of nature, which can only be attributed to divine power" (Catechism, glossary). The miracles recorded in the Bible need to be viewed from the perspective of faith.

In the days of Jesus, a miracle was considered a "sign" of God's power, love, and presence. When the Gospel writers record that Jesus worked miracles, they are saying that something extraordinary was happening through Jesus. God the Father's power was at work in Jesus. Jesus made him real to people in ways they had never before experienced. The Gospel writers are also affirming that Jesus is divine, for only God has the power to work miracles. Jesus' miracles can be classified into four types.

Jesus raised his friend Lazarus back to life.

Healing miracles	Exorcisms	Raising the dead	Nature miracles
Someone is cured of illness or a disability through the action of Jesus. One example is Jesus healing the ten lepers. (See Luke 17:12–19.)	In an exorcism, the devil (or an evil spirit) is driven out of a possessed person. An example of this type of miracle is Jesus' healing of a boy with a demon. (See Matthew 17:14–21, Mark 9:14–29, and Luke 9:37–43.)	In this type of miracle, a dead person is restored to life. Eventually the person will die again. The most well-known miracle is Jesus bringing Lazarus back to life, found in John 11:1–44.	In this type of miracle, Jesus shows that he has power over nature itself, such as when he calms the storm. (See Matthew 8:23–27, Mark 4:35–41, and Luke 8:22–25.)

The Gospels record many miracles, and a list of these miracles and where they can be found in the Gospels is included in the Catholic Source Book (page 235). The Gospel writers included numerous miracles in their Gospels to get across a basic truth: that Jesus is the Son of God and that something amazing happened in and through the life of Jesus.

Many people do understand the message of Jesus' miracles. They see God's loving presence not only in the miracles of the Bible but also in the events of the modern-day world. As one contemporary author explains, "If you truly have faith in God, you do not need a miracle as proof of anything. If you do not have faith, no seemingly miraculous event will persuade you that faith makes sense." God continually loves us and cares for us. He *does* act in our lives in miraculous ways. For him, nothing is impossible with God.

Let's Talk!

1. What is your attitude toward miracles?

2. How do miracles help people believe in God?

3. Do you believe in God's love, whether or not you have experienced a miracle? Explain.

The Messiah and Son of God

Jesus revealed himself as God—the Messiah and the Son of God. All four Gospels record that Jesus acknowledges his divine and human nature. The early Church knew him to be the Son of Man, the Son of God, and the promised Messiah of God. In one incident Jesus reveals himself to his disciples as light and glory—two aspects of his divinity.

> " Jesus took with him Peter and James and his brother John and led them up a high mountain, by themselves. And he was transfigured before them, and his face shone like the sun, and his clothes became dazzling white. "
>
> MATTHEW 17:1–2

As we noted in the previous chapter, the event in which Jesus reveals his divine glory to his Apostles is called the **Transfiguration.** The Church celebrates this feast on August 6. In the Transfiguration, the Apostles get a foretaste of the Risen Lord in all his glory, but at the time they fail to understand what it means. It is only after the Resurrection of Jesus that they come to understand the full significance of the Transfiguration. The clouds, light, glorious whiteness, and mountain are traditional biblical symbols of the tangible presence of God.

In addition to the witness of the Gospels and the letters, another New Testament book—the Acts of the Apostles—attests to the Apostles' and disciples' faith in Jesus. "And every day in the temple and at home they did not cease to teach and proclaim Jesus as the Messiah" (Acts 5:42). "Therefore let the entire house of Israel know with certainty that God has made him both Lord and Messiah, this Jesus whom you crucified" (Acts 2:36). Over the centuries, this message has been heard. It is now our turn to embrace this part of the Church's creed and pass it along to others: "Jesus Christ . . . is Lord of all" (Acts 10:36).

Activities

1. Do a dramatic presentation of one of the miracles of Jesus found in Scripture. Discuss the experience from the perspective of each of the persons involved in the miracle.

2. Read the Scripture readings for the feast of the Transfiguration (Daniel 7:9–10, 13–14; Psalm 97:1–2, 5–6, 9; 2 Peter 1:16–19; and Matthew 17:1–9). Draw or sketch the readings and put the illustrations into four panels, side-by-side. After studying the illustrations, tell how all the readings are connected. What do you think is their essential message? What is the significance of this feast for your life?

TEACHER AND PREACHER

Jesus taught people about God's love and how they could live in the **kingdom of God.** He did this especially through stories called *parables*. In the Gospels according to Matthew, Mark, and Luke, there are fifty-three passages that may be classified as parables. The list would be longer if every figurative expression of Jesus were included. Basically, Jesus described the kingdom of God, not as a geographic place or an earthly kingdom, but as a relationship with God and other people that is one of justice, love, and peace. Here are four key points Jesus made about God's kingdom:

The message of Jesus is proclaimed at every liturgy.

- ". . . the kingdom of God has come near" (Mark 1:14). The kingdom of God is a central teaching of Jesus. The kingdom is present in him. Jesus reveals God's kingdom through his life, death, and Resurrection. The kingdom is present whenever God is present, especially in the Eucharist and the Church. You can live in God's kingdom when you show love for him and other people in your daily life. His kingdom is present incompletely now and will be realized fully at the end of time.

- God calls everyone to enter the kingdom, people of all nations, those who are poor, lowly, and sinners. According to Jesus, his kingdom especially belongs to those who are poor and lowly. These people are without worldly influence or the means to protect themselves against injustice and oppression. Jesus teaches that anyone wishing to enter the kingdom must first show an active love toward those who are poor.

- To enter the kingdom of God, one must truly seek it. Words are not enough; deeds are required *(see Matthew 21:28–32)*. Faith in God calls us to make a radical choice. We must not only turn away from sin; sometimes we must also sacrifice earthly goods in order to follow Jesus. We must "sell all" in order to purchase the "pearl of great price."

- We can gain access to the kingdom of God through the Church. Jesus gives the keys to God's kingdom to Peter, who is to be the leader of his Church *(see Matthew 16:19, 18:18)*.

Activities

1. Use magazine pictures to make a collage that expresses what the kingdom of God is to you.
2. Read and discuss each of the parables assigned. Then, based on your understanding of the parable, make a list of modern symbols that describe the kingdom of God. (A symbol is something that stands for, or represents, something else—a dark cloud symbolizes a storm, or rain, and so on.)

1. Write about a time when you obeyed a commandment with your actions but not in your words or attitude. What change(s) do you think Jesus is challenging you to make in the future?

2. Why will these changes be easy or difficult for you?

The Implications of Jesus' Teaching

Jesus taught about his Father and the Holy Spirit. He revealed God's plan for salvation. He challenged people to live in a new way—to change their attitudes and behavior.

You have already learned how Jesus restated the first three commandments in terms of loving God with one's whole heart and soul. He also taught the fourth through the tenth commandments:

4. Honor your father and your mother.
   - Respect and obey parents, guardians, and others who have proper authority.
5. You shall not kill.
   - Respect and protect your life and the lives of others.
6. You shall not commit adultery.
   - Be faithful to spouses, friends, and family
   - Respect God's gift of sexuallity, and practice the virtue of chastity.
   - Learn to appreciate the gift of sexuality by practicing self-mastery.
   - Be aware of sins contrary to chastity: masturbation, fornication, pornography, and homosexual acts.
7. You shall not steal.
   - Respect the things that belong to others.
   - Share what you have with those in need.
8. You shall not bear false witness against your neighbor.
   - Be honest and truthful.
   - Avoid bragging.
   - Don't say untruthful or negative things about others.
9. You shall not covet your neighbor's wife.
   - Don't lust after another person's spouse.
   - Practice modesty in thoughts, words, dress, and actions.
10. You shall not covet your neighbor's goods.
    - Rejoice in others' good fortune.
    - Don't be jealous of others' possessions.
    - Don't be greedy.

Jesus summarized the overall message of the fourth through tenth commandments by saying, "You shall love your neighbor as yourself" (Matthew 22:39). In other words, if we truly have faith, we will love God. If we truly love God, we will love other people as much as we love ourselves.

Activity

Formulate a list of questions that teens could use to examine their conscience in terms of the fourth through tenth commandments.

"Rich Man Who Went Away Sorrowful" by Heinrich Hoffman.

Research

1. One day a rich young man approached Jesus. He wanted to know what he had to do to gain eternal life. Read Matthew 19:16–26.

2. Discuss:
   • Think about the story of the rich young man. Do you think Jesus is saying that rich people cannot get into God's kingdom? Explain.
   • What "riches" in the lives of today's teens might be considered obstacles to God's kingdom? Why?

Living One's Faith

The rich young man was both surprised and disturbed by Jesus' words. If he was like most people in those days, he believed that God favored him by giving him riches. However, Jesus was saying that entrance into God's kingdom is not at all related to one's economic situation in life. Nor is it dependent on merely external observance of the Ten Commandments. A modern-day business executive, for example, might seem righteous because he or she doesn't steal money from the company, but that person may be getting rich by exploiting people in other countries, hiring them to work for ridiculously low pay.

Jesus taught us that God wants us to obey the commandments with our actions *and also* with our hearts. That means that keeping the fourth through the tenth commandments should lead to greater love of others. A commitment to honesty rather than stealing should extend to genuine concern for the people employed. Obedience to parents should include words and an inner attitude of sincerity.

Indeed, salvation is about holiness and wholeness. Christianity is a religion about complete personal involvement. Jesus invites all to follow him, to enter into a *relationship* with him, just as the Apostles did. Christians are to make Jesus a priority in their lives by making love of others a priority. Such love means more than giving alms to people who are poor; it also means becoming involved in charitable work. It means giving of oneself, as Jesus gave of himself. That is what Jesus meant when he said, ". . . and if anyone forces you to go one mile, go also the second mile" (Matthew 5:41). "Just as I have loved you, you also should love one another" (John 13:34).

Reflection

Imagine that you are the rich young man in the story. What "riches," possessions, or dreams would you find difficult to give up in order to follow Jesus more completely?

— THE SCRIPTURES PROCLAIMED —

In Scripture, "God speaks to them [humans] in human words" and that "through all the words of Sacred Scripture, God speaks only one single Word, his one [Word] in whom he expresses himself completely"—Jesus Christ (Catechism, #s 101-2). Jesus is the Word of God. For that reason, the letters and Gospels of the New Testament have an important place in Catholic liturgy. Selections from the letters and Gospels are read at every celebration of the Mass and the other sacraments.

The Mass itself has two main parts: the Liturgy of the Word and the Liturgy of the Eucharist. In the Liturgy of the Word, the first main part of the Mass, readings from Scripture are proclaimed; a reading from one of the Gospels is always read.

The Liturgy of the Word at Mass

Before the Liturgy of the Word begins, there are Introductory Rites. The people sing an entrance song as the presider and other liturgical ministers process toward the altar. The presider, or celebrant, is a priest; he is the leader of the assembly, the people who have gathered for the celebration of the Mass. The presider begins the Mass with the Sign of the Cross and greets the assembly. Next there is a penitential rite. The assembly prays that God will send his mercy to those gathered and make them worthy to participate in this holy sacrament. During the penitential rite, the priest may bless and sprinkle the assembly with holy water. More frequently, the assembly prays, "Lord, have mercy." This is followed by a song of praise in the "Glory to God." Then the priest prays an opening prayer.

The Liturgy of the Word begins when a reader goes to the lectern to read a Scripture passage from a special book called the lectionary. The assembly is seated to hear the word of God proclaimed. At Sunday Mass, the first reading is often from the Old Testament, though sometimes from the Acts of the Apostles. At the end of the reading, the reader says, "The Word of the Lord." The assembly responds, "Thanks be to God."

After a brief period of reflection, the cantor (song leader) leads the assembly in a responsorial psalm. The psalm helps those gathered to respond personally to the first reading. During every Sunday Mass and on special feasts, there is a second Scripture reading, usually from one of the New Testament letters.

Next, there is an Alleluia and gospel acclamation. While the assembly sings, the priest may incense the Book of the Gospels. This song and action is a reminder of the importance of the gospel in Christian life. At every Mass, the priest or deacon proclaims a passage from one of the Gospels; the assembly stands in reverence. After reading the Gospel passage, the priest or deacon says, "The gospel of the Lord." The assembly responds, "Praise to you, Lord Jesus Christ." The people then sit as the priest or deacon gives a homily that is a reflection on the meaning of the gospel and how it applies to life today.

The Liturgy of the Word concludes with the Nicene Creed and the general intercessions.

Activities

1. Read the Scripture passages that will be proclaimed at Mass this Sunday. In a small group, discuss what you think God is saying to Christians today through these passages.

2. Write a possible "homily" for teens based on the Scripture readings for this coming Sunday.

Order of Readings

Which Scripture passages are read at Mass is determined by a calendar of readings known as the *Ordo* (this Latin word means "order"). The Catholic Church all over the world follows the same *Ordo,* so that the same readings are read on each day regardless of the country in which the Mass is being celebrated. (Lutherans and Episcopalians also follow this same *Ordo,* with some minor differences.)

The *Ordo* is divided into two main parts, the Sunday readings and the weekday readings. With all the readings in these two parts, the assembly hears a great deal of the Bible over an extended period of time. In short, people learn more about the Bible and what God reveals through it.

The *Ordo* arranges the Sunday readings in a three-year cycle. In Year A, most of the Gospel readings are from the Gospel according to Matthew; in Year B, most are from the Gospel according to Mark; in Year C, most are from the Gospel according to Luke. Readings from the Gospel according to John are spread over all three years. Sunday readings are further divided into the seasons of the Church year: Advent, Christmas, Lent, Triduum, Easter, and Ordinary Time.

The first reading at Sunday Mass correlates with the Gospel passage for that Sunday. This first reading helps those gathered to see the ways God remembered and acted in the lives of his people and how the Old and New Testaments are related. The second reading at Sunday Mass, usually from the New Testament letters, tends to be consecutive in order so that after three years all the letters will have been read.

The *Ordo* arranges the weekday readings in a two-year cycle—Year I and Year II. Usually there are only two readings at weekday Masses. The first reading is either from the Old Testament, a New Testament letter, the Acts of the Apostles, or the Book of Revelation. The second reading is always from one of the Gospels.

There is also a third arrangement found in the *Ordo* that is based on a one-year cycle. This arrangement features the feast days of saints and important events in the life of Jesus, such as the Epiphany and Transfiguration.

Let's Talk!

1. How does your school or parish celebrate the seasons of the Church year?
2. Which saints' feasts does your school or parish celebrate? How are the feasts celebrated?

Activity

Some feasts in the Church year fall on a different date each year. Consult a Church calendar, lectionary, or *Ordo* to find out when the following feasts will occur this school year: Epiphany, Baptism of the Lord, First Sunday of Lent, Easter, Pentecost, and First Sunday of Advent.

JESUS AND SCRIPTURE

The Scriptures do not tell exactly when Jesus prayed each day. But it is clear that he prayed in many different settings and that he experienced an intimate relationship with his Father. Remember, prayer is conversation with God. Jesus, the Son of God, was in constant internal communication with his Father and the Holy Spirit. Thus we can assume that he prayed always.

We learn from the Gospels that one of the ways Jesus prayed was with Scripture. Obviously, Jesus must have first engaged in this type of prayer in early childhood. For by the time he was twelve, he was able to converse knowledgeably with Scripture scholars in the temple in Jerusalem. *(See Luke 2:46.)*

Jesus undoubtedly learned the Scriptures from his parents. Like all devout Jews, the Holy Family probably went to the synagogue each Sabbath (Saturday) to pray and study the Scriptures. The Gospel according to Luke indicates that Jesus continued this practice in adulthood.

"Jesus in the Synagogue" by James J. Tissot.

❝ When he came to Nazareth, where he had been brought up, he went to the synagogue on the sabbath day, as was his custom. He stood up to read, and the scroll of the prophet Isaiah was given to him. He unrolled the scroll and found the place where it was written:

'The Spirit of the Lord is upon me,

because he has anointed me
to bring good news to the poor.

He has sent me to proclaim release to the captives
and recovery of sight to the blind,
to let the oppressed go free,
to proclaim the year of the Lord's favor.'

And he rolled up the scroll, gave it back to the attendant, and sat down. The eyes of all in the synagogue were fixed on him. Then he began to say to them, 'Today this scripture has been fulfilled in your hearing.' All spoke well of him and were amazed at the gracious words that came from his mouth. ❞

LUKE 4:16–22

Jesus not only knew the Hebrew Scriptures and prayed with them, he lived them. He ministered to those who were poor and oppressed, blind and lame—the "rejects" of his society, and he told his followers to do the same.

Throughout the Gospel accounts of Jesus' public ministry, there are many additional references to his love for and familiarity with Scripture. Here are some examples:

- When Jesus encountered the devil in the desert, he quoted Scripture to stand up against temptation.
- In his Sermon on the Mount, Jesus quoted several commandments by heart and interpreted them in terms of sincere love for God and neighbor.
- On several occasions Jesus explained, by his own actions, the true meaning of obeying the Third Commandment.
- Jesus knew the Law of Moses and condemned some of the Pharisees for obeying this law only with their actions and not with their hearts.
- Jesus knew the writings of the prophets, especially those that pertained to the messiah.
- Jesus observed the annual ritual of the Passover meal, which would have included readings from the Book of Exodus.
- Jesus prayed by singing psalms with his disciples.

"Christ Healing the Paralytic at the Pool of Bethesda" by Bartolomé Esteban Murillo, late 1600s

Repeatedly, Jesus explained to his followers that he had not come to abolish the Scriptures (the Law and the prophets), but to fulfill them. He came to teach people what it truly meant to *live* the Scriptures.

Jesus was a teacher like no other. His parables and sayings were both descriptive and challenging. In his Sermon of the Mount, Jesus held the crowds' attention with one of his most famous teachings known as the Beatitudes. The **Beatitudes** are the foundation of Jesus' message and of the Christian life. The word *beatitude* means blessed or happy, and in the Beatitudes Jesus teaches about the meaning and path to true happiness. The Beatitudes depict the attitudes and actions that followers of Christ should have and the way to live in God's kingdom today. They describe the way to attain the eternal holiness or blessedness to which God calls all people. Begin today to reach out to others and to live the values that the Beatitudes demand.

Reflection

On a scale of 1 to 10, how would you rate your present knowledge of the New Testament letters and Gospels? Write down three actions that could help you get to know the New Testament better. Try to follow through on your ideas.

Activity

Work in small groups to find in the Gospels an example of each of the bulleted items in this section. Share your examples with the class.

THE BEATITUDES

Blessed are the poor in spirit,
  for theirs is the kingdom of heaven.

Blessed are those who mourn,
  for they will be comforted.

Blessed are the meek,
  for they will inherit the earth.
Blessed are those who hunger and thirst for righteousness,
  for they will be filled.

Blessed are the merciful,
  for they will receive mercy.

Blessed are the pure in heart,
  for they will see God.
Blessed are the peacemakers,
  for they will be called children of God.
Blessed are those who are persecuted for
    righteousness' sake,
  for theirs is the kingdom of heaven.

MATTHEW 5:3–10

- You depend on God rather than on things, and you believe that helping others is more important than acquiring things.
- You are aware of the sufferings of others and walk with them in their grief; your grieving is not dominated by selfishness.
- You are humble, patient, and gentle with yourself and with others.
- You stand up for what is right and for the rights of others; you work for a more just world and the fullness of God's kingdom.
- You readily forgive others from the heart, refusing to hold a grudge, and you forgive yourself as you seek God's forgiveness and the forgiveness of those you have hurt or harmed.
- You recognize God's image in yourself and in those around you, and you treat others with reverence.
- You live peacefully with others and promote peace between people and groups.
- You make a stand for what you believe in, even when you suffer emotional or physical pain as a result of your decision.

Learning How to Pray with Scripture

For centuries, many Christians have prayed with Scripture. The Church calls this ancient form of prayer *lectio divina* (divine, or spiritual, reading). There are four basic steps in this type of prayer:

1. **Read a specific Scripture passage, especially from a Gospel.** Get to know the passage, the characters, the setting, the circumstances, and so forth. Put yourself in the scene. Make it seem real. Ask yourself: What does the text say literally?

2. **Meditate in a quiet place.** Think about the passage in silence. Ask yourself: What is God saying to me through this passage? What does the text say spiritually? What is its overall message? Become still so that you can hear God speaking to your heart.

3. **Pray simply by talking to God.** Ask yourself: What do I want to say to God in response to this passage? For example, you may wish to adore God. You may wish to thank God for a favor. Or you may wish to ask for something you need.

4. **Act.** Ask yourself: What difference should this passage make in my life? How is it calling me to think, speak, or act in a new way? Once you have identified a plan of action, follow it!

Activity

Make a bookmark with one of the Beatitudes, one that is especially meaningful to you. On the back, write a sentence explaining in your own words the meaning of that Beatitude.

A Faith Testimony

In our own day, many Christians continue to apply the gospel message of Jesus to their daily lives. Among such people is the Most Reverend Patrick E. Flores, at the time of this writing, archbishop of San Antonio, Texas. Here is what he says about prayer and about following Jesus:

" I find God by falling on my knees early in the morning and at the end of the day. In silence I pray, 'Lord, help me to see you more clearly in what I say, in what I do, and in the people whom I meet from day to day.'

I find God in the poor, the abandoned, the elderly, the rejected. I always bear in mind that Jesus has assured us, 'Whatever you do to the least of my brethren you do to me. For I was hungry and you gave me food. I was thirsty and you gave me drink. I was homeless and you took me in. I was naked and you clothed me. I was sick and you cared for me. I was in prison and you visited me.' I find God most of all when I offer a helping hand to people in such circumstances, and I thank God that I am able to find him in the people I meet each day. "

JAMES MARTIN, "HOW CAN I FIND GOD?" *AMERICA* (30 SEPTEMBER 1995).

Here are a few ideas on how you can choose to follow Jesus in your life, especially when it comes to helping those who are poor.

1. Work with others to raise money for a worthy charitable cause. Organize a car wash, bake sale, walkathon, dance, craft show, international food festival, raffle, concert, and so forth. Donate the money to your chosen cause.

2. Exchange letters and information with students from poor or war-torn countries. Remember, such students will probably not have access to computers and e-mail.

3. Contribute ideas for a weekly column in your school newspaper about problems afflicting people around the world.

4. Learn more about worldwide poverty by talking to returned Peace Corps volunteers or young adults who have worked with AmeriCorps or VISTA (Volunteers in Service to America) or one of the many Catholic volunteer organizations.

Let's Talk!

After reading about Katharine Drexel on page 82, discuss the following questions:

What would you do if you inherited a fortune of $1,000 a day? Be honest! How easy or difficult would it be for you to give this money to those who are poor?

Activities

1. Using the handout your teacher will provide, find out more about one of the resources. Compile a list of practical ways teens can help others through this organization. Then contribute your ideas to a class list.

2. Choose one or more projects to help those who are poor, based on your research in Activity 1.

A PERSON OF FAITH

Katharine Drexel

Since the time of Jesus, Christians have attempted to follow in his footsteps. The stories of countless saints attest to these attempts. Their stories too have inspired others to follow Jesus. Through twenty centuries Jesus has called out to saints and sinners alike: "Come, follow me." Here is the story of one woman who accepted that challenge.

Katharine Drexel was born on November 26, 1858, into a wealthy Philadelphia banking family. Her mother died five weeks later. Her father later married a Catholic, who proved to be an excellent mother and role model for Katharine. The Drexels gave time and money to charitable activities. Katharine helped conduct a Sunday school for children during the summer and spent two afternoons a week helping her stepmother serve people who were poor.

When her father and stepmother died in 1885, Katharine and her two sisters inherited a fortune. From the income of their trust fund, they each received $1,000 a day. Katharine took to heart Jesus' teaching: "Love God and love your neighbor. Love others as I have loved them." Katharine decided to apply Jesus' words to the poorest and most oppressed people in the United States and its territories—the African Americans and Native Americans who lived in extreme poverty. At first, she simply donated money. Then she realized personal involvement was also needed.

In 1891 Katharine started her own religious community to help native peoples and blacks. Because of her devotion to Jesus in the Eucharist, she called her community the Sisters of the Blessed Sacrament. These were white religious women who taught the Catholic faith to, and served the needs of, African Americans and Native Americans.

Katharine's work took place in a time when there was a great deal of discrimination against people of minority races. Most people thought that whites should live apart from people of other races. For this reason, Katharine met fierce opposition in her mission to improve the lives of African Americans and Native Americans. But she never faltered in her resolve. Throughout her life, Katharine lived in poverty, spending her entire inheritance—$20 million—on the sisters' work. Here is a brief summary of her work:

- In 1894 she opened St. Catherine's Boarding School for Pueblo Indians in Santa Fe, New Mexico, the first mission school for Native Americans.

- In 1902 she opened St. Michael's School on the Navajo Indian reservation in northeast Arizona. Sixty other schools followed, for Native Americans west of the Mississippi River and for African Americans in the southern part of the United States.

- In 1925 she founded Xavier University in New Orleans, the only Catholic university for African Americans.

In 1935 Katharine had a heart attack and never fully recovered. She retired from her leadership position but continued contributing her time, prayers, and money to the sisters' work. Her health gradually deteriorated, and she was confined to a wheelchair. When she died on March 3, 1955, there were five hundred sisters teaching in sixty-three schools throughout the country. In 1959 the order admitted its first black sister.

In order for the Church to canonize someone as a saint, two miracles must be proved to have occurred through the person's intercession (unless the person was martyred). In 1964 a fourteen-year-old boy was healed from deafness in one ear after his parents prayed to Katharine Drexel. In 1972 a seven-year-old girl who was born deaf also was cured through Katharine's intercession. The Church beatified Katharine (declared her "blessed") on November 20, 1988. She was canonized (recognized as a saint) on October 1, 2000. Her feast day is March 3.

Celebrating Faith

This prayer service follows the basic pattern for the Liturgy of the Word on weekdays.

Opening Song: "With You by My Side"

Leader: Let us begin: In the name of the Father, and of the Son, and of the Holy Spirit.

All: **Amen.**

Leader: Lord Jesus, you are Mighty God and Prince of Peace: Lord, have mercy.

All: **Lord, have mercy.**

Leader: Lord Jesus, you are Son of God and Son of Mary: Christ, have mercy.

All: **Christ, have mercy.**

Leader: Lord Jesus, you are Word made flesh and splendor of the Father: Lord, have mercy.

All: **Lord, have mercy.**

Leader: Lord God Almighty, place in our hearts a desire to please you. Fill our minds with insight into real love, so that all our thoughts may grow in wisdom and all our efforts may be filled with your peace. We ask this through Christ our Lord.

All: **Amen.**

Based on the opening prayer for the Twenty-second Sunday in Ordinary Time.

Reader 1: *Jeremiah 31:31–34*

Response: **Create in me a clean heart, O God.**

Side 1: **Create in me a clean heart, O God,
and put a new and right spirit within me.**

Side 2: **Do not cast me away from your presence,
and do not take your holy spirit from me.** *(Response)*

Side 1: **Restore to me the joy of your salvation,
and sustain in me a willing spirit.**

Side 2: **The sacrifice acceptable to God is a broken spirit;
a broken and contrite heart.** *(Response)*

Psalm 51:10–12, 17

Reader 2: *Matthew 16:13–20*

Leader: Let us share our reflections on what God may be saying to us through these Scripture readings. *(Time for sharing)* Let us now offer our prayers to God, for our own needs and the needs of others. *(Spontaneous petitions and intercessions)* Lord God, we ask you to hear these prayers through the intercession of Jesus Christ and the Holy Spirit.

All: **Amen.**

Review

1. What does the name *Jesus* mean? What does the title *Christ* mean? What does the title *Son of God* mean in reference to Jesus? What does the title *Lord* mean?

2. What are the four Gospels that are included in the New Testament? Why are there differences, and sometimes seeming contradictions, among these Gospels?

3. What is the Incarnation? When does the Church celebrate this mystery of faith?

4. According to the Catechism, what are four major reasons that the Son of God became human?

5. What does the Church teach us about Mary, the mother of Jesus?

6. As told by the writers of the Gospels according to Matthew and Luke, what were the major events in the childhood of Jesus?

7. What are four key points Jesus taught about the kingdom of God?

8. What are miracles? What are the four types of miracles that Jesus worked?

9. What were the Gospel writers showing us about Jesus when they wrote about the Transfiguration?

10. What is the basic outline of the Liturgy of the Word at Mass?

11. What are the four steps to use when praying with Scripture (*lectio divino*)?

12. What are the Beatitudes?

WORDS OF FAITH

Annunciation—the announcement of the angel Gabriel that through the power of the Holy Spirit, Mary, though a virgin, was to be the mother of the Son of God, who would be called Jesus. The Church celebrates the feast of the Annunciation on March 25.

Assumption—the Church teaching that, at the end of her life, Mary, body and soul, was "taken up" (assumed) into heaven. The Church celebrates the feast of the Assumption on August 15.

Beatitudes—Jesus' eight teachings about the meaning and path to true happiness which depict the attitudes and actions that followers of Christ should have and the way to live in God's kingdom today. They describe the way to attain the eternal holiness or blessedness to which God calls all people.

Christ—the Anointed One, the Messiah, Jesus Christ. As Messiah, Jesus restored all people to communion and friendship with God through his life, death, and Resurrection.

Epiphany—a revealing or showing; after Jesus' birth, God revealed to people other than the Jews, represented by the magi, that Jesus was the long-promised Messiah.

gospel—the good news—the message of Christ, the kingdom of God, and salvation. In the New Testament of the Bible, there are four Gospels—Matthew, Mark, Luke, and John—four accounts of Jesus' life, teachings, death, and Resurrection.

Enrichment

Choose one of the following to present to the class.

1. Create a collage, booklet of pictures, or musical presentation that represents each of the Beatitudes. Be sure to identify each picture with the Beatitude it represents.

2. Imagine what Jesus was like as a child. Write a short descriptive essay or do a dramatic presentation about Jesus growing up in Nazareth. What kinds of things interested him? What activities did he enjoy? What challenges did he meet?

3. Choose a saint (perhaps your own patron saint), and read about his or her life using the Internet or library. Find out how Jesus made a difference in the saint's life. How was the saint able to make Jesus present to others? Prepare a presentation for the class.

4. Draw or sketch a picture of one of the events in Jesus' public life: his baptism, temptation, Transfiguration, a miracle, or a teaching. Display your completed work in the classroom.

holiness—a state of becoming more God-like, living in his presence, or with his love

Immaculate Conception—The Church teaching that God favored Mary by preserving her from all stain of original sin from the first moment of her conception.

Incarnation—the Second Person of the Blessed Trinity, while remaining God, assumed a human nature and became man. The Son of God became true man while remaining true God.

Jesus—name that means "God saves"; Jesus of Nazareth is the Savior God sent to redeem people from sin and eternal death.

kingdom of God—God's reign of justice, love, and peace

Mary—the mother of Jesus, thus the Mother of God

reconcile—to restore to friendship. Jesus reconciled all people to God through his life, death, and Resurrection.

Transfiguration—the event in which Jesus reveals his divine glory to his Apostles. This event prefigures or points to the Resurrection of Jesus.

Truth and Light

"[T]he light has come into the world, and people loved darkness rather than light because their deeds were evil. For all who do evil hate the light and do not come to the light, so that their deeds may not be exposed. But those who do what is true come to the light, so that it may be clearly seen that their deeds have been done in God."

JOHN 3:19–21

In this chapter, you will:

- examine your thoughts and attitudes toward the mystery of human suffering.

- recognize that Jesus willingly suffered and died to redeem humanity from the power of sin and eternal death.

- articulate the significance of the different events of the Paschal mystery.

- examine sin, moral decision making, conscience, and virtue.

- explore the liturgies of Holy Week.

- learn the history and spirituality of some traditional prayers.

WORDS OF FAITH

Ascension	Holy Thursday	sacramental
blasphemy	mortal sin	second coming
capital sins	Paschal mystery	sin
crucifixion	passion	suffering servant
Easter Vigil	Redemption	venial sin
Good Friday	Resurrection	

THE MYSTERY OF LIFE

It does not take long to realize that life is not all "sugar and spice and everything nice." Very often, life is difficult. Everyone experiences challenges in life, such as getting good grades, earning a living, choosing a spouse, or having a happy family life. There are times of suffering, either physically or mentally or both. At times, there is little one can do about the suffering, one's own or that of others.

Just think about the number of people who spent days or weeks in the hospital this past year. Or think about the teens who died in car accidents or the children who contracted terrible diseases because their parents could not afford to get them vaccinated. Unfortunately, accidents are the leading cause of death in the United States for people under forty-four years of age; they account for three-fourths of the deaths in the 15–24 age group. In older age groups, cancer and heart disease are the leading causes of death.

Think about the many people who go to bed hungry each night, or the children who are abandoned, or the people who spend many years in a convalescent home, or the homeless who live on the streets.

The list goes on and on. The *truth* is that suffering is part of being human. The *problem* is we don't understand why. Why does one person get sick and another person doesn't? Why do bad things happen to good people? Why do innocent people die of hunger, disease, and war? If you've ever asked these questions, you are not alone.

It's very difficult to understand suffering. It seems so unfair. One thing does seem certain, however. Suffering and faith are somehow related. Suffering either causes one to turn away from God, or suffering brings one closer to God and helps make faith stronger.

The question of suffering is one of life's great mysteries.

Research

From the handout your teacher will provide, select a present-day situation of suffering. Use the library or the Internet to research this topic. Prepare a report of your findings and present it to the class in a written or oral format or as an electronic slide presentation.

THE DARKEST DAY

On the morning of September 11, 2001, two hijacked airliners crashed into the North and South towers of the World Trade Center in New York City. Nearly three thousand people died, but many bodies were never recovered. Phillip and Matthew, two high school boys in the city, found that suffering can be mental, psychological, spiritual, as well as physical. The horrible event shook them in ways that nothing else had ever done before. It forced them to take a fresh look at God's gifts of life and faith.

It was a gorgeous morning. Phillip looked out the window and saw paper flying everywhere. Strange, he thought. But then, when your school is in downtown Manhattan, strange sights aren't all that uncommon.

In another classroom on the tenth floor, Matthew thought he smelled something burning. But again, in Manhattan, strange smells aren't so unusual, either. But then something terribly unusual did happen.

"It sounded like an explosion," says Matthew, 15, "and the floor shook as if it was an earthquake."

Of course, it wasn't an earthquake. It was a commercial jet, hijacked by terrorists, crashing into the World Trade Center, just three blocks away from Phillip and Matthew's school. Immediately, students were running for their lives. Students and teachers headed toward the lower tip of Manhattan, ending up with thousands of others in the Battery Park area, about ten blocks away from the World Trade Center. Most of them were staring upward in disbelief: Twin towering infernos, the upper floors of both buildings were swallowed up in flames.

Moments later, first one tower, then the other, came crashing down. Massive walls of dust, debris, and smoke surged in all directions through the canyons of Manhattan's streets, sending thousands running for refuge.

When the smoke and debris overtook them, they couldn't see and could hardly breathe. That's when Matthew thought he might die. "I was just thinking, God, help me, please help me..." he says. "I wanted to get out of there and get to a safe place." For Matthew, that safe place was the church where his father is the pastor. "We covered our mouths with our T-shirts so we could breathe. We just walked 'til we got to the church. My dad hugged me and he started crying." Matthew said a prayer of thanks on the spot.

Meanwhile, Phillip, a friend, and two teachers were also trying to get away from the deadly cloud of dust and debris. They piled into an unlocked parked car to catch their breath and dust off. Then they were on the way again, running to Phillip's home.

As Matthew and Phillip look back on the incident, they talk about how it changed their lives forever.

"It has actually increased my faith," says Matthew. Phillip says, "This has changed my whole perspective on life. Now I love God even more. Now I'm starting to live day to day, instead of month to month and year to year, because you never know what might happen."

Shortened from Mark Moring, "The Nightmare of September 11 . . ." Campus Life (January–February 2002).

Let's Talk!

1. How do you think you would have reacted if you had been near the World Trade Center on September 11, 2001?

2. Why do you think Phillip and Matthew both say their faith was deepened as a result of the disaster?

3. What do you think Phillip meant when he said, "I'm starting to live day to day instead of month to month and year to year"?

4. How do you think Phillip and Matthew will respond to suffering as they live out their lives?

Reflection

Describe the darkest time in your life. What happened? What were your feelings at the time? How did this experience affect your faith?

A Suffering Messiah

At the time of Jesus, some of the Jewish people were expecting a messiah. In general most of these people thought the messiah would be a rich king or powerful military leader. Instead, Jesus is both the Messiah and the **suffering servant** described in the Book of the Prophet Isaiah—one who would unjustly, but willingly, suffer and die for others. The suffering servant image describes the messiah in terms of his role as redeemer:

" [H]e had no form or majesty that we should look at him,
    nothing in his appearance that we should desire him.

He was despised and rejected by others;
    a man of suffering and acquainted with infirmity;

and as one from whom others hide their faces
    he was despised, and we held him of no account.

Surely he has borne our infirmities
    and carried our diseases;

yet we accounted him stricken,
    struck down by God, and afflicted.

But he was wounded for our transgressions,
    crushed for our iniquities;

upon him was the punishment that made us whole,
    and by his bruises we are healed.

All we like sheep have gone astray;
    we have all turned to our own way,

and the Lord has laid on him
    the iniquity of us all.

He was oppressed, and he was afflicted,
    yet he did not open his mouth;

like a lamb that is led to the slaughter,
    and like a sheep that before its shearers is silent,
    so he did not open his mouth.

By a perversion of justice he was taken away.
    Who could have imagined his future?

For he was cut off from the land of the living,
    stricken for the transgression of my people.

They made his grave with the wicked
    and his tomb with the rich,

although he had done no violence,
    and there was no deceit in his mouth. "

ISAIAH 53:2B–9

During the time of Isaiah and the other prophets, reconciliation with God was associated with atonement (sacrifice) for human sins. Each year the ancient Israelites celebrated a day of atonement during which they offered sacrifices to God and asked him to take away their sins. Jewish people today still celebrate this Day of Atonement; Yom Kippur is the holiest day of the Jewish year. Rosh Hashanah, which celebrates the inscription of names by God in the Book of Life, is celebrated eight days before Yom Kippur. The days between the two feasts, the Days of Awe, are a time of self-denial as preparation for God's cleansing the people of their sins. On Yom Kippur judgment is entered and the Book of Life sealed.

"Yom Kippur in the Synagogue" by Antonietta Raphael Mafai (1931).

Activity

Read Leviticus, chapter 16, and Numbers 29:7–11 to find out more about the Day of Atonement. Then, in small groups, discuss:

- How does this ritual reminds you of the suffering and death of Jesus?
- Why is Jesus' death a sacrifice of redemption?
- How is the suffering servant like the scapegoat?

"Judas Betraying Jesus with a Kiss" by James J. Tissot.

The Passion of Jesus

Jesus identified with the suffering servant. He interpreted his life and death in terms of the suffering servant, explaining to his followers that he came to give his life as a ransom, a payment, for many (see Matthew 20:28). Paul writes, "Christ died for our sins in accordance with the scriptures" (1 Corinthians 15:3). That is how totally God, in Jesus, became *one with us.* Jesus experienced death to show God's oneness with humans in *every* event of human existence, in death as well as life. Therefore, ". . . neither death, nor life, nor angels, nor rulers, nor things present, nor things to come, nor powers, nor height, nor depth, nor anything else in all creation, will be able to separate us from the love of God in Christ Jesus our Lord" (Romans 8:38–39).

The Gospel according to Matthew describes Jesus as someone who knows ahead of time that he must suffer and die. In fact, the Gospel mentions that Jesus, on three separate occasions during his ministry, predicted his own **passion,** his suffering and death. Knowing that he would die in the near future must not have been easy for Jesus. Knowing that he would first have to suffer physically and mentally must have been even more difficult. Even in his agony, nearing the end of his life, he turned himself over to his heavenly Father.

Jesus' passion, death, **Resurrection,** and Ascension are called the **Paschal mystery.** This term relates to the *Pasch* (in Hebrew, *pesah*), the Passover event of the Exodus (Exodus 12—13:16). Just as God delivered the ancient Hebrews from slavery and death in Egypt, so he saves us from the power of sin and eternal death. God the Father sent his own Son to redeem all of humanity. Jesus freely offered himself for the salvation of all through his suffering, death, Resurrection, and Ascension, and through the sending of the Holy Spirit. The sending of the Holy Spirit will be studied more thoroughly in the next chapter.

Let's Talk!

1. Why would you want to know ahead of time or not know the *date* of your death?
2. Why would you want to know ahead of time or not know the *manner* in which you will die?

Activity

Look up Matthew 16:21, 17:22–23, and 20:17–19, and tell why these passages are used to support the idea that Jesus knew he would have to suffer and die.

Empathy for Those Who Suffer

The fact of Jesus' passion and death does not, in itself, explain why God allows suffering to exist, but it does remind us that he suffers with us when we suffer. Human suffering takes on deeper meaning and significance because of Jesus' suffering and death. Furthermore, Christians are called to work to alleviate human suffering.

On this page is a real-life story of teens who freely chose to participate in Christ's passion. They made this courageous choice to learn the truth about suffering and to open their eyes to the pain of people in their city.

Christians suffer with those who suffer, just as all parts of the human body suffer when one of its parts suffers (see 1 Corinthians 12:26). God is with them when they suffer. They empathize with and to alleviate the suffering of others.

Apostles' Creed: He [Jesus] suffered under Pontius Pilate, was crucified, died, and was buried. He descended into hell. On the third day he rose again. He ascended into heaven and is seated at the right hand of the Father. He will come again to judge the living and the dead.

Nicene Creed: For our sake he was crucified under Pontius Pilate; he suffered, died, and was buried. On the third day he rose again in fulfillment of the Scriptures; he ascended into heaven and is seated at the right hand of the Father. He will come again in glory to judge the living and the dead, and his kingdom will have no end.

ANOTHER CHRISTMAS STORY

Whenever I recall the birth of Jesus, a sign of God's love for the human family, I remember another Christmas story. When I was a boy, our family owned a small dry-goods store in the West End of Cincinnati. It was a happy place where neighborhood folks laughed and cried together. People bought merchandise there, knowing that all—including poor African-American and white people—were welcome.

One Christmas stands out above the rest. In early December, a delegation from the black Holiness church came into the store and asked for my father. I knew this was no ordinary meeting, because Dad listened with a worried smile. When they left, he proudly told me they invited him to preach the Christmas sermon at their church. "Dad," I asked, what did you tell them?" He replied that he wanted to talk it over with Mom before giving them an answer.

I sensed what his decision would be—that the only sermon he could preach was in the store. The following Thursday, he confirmed my suspicions. Up the street he went to tell the church members that he couldn't do it. He returned shortly, hoping they understood him.

Two weeks passed, and it was the day before Christmas. Right before noon, Dad found out how well the people understood him. The church people came into the store carrying chicken dinners—a delicacy they occasionally brought us on busy days. Dad was overjoyed. As he thanked them, we gathered around the potbellied stove. Dad threw in several large lumps of coal. The warmth of Christmas Eve melted the chill in the store, as everyone laughed, reminisced, and ate their chicken dinners.

Before the church people left, Dad moved about the store picking out a very nice selection of gifts, clothes, and household items for the church's poor who might not receive much on Christmas Day. As the coal turned to ashes, the black and white brothers and sisters, who exchanged best wishes for peace, joy, and goodwill around the old potbellied stove, preached the real Christmas sermon.

The old store and church are gone now, but memories live on. Whenever I drive past the spot where the store once stood, I remember the special Christmas that taught me the real reason for Jesus' birth.

The Christmas experience in my father's store, a symbol of God's love as demonstrated in Jesus' birth, helped me appreciate why Jesus was born in simplicity in the midst of poverty, uncertainty, and struggle. Jesus' birth, a paradigm of family life, shows how God's love can overcome human obstacles and bring new life. In recalling past Christmases, the only sermon I remember is the one preached in my family's store. This old store was my cave of Bethlehem. From it, I learned the real meaning of Jesus' birth.

Fr. Robert Hater
from The Catholic Family in a Changing World
(Harcourt Religion Publishers, ©2005)

THE PASSION NARRATIVES

Activities

1. Prepare a presentation comparing one of the passion accounts with the corresponding Old Testament passages listed in the text. Present your findings to the class. Explain what the Gospel writer was saying about the passion of Jesus.

2. The passion narratives in the Gospels are the source of a traditional devotion known as "the Seven Last Words of Jesus." Search through all four passion narratives to find the seven last words of Jesus. Make a list of these words, with their scriptural citations. Discuss what the list tells about Jesus and his role as Redeemer.

3. Compare the passion accounts using the two handouts your teacher will provide. Take notes on how the accounts are similar and different.

All four Gospels contain accounts of the passion of Jesus. These accounts were written from the perspective of a post-resurrection faith, that is, a faith that had been deepened through the experience of the Resurrection of Jesus. The Gospel writers knew that Jesus' death was not the end of the story. Since they each had a specific purpose in telling the passion story as they did, their accounts, though similar, differ somewhat.

- Matthew 26–27 shows that Jesus is the suffering servant of Isaiah. *(See Isaiah 52:13–53:12.)* His death and Resurrection lead to his eternal presence in the Christian community.

- Mark 14–15 shows Jesus is the Son of God, the mediator between God and man. His cross is a paradox of kingship and humiliation, of death and Resurrection. Jesus is the high priest, after the order of Melchizedek. Jesus gives his life as a sacrifice for sin.

- In Luke 22–23 Jesus is portrayed as one who is unjustly condemned to death. With his dying breath, he forgives his persecutors and accepted his Father's loving plan. Jesus is the righteous one of the Old Testament who is persecuted unjustly but later vindicated by God the Father.

- In John 18–19 the passion and death are moments in Jesus' triumphal return to the Father. Jesus is in control of his fate. It is his hour of glorification. Jesus' death is like the Passover sacrifice. *(See Exodus 12:1–28, 1 Corinthians 5:7.)* Jesus himself is the Passover lamb. *(See John 1:29.)*

In short, all four Gospels show how Jesus' death was part of God's loving plan of **Redemption.** "No one has greater love than this, to lay down one's life for one's friends" (John 15:13). Jesus fulfilled the Old Testament prophecies. He was the long-promised Messiah, sent to save us from sin and show us God's forgiving love.

Wood crucifixion scene in Madrid, Spain. Artist: Rogier van der Weyden, fifteenth century.

Celebrating the Passover

Each spring, devout Jewish people celebrate Passover. In Jesus' day, families were encouraged to travel to Jerusalem for this eight-day feast. The temple was in Jerusalem, so the city was the religious center of Judaism. At the time of Passover, families or groups of families procured a lamb that was sacrificed in the temple area. The families then shared a meal. The meal included roast lamb, bitter herbs, wine, and unleavened bread—the same as the ancient Hebrews ate before fleeing Egypt. The Passover meal was a formal ritual with a certain order. The participants ate certain foods accompanied by specific prayers and readings from Scripture, especially from the Book of Exodus.

The Passover meal is usually celebrated in a family setting.

The Gospel according to Luke indicates that the child Jesus and his family traveled to Jerusalem for Passover. It is likely that, as an adult, Jesus continued this tradition with his family members, friends, and Apostles. Indeed, all four Gospels recount that in the third year of his public ministry, Jesus traveled to Jerusalem for the feast of Passover, fully aware that in Jerusalem he would suffer a brutal death. By doing so, he himself would be the sacrificial lamb, "the Lamb of God who takes away the sin of the world" (John 1:29).

According to the Gospels, Jesus' entry into the city was humble, in that he rode a colt or a donkey. But it was also triumphant as the people greeted him by waving palm branches and singing one of the psalms:

> " Blessed is the one who comes in the name of the LORD.
>   We bless you from the house of the LORD.
>
> The LORD is God,
>   and he has given us light.
>
> Bind the festal procession with branches,
>   up to the horns of the altar. "
>
> PSALM 118:26–27

The paradox of the scene becomes clear only after Jesus' Resurrection. Jesus is the Son of David and the King of Glory, and yet he is not the usual earthly king. God's kingdom is among those who are poor—those who walk by foot to Jerusalem and need to borrow a colt or donkey from others.

Each year during the celebration of Passion (Palm) Sunday, Catholics recall in a special way Jesus' entry into Jerusalem. And at every celebration of the Mass, we say "Blessed is he who comes in the name of the Lord. Hosanna in the highest." These words are the same words in Matthew spoken by the crowds who welcomed Jesus on the road to Jerusalem.

Activity

In small groups compare the four Gospel accounts of Jesus' entry into Jerusalem (Matthew 21:1–11, Mark 11:1–10, Luke 19:28–40, John 12:12–19). How are they similar? How are they different? What do you think the Gospels are saying about Jesus?

Salvador Dali's representation of the Last Supper.

Research

Today the Passover is celebrated by Jews around the world very much as it was celebrated centuries ago. Using the library or the Internet, find out more about the celebration (traditional and current) of the Passover meal. What recipes are used? What prayers are said? What Scriptures are read? Report your findings to the class.

Activity

Compare the three scriptural accounts of the agony in the garden. How are they the same? How are they different? What do you think is the overall message the Gospels are conveying?

The Last Supper

In Jerusalem on the night before he was to die, Jesus shared the traditional Passover meal with his Apostles, family members, and friends. Christians call this the *Last Supper* and remember it each year on Holy Thursday. Details of the institution of the Eucharist at the Last Supper can be found in Matthew 26:26-29, Mark 14:22-25, Luke 22:14–20, and 1 Corinthians 11:23–26. These passages give an account of how at this meal Jesus established God's new covenant with humanity. Jesus changed the unleavened bread and the wine into his own Body and Blood that he would offer to his Father on the cross the next day. Jesus let his disciples know that he was voluntarily laying down his life for them. He established the Eucharist—a meal and a sacrifice combined—which they were to continue for all time. Catholics celebrate this Eucharist at every Mass.

“ [T]he Lord Jesus on the night when he was betrayed took a loaf of bread, and when he had given thanks, he broke it and said, 'This is my body that is for you. Do this in remembrance of me.' In the same way he took the cup also, after supper, saying, 'This cup is the new covenant in my blood. Do this, as often as you drink it, in remembrance of me.' For as often as you eat this bread and drink this cup, you proclaim the Lord's death until he comes. ”

1 CORINTHIANS 11:23–26

After the Last Supper, Jesus went with Peter, James, and John to pray in a garden at the Mount of Olives. This event, which is found in Matthew 26:36–46, Mark 14:32–42, and Luke 22:39–46, shows us the extent of Jesus' mental suffering. These passages also show that Jesus submits to the Father's will despite the painful death he knows he will soon undergo.

“ He came out and went, as was his custom, to the Mount of Olives; and the disciples followed him. When he reached the place, he said to them, 'Pray that you may not come into the time of trial.' Then he withdrew from them about a stone's throw, knelt down, and prayed. 'Father, if you are willing, remove this cup from me; yet, not my will but yours be done.' Then an angel from heaven appeared to him and gave him strength. In his anguish he prayed more earnestly, and his sweat became like great drops of blood falling down on the ground. ”

LUKE 22:39–44

BETRAYAL, SUFFERING, AND DEATH

While Jesus was still praying, Judas arrived with the chief priests, temple guards, religious elders, and high priest's servants—some armed with swords and clubs. They arrested Jesus under cover of darkness, while his disciples fled in fear for their lives. Judas—one of Jesus' own disciples—had betrayed Jesus for thirty pieces of silver.

Jesus on Trial

After Jesus was arrested, he was led away for a mock trial, which took place in secret late at night. First, Jesus was taken to the house of the high priest, where he was beaten and ridiculed. At daybreak, Jesus was taken to the Sanhedrin, a council of Jewish elders, who decided that he had indeed committed the sin of **blasphemy,** that is, showing contempt or lack of reverence for God and his name, because he called himself God's Son. They decided he should receive the ultimate punishment—death.

"What Is the Truth? (Christ Before Pilate)" by Nikolai Ge; Tretyakov Gallery, Moscow, Russia.

There was only one problem with their decision: The law did not permit them to carry out a sentence of capital punishment. Only the Romans were allowed to execute criminals. So Jesus was next taken to Pontius Pilate, the Roman governor of Judea. Pilate found Jesus innocent. When the religious leaders loudly objected, Pilate had Jesus sent to King Herod, who held official jurisdiction in the matter. Herod mocked Jesus and tried to get him to perform a miracle. When Jesus refused, Herod returned him to Pilate. The Gospel according to John recounts the following dialogue between Jesus and Pilate:

" [Pilate] summoned Jesus and asked him, 'Are you the King of the Jews?' Jesus answered, 'Do you ask this on your own, or did others tell you about me?' Pilate replied, 'I am not a Jew, am I? Your own nation and the chief priests have handed you over to me. What have you done?' Jesus answered, 'My kingdom is not from this world. If my kingdom were from this world, my followers would be fighting to keep me from being handed over to the Jews. But as it is, my kingdom is not from here.' Pilate asked him, 'So you are a king?' Jesus answered, 'You say that I am a king. For this I was born, and for this I came into the world, to testify to the truth. Everyone who belongs to the truth listens to my voice.' "

JOHN 18:33–37

This dialogue with Pilate is the last time the word *truth* is used in the Gospel according to John. Jesus had spent his life telling people the truth about God's redeeming love. But many people could not hear what Jesus had to say. Although Pilate was of the opinion that Jesus was innocent, he allowed himself to be pressured into changing his mind. Eventually, Pilate "handed Jesus over as they wished" (Luke 23:25).

Activities

1. On the Internet, look for a virtual tour of or read about Jerusalem or some of the other places associated with Jesus' death.

2. Reenact one of the Gospel accounts of the betrayal of Jesus. Discuss what you think Judas might have been thinking when he betrayed Jesus.

"Jesus and the Adulteress" by Fortunino Mantania. Jesus refused to condemn the woman caught in the act of adultery. He saw the woman as more important than the law that required she be stoned to death. Instead, he asked her to sin no more.

Reflection

Pilate could not stand up to peer pressure during the trial of Jesus. Think about your own life. Write about times when you have had to face negative peer pressure. Did you stand by your convictions, or did you go along with the crowd? How do you feel about that now? If given a second chance, would you do anything differently? Why?

Why Was Jesus Put to Death?

Historical records indicate that Jesus died as a prisoner. He was sentenced to death by **crucifixion,** that is, being tied or nailed to a cross. Crucifixion is torturous; only after great pain does the person die.

From the New Testament, we learn that certain influential Jews supporting King Herod plotted with the priests and scribes to kill Jesus. They saw Jesus as a threat to the *status quo,* to things as they were. First of all, they thought Jesus had the potential to stir up the Jewish people and perhaps lead a riot against Rome. The Jews involved knew that if this happened, Rome would retaliate and would be even more oppressive toward the Jewish people. Second, some of them thought Jesus was making a mockery out of the Jewish religion. He seemed to ridicule aspects of the Mosaic law dealing with purity and requirements of Jewish behavior—something these Jews considered very important, believing that faithfulness to even the smallest law made it easier for people to keep the more important laws.

The accusers of Jesus felt justified in their assessment of him. Jesus performed miracles on the Sabbath, even though all work was forbidden then. He spent time with "unclean people," such as public sinners, women (unclean during menstruation and for a time after childbirth), lepers, and tax collectors. Worst of all, his accusers thought he was guilty of blasphemy. While the Jewish law taught that only God could forgive sins, Jesus presented himself as God's equal by forgiving the sins of others. Saint Thomas Aquinas, in the thirteenth century, explained blasphemy as a sin against faith. The sinner either attributes to God something that does not belong to him or denies God something that is his due.

In truth, Jesus' mission was not to destroy the Romans or start a revolution against them. Neither did Jesus come to abolish the Law of Moses established at Mount Sinai. Instead, he explained to people what it really meant to keep the Ten Commandments and the Law of Moses. Jesus fulfilled the law, showing people that its main purpose is to love God and love other people. In fact, Jesus fulfilled the Law of Moses perfectly and redeemed people from all the sins committed against it.

So what about all these charges against Jesus? Why were the people in power so against him? Because he had a power they didn't have, and he threatened their power, authority, and interpretation of Mosaic law.

Jesus' Crucifixion and Death

All four Gospels mention Jesus' torturous journey through Jerusalem to a hill called Golgotha (place of the skull). The soldiers forced Jesus to carry his cross, the instrument of his death. Then, when Jesus could no longer do so, the soldiers forced a man named Simon to assist him in carrying the cross. On the hill of Golgotha, Jesus was crucified.

The death of Jesus is recorded in all four Gospels (Matthew 27:45–56, Mark 15:33–41, Luke 23:44–49, John 19:28–30). These passages are key to understanding the significance of the Paschal mystery. Jesus, fully human and the Son of God, truly died. He did not fake his death or fall into a death-like coma. He really died, just as every human will one day die. Most of the twelve Apostles fled when Jesus was arrested. From the accounts in the Gospels, it is not known whether any of the Apostles were present at the crucifixion, except for the Apostle John, along with some of the women disciples of Jesus. As the Gospels tell us, Mary, the mother of Jesus, and the Apostle John were at the foot of the cross when Jesus died.

Placing the Blame

Who is to blame for the death of Jesus? For many centuries, some Church members have blamed the Jews. They use this blame to rationalize sentiments and actions of hatred against Jewish people, simply because they are Jewish. Such hatred and discrimination is sometimes called anti-Semitism (from *Semite*, Jewish). The Jews were not responsible for Jesus' death. To blame them for his death is an instance of anti-Semitism. Tragically, anti-Semitism runs through history, horribly so in the Holocaust, the mass slaughter of six million Jews by Hitler and the Nazis. Tragically, too, anti-Semitism continues today in the Middle East and among many Muslims and Christians in other parts of the world.

After one of Jesus' Apostles, Judas, betrayed him, some influential Jews became involved in discussing the fate of Jesus. Ultimately, however, Roman officials made the decision to put Jesus to death. One was Pilate, the Roman governor of Judea. Another was Herod, himself a Jew and a nominal king under Roman authority. In the end, all sinners are to blame, for without sin, humans wouldn't need a savior. Thus, from the viewpoint of faith, *all* sinners must assume some responsibility for Jesus' death.

Let's Talk!

1. What do you think the Apostles were thinking and feeling at the time of the crucifixion? What do you think Mary and the Apostle John were thinking and feeling? How do you think the crucifixion affected their faith in Jesus?

2. Imagine that a friend of yours is suddenly arrested for a major crime, such as grand theft, murder, or child abuse. You know your friend is innocent. What would you be thinking and feeling? How will your friendship survive?

La Pieta, *by Michelangelo, St. Peter's Basilica, the Vatican.*

Activity

Read about the Holocaust: *The Diary of Anne Frank, My Secret Camera: Life in the Lodz Ghetto* (Harcourt), or the Vatican's 1998 document, *We Remember: A Reflection on the Shoah.* Report your findings to the class. Be prepared to discuss why anti-Semitism is morally wrong.

Jesus' Burial

The Gospels tell us that after Jesus died on the cross, his body was taken down and laid in a tomb that was given by Joseph of Arimathea, who was a leading Pharisee of the Sanhedrin. Jesus' followers had to attend to the burial quickly because the Sabbath was about to start and the law required them to do no work on the Sabbath. So the body of Jesus was laid on a slab in a tomb, but he was not washed or anointed according to Jewish burial custom. Women would return after the Sabbath to perform these rituals. In the days of Jesus, Jews who died were usually buried the same day. Many times, the burial took place in a cave or underground passageway. The entrance was then sealed with a large stone.

What happened to Jesus during the time between his death and his Resurrection on the third day? The Church explains this mystery of faith by saying that "In his human soul united to his divine person, the dead Christ went down to the realm of the dead" (CCC, #637). He descended to this realm "as Savior, proclaiming the Good News to the spirits imprisoned there" (CCC, #632). In other words, "he opened heaven's gates for the just who had gone before him" (CCC, #637).

Where is the "realm of the dead"? One version of the Apostles' Creed says that Jesus "descended into hell." (Today the version used in liturgy reads: "descended to the dead.") In Scripture, *hell* is the name for the realm of the dead (*Sheol* in Hebrew, *Hades* in Greek). Jesus went to the place of the dead to free the just who had lived and died before him, to "open heaven's gate" for them. The souls of the just were separated from God not because they chose to be but because Jesus had not yet redeemed them.

In Chapter 8 the mysteries of death, heaven, hell, and judgment will be discussed in more detail. For now, what is important to remember about this part of the creed is its overall message: The Redemption Jesus won applies to all people of all times in history, not just to those who lived on earth after him.

"Descent into Hell," Bridge Building Images.

JESUS' RESURRECTION

When the women returned to the grave on Sunday morning to perform the ritual anointing, they found that the huge stone covering the entrance had been moved aside. Inside, the body of Jesus was missing; all that remained were the burial cloths that had covered him. Then two men in dazzling clothes (or angels) told them that Jesus had been raised from the dead. Imagine the surprise, fear, confusion, and joy the women must have felt.

Now imagine how the Apostles who had gone into hiding must have reacted when the women told them what the angels had said. Remember, the Apostles feared that the death of Jesus would mark the beginning of their own persecution by the temple leaders and the Romans. The Apostles also, like most Jews at the time of Jesus, did not have a firm belief in or clear understanding of life after death. Many people at the time of Jesus thought that resurrection from the dead was linked to the end of the world. When Jesus was raised from the dead, people were both astonished and fearful, thinking that the end of the world had arrived.

The Resurrection is a central truth of our faith in Jesus. It is an unparalleled intervention of God into human history. In the Resurrection we can see the three persons of the Trinity working together as one. The power of the almighty Father raised up his Son. Jesus is decisively revealed as the Son of God because it was impossible for him to be held in death's power (Acts 2:24). And the Holy Spirit breathed life into Jesus' dead humanity and seated him at the right hand of the Father in heaven, "above every name that is named, not only in this age but also in the age to come" (Ephesians 1:21).

"Resurrection," from "The Life of Christ" triptych by Emil Nolde.

Research

Compare the Gospel accounts of the Resurrection (Matthew 28:1–10, Mark 16:1–8, Luke 24:1–10, John 20:1–18).

- How are they similar or different?
- What do you think is the overall message?

Let's Talk!

Imagine that you were one of the women or one of the Apostles. What would be your reaction to the empty tomb?

"Resurrection of Christ," from the Isenheim altarpiece, by Mathias Gruenwald; now in Musée Unterlinden, Colmare, France.

Post-Resurrection Appearances

On Easter Sunday night, the risen Jesus appeared to the Apostles and told them not to be afraid. Slowly they began to realize the enormous truth. God the Father had raised up Jesus—the innocent one—from the darkness of death and "abolished death and brought life and immortality to light through the gospel" (2 Timothy 1:10). The Messiah had really come and had saved humanity from the power of sin and eternal death.

Even though skeptics accused the Apostles of making up the story of the Resurrection, the Apostles kept insisting that the event was real. To verify that Jesus had really been raised from the dead by the Father, the apostles cited the many times the risen Jesus appeared to them. As the Gospels themselves bear witness, Jesus appeared to disciples in Galilee and to disciples in Jerusalem. Saul (Paul) himself, a Pharisee intent on persecuting those who believed in Jesus, had a vision of the risen Jesus. The experience led to his conversion and Baptism. After that time, he became an ardent preacher of the Resurrection.

Activity

Do a dramatzation of one of the Gospel accounts of the appearances of the Risen Lord (Matthew 28:9–10, 16–20; Mark 16:9–15; Luke 24:13–49; John 20:11–29). Afterward, discuss the similarities and differences among the accounts. What do you think is the overall message?

Believing in the Resurrection

God's gift of faith helps us believe in Jesus' Resurrection. This belief, however, often leads to many questions. As the Gospels imply, the body of the Risen Christ is the "same" body in which he suffered and died. It is "different" in how it was changed by the Resurrection. After his Resurrection, Christ eats and drinks as humans do, but he also enters locked rooms. Furthermore, in analyzing Jesus' actions after the Resurrection, one can conclude that the Resurrection of Jesus is different from resuscitation. The risen Jesus will not die again. "In his risen body he passes from the state of death to another life beyond time and space" (CCC, #646). At the moment of his Resurrection, Christ becomes the "first-born from the dead" (Colossians 1:18). Jesus' Resurrection hints at what will happen to all believers at their own resurrection.

Both the Gospels and Church Tradition maintain that Baptism unites Catholics not only with the death of Jesus but also with his Resurrection. The Risen Lord is present in every Eucharist that is celebrated. The Catholic Church celebrates the Resurrection of Jesus at every Mass, and especially on Easter Sunday.

Reflection

Read John 20:24–29. In what ways are you like the Apostle Thomas? What doubts do you have regarding the Resurrection of Jesus or faith in general?

The Easter liturgies are the most joyful of the Church year.

Activity

Read and summarize the Scripture passages from the handout your teacher will provide. Then write one or two paragraphs explaining your own understanding of what the Church teaches about the Resurrection of Jesus. Be prepared to share your thoughts in class.

The Ascension

The Resurrection of Christ and his subsequent manifestation were historically verified in New Testament accounts. This event is attested to by his Apostles and disciples. During Jesus' final apparition to them, he ascends into heaven and is now seated at the right hand of the Father.

> " Then he led them out as far as Bethany, and, lifting up his hands, he blessed them. While he was blessing them, he withdrew from them and was carried up into heaven. "
>
> LUKE 24:50–51

This departure of Jesus is known as the **Ascension.** Ascending into heaven is an image present in the Old Testament. Ancient holy figures, such as Enoch, Elijah, Moses, Baruch, and Ezra, were thought to have ascended to God in heaven after their earthly lives. Indeed, ascension was a somewhat common literary device to show the greatness of certain individuals (Greco-Roman heroes, as well as Old Testament figures). Ascension to the heavens indicated divine approval or favor of the person, as well as his or her rise to heavenly power.

Like the Resurrection, the Ascension of Jesus is a mystery of faith. As the Catechism states, the Ascension "marks the definitive entrance of Jesus' humanity into God's heavenly domain, whence he will come again (cf. *Acts* 1:11)" (#665). From now on, until the end of the world, the Risen Lord is seated at the right hand of God the Father. Christ is "the King of kings and Lord of lords . . . and dwells in unapproachable light" (1 Timothy 6:15, 16). He exists as Son of God before all ages, one with the Father and the Holy Spirit.

Activity

Compare the story of the Ascension of Jesus (Mark 16:19, Luke 24:50–53, and Acts 1:9–12) to other scriptural stories of possible ascension (Enoch—Genesis 5:24, and Elijah— 2 Kings 2:1–11). What do you think is the overall message of the accounts of Jesus' Ascension? Be prepared to discuss your ideas in class.

Italian bone carving of "Ascension of Jesus Christ."

Early Christian mosaic of Christ separating the sheep from the rams, found in S. Apollinare Nuovo, Ravenna, Italy.

The Second Coming

The Apostles themselves believed that the Risen Christ would someday return. Jesus himself taught about the final judgment in a teaching that begins: "When the Son of Man comes in his glory . . ." (see Matthew 25:31–46). Like a triumphant monarch returning home in glory after a great battle, Christ will come again at the end of time. Then all will receive justice. Like the triumphant monarch who rewards those who have served him faithfully and punishes those who have acted against him, Christ will judge the living and the dead. The reward is eternal life—the punishment, eternal death. This expected event at the end of time is called the **second coming** of Christ.

Many early Christians, including the Apostles and Paul, first believed that the second coming would happen in their lifetimes. In other words, they believed the end of the world would take place some time in the first century. Obviously, this did not happen. The Apostles and first disciples began to die, and the second coming did not happen. This delay challenged the faith of some believers until the Church clarified what was truly important. Christ would indeed come again, but we do not know when it will occur. What is important to remember for now is the overall message: Christ is the ultimate victor over the power of sin and everlasting death. Through his Paschal mystery, he redeems humanity and makes accessible to everyone God's infinite mercy and justice.

Even today, at every Mass, after the consecration of the bread and wine, those gathered summarize their beliefs in the events of the Paschal mystery with an acclamation of faith: "Christ has died; Christ is risen; Christ will come again."

Activities

Interview five people on their views of the end times. Then compare their responses with those obtained by your classmates. What views seem to be contrary to Catholic teaching? What views are in agreement with Catholic teaching?

SIN AND VIRTUE

One fact clearly emerges from Jesus' life: he always did what was pleasing to the Father. Two ways we follow Jesus' example are by avoiding sin and by making moral decisions that are pleasing to the Father.

Sin is an offense against God; it breaks or damages our communion with him and with the Church. Sin wounds our human nature and the solidarity and community among people. It "is an offense against reason, truth, and right conscience" (CCC, #1849)

There are two types of sin for which we are personally responsible. The Church has traditionally taught that a **mortal sin** has three characteristics: (1) The matter involved is seriously wrong (contrary to God's law) or believed to be seriously wrong. (2) The person acting sufficiently reflects on the fact that it is seriously wrong, but (3) freely chooses to commit the wrong anyway. The effect of mortal sin—if unrepented—is the eternal death of hell, that is, separation from God forever. A **venial sin** is a less serious wrong that weakens but does not destroy a person's relationship with God, or a serious wrong without full knowledge or free will.

Social sin results from the effects our individual sins have on a community. People who have been sinned against may sin in return. Violence, injustice, and other wrongs may develop within a community. As a result, there may be sinful social structures that perpetuate the social sin.

Capital Sins

All sins stem from sinful attitudes or tendencies within the human person. The Church names these as **capital sins** because they lead to other sins. The Church has traditionally numbered the capital (major) sins as seven: pride, envy, anger, sloth, greed, gluttony, and lust. These "deadly" attitudes can lead to seriously sinful thoughts, behaviors, and omissions. They can lead us to commit mortal (deadly) sins, which, if unrepented, can result in eternal separation from God.

Human morality is not based on external actions alone. The U.S. justice system may be able to distinguish felonies (serious crimes) from misdemeanors (less serious crimes) on actions alone. But Christian morality involves more than the judgment of external actions. It also includes a person's inner attitudes and motivations. Jesus alluded to this when he said,

> " Do not judge, so that you may not be judged. For with the judgment you make you will be judged, and the measure you give will be the measure you get. Why do you see the speck in your neighbor's eye, but do not notice the log in your own eye? Or how can you say to your neighbor, "Let me take the speck out of your eye," while the log is in your own eye? You hypocrite, first take the log out of your own eye, and then you will see clearly to take the speck out of your neighbor's eye. "

MATTHEW 7:1–5

Activity

Prepare a report for the class or an electronic slide presentation on the seven deadly sins. Explain what each sin is and why it can lead to other sins.

Moral Decision Making

We have the freedom and the wisdom to judge whether an act is good or bad, whether it will lead us toward goodness or toward sin. Much of that wisdom comes from God, who has placed his natural law within us, endowed us with a conscience, and has given us the Ten Commandments and the witness of his Son. God has also given us the Church to teach us about faith and morals. To help us judge the goodness or evil of an act, the Church provides us three traditional sources of morality: the object chosen, the intention, and the circumstances surrounding the act to help us judge the goodness or evil an act.

The "object chosen" refers to the act we have chosen. Good acts involve something we know is good—feeding the poor, refusing to ridicule a classmate, visiting the sick, telling the truth, and so on. Bad acts involve matter that we know is bad—selling drugs, killing an innocent person, stealing, deliberately harming another person's reputation, and so.

"Intention" refers to our motive or intention in performing an act. Giving a blanket to a homeless person because you are concerned for her well-being is a good act with a good intention. Cleaning a neighbor's house because you want to steal from that neighbor is an example of a good act done with an evil motive. Murdering a tyrannical dictator because you want to free a nation from oppression is an evil act for what appears to be good reasons. But we cannot justify an evil act performed for good reasons.

The "circumstances" of an act refers to conditions surrounding the act that affect its goodness or evil. Certain factors can "contribute to increasing or

---

CONSCIENCE

Conscience is the God-given ability to know right from wrong and choose what is right. In everything we say and do, we are obliged to follow the "certain judgment" (CCC, #1800) of our conscience. To do this we need to have an informed conscience, otherwise the conscience can be ignorant and thus liable to make wrong judgments. Forming an informed conscience, then, is a lifelong task. Some steps that will help in this task are:

- Pray for the guidance of the Spirit.
- Educate and develop it through constant use and examination.

- Know the Church's teachings.
- Seek advice from good moral people.

Examining your conscience should be done daily and in preparation for the Sacrament of Reconciliation.

1. Pray to the Holy Spirit to help you examine your conscience.
2. Look at your life in light of the Beatitudes, the Ten Commandments, the Great Commandment, and the precepts of the Church.
3. Ask yourself questions such as these: Where have I fallen short of what God wants for me? Whom have I hurt? What have I done that I knew was wrong? What have I not done that I should have done? Have I done penance and tried as hard as I could to make up for past sins? Am I working to overcome my bad habits? In what areas am I still having trouble? Am I sincerely sorry for all my sins?
4. In addition to confessing your sins, you may wish to talk with a priest about one or more of the above questions.

"The Table of the Seven Deadly Sins," around the figure of Christ; Museo del Prado, Madrid, Spain.

diminishing the moral goodness or evil of human acts (for example the amount of a theft). They can also diminish or increase the agent's responsibility (such as out of a fear of death)" (CCC, #1754). Thus, there are factors that come into play when judging the goodness and evil of an act. The consequences of the act, fear, ignorance, and pressure, are some examples of these mitigating factors.

It is important to realize that a morally good act has three requirements: the goodness of its object, the goodness of its intentions, and the goodness of its circumstances. However there are certain acts that are always wrong to choose. These acts include blasphemy, perjury, murder, and adultery. Evil cannot be done so that good may result from it.

Virtue

We are all acquainted with good dietary and hygienic habits. These habits generally lead us to good health and a pleasing appearance. Virtues are good moral and spiritual habits that help us make good moral decisions and avoid sin. There are two types of categories of virtues: theological virtues and cardinal virtues.

The theological virtues are the pivotal virtues of faith, hope, and charity. They are called the theological virtues because they are rooted in God, directed toward him, and reflect his presence in our lives. (In Greek "theos" means "god.") The theological virtues are gifts from God. They do, however, call for a response on our part. That is, by living faithfully, hopefully, and lovingly, we cooperate with God's gifts of faith, hope, and charity. Faith means believing in him and all that he has revealed to us and that the Church proposes for our belief. Hope is the desire, bolstered by trust, to do his will, achieve eternal life and the graces that make this desire come true. "By charity, we love God above all things and our neighbor as ourselves for love of God" (CCC, #1844).

The cardinal virtues are the principal moral virtues that help us lead a moral life by governing our actions, controlling our passions and emotions, and keeping our conduct on the right tract. These virtues are prudence (careful judgment), fortitude (courage), justice (giving God and people their due), and temperance (moderation, balance). With the help of God's grace, we develop the moral virtues by means of education, practice, and perseverance.

THE PASCHAL MYSTERY

People of faith see all times as opportunities to experience God's presence. All times are opportunities to grow in friendship with God, self, and others. The Catholic Church celebrates its relationship with God throughout the year in a liturgical calendar known as the Church year. The Church divides its year according to different seasons of faith. Each season celebrates the Paschal mystery with an emphasis on a different aspect of Christ's life and saving work.

Advent	This season of waiting helps Catholics prepare for the second coming of Christ. Advent, the first season of the Church year, lasts up to four weeks; there are always four Sundays. During this time, Catholics celebrate the faith of all the people before Christ who believed that God would send them a messiah. With great joy, the first coming of the Son of God is celebrated and the second coming of Christ is anticipated.
Christmas	During this season Catholics celebrate the birth, Epiphany, and baptism of Jesus. Catholics celebrate the fact that Jesus is the promised Messiah and the Light of the World that overcomes all darkness.
Lent	This season of fasting, prayer, and almsgiving—which lasts approximately six weeks—helps Catholics remember that they are not always faithful to God's covenant. It is a time of penance, renewal, and recommitment to living one's faith by putting it into action.
Triduum	From the Mass of the Lord's Supper on Holy Thursday through Good Friday and the Easter Vigil, to evening prayer on Easter Sunday, the Church celebrates the death and Resurrection of Christ with ancient and solemn liturgies. These are the holiest days of the Church year.
Easter	This season celebrates Jesus' Resurrection and victory over the power of sin and eternal death. The season lasts seven weeks, through Pentecost.
Ordinary Time	This season is the longest in the Church year. It is a reminder of the actions and teachings of Jesus and that every time is a good time to grow in faith. This season is celebrated twice; a short period falls between the Seasons of Christmas and Lent, and a much longer period begins after the Easter Season and concludes the Church year with the Solemnity of Christ the King.

Let's Talk!

1. What is your favorite liturgical season of the Church year? Why? What makes this season so special for you?
2. In your own life, how have you celebrated important events with your family and friends? What kind of rituals do you do to recall these important moments in your life?

Liturgical colors are used in vestments and church decorations, such as banners.

Holy Week

The Catholic Church celebrates the Paschal mystery at every Mass. However, during Holy Week the Church celebrates the events of Jesus' passion and death in a special way.

Holy Week spans the Season of Lent and the Triduum. It begins with a Sunday known as Passion Sunday, or Palm Sunday. The priest blesses palm branches and distributes them to the gathered people. Before the joyful entrance procession, he reads the Gospel passage of Jesus' humble yet majestic entry into Jerusalem. During the Liturgy of the Word, the entire passion of Jesus Christ is proclaimed. In many parishes, the assembly participates in this reading, sometimes taking the role of those who falsely accused Jesus. This participation reminds us of how our own sins have contributed to Jesus' crucifixion and death.

The last three days of Holy Week are known as the Easter Triduum (a word that means "three"). The Triduum begins with evening Mass on the Thursday before Easter, known as **Holy Thursday.** The Church's liturgy on this day is called the *Mass of the Lord's Supper* because it focuses on the Last Supper of Jesus and the institution of the Eucharist. The Holy Thursday readings recount the Passover event of the ancient Israelites, how Jesus washed the feet of his disciples at the Last Supper, and the institution of the Eucharist. In imitation of Jesus, the priest may then wash the feet of twelve parishioners. The overall message of the liturgy is clear: We are to serve others as Jesus did. At the conclusion of the Mass, the altar is stripped bare. The Eucharist is taken to a specially prepared altar or chapel. Just as Jesus told Peter, James, and John to stay awake and pray with him in the garden of Gethsemane, so we are invited to stay at the special chapel or altar, adoring Jesus in the Blessed Sacrament.

Holy Thursday moves into **Good Friday,** during which the passion and death of Jesus on the cross is celebrated. We hear the passion story from the Gospel according to John. We join with others in showing reverence toward the cross. The liturgy that day does not consist of a usual Mass. Instead, there is a Communion service, using hosts that were consecrated the night before.

During the day of Holy Saturday, there is no Mass or Communion service; this is a reminder of the time that Jesus spent in the tomb. Visits to the Blessed Sacrament are encouraged.

The Easter candle is lit from the new fire at the Easter Vigil.

The celebration of Easter begins after dark on Saturday night with the **Easter Vigil** service. This beautiful ritual consists of four main parts:

- **The Service of Light.** This ceremony recalls that Jesus is the light of the world. All the lights in the church building are turned off. Many times the people go outside, where the priest and ministers gather around a pile of wood. The priest lights the wood and blesses the fire. Then he lights the Easter candle from the new fire. The Easter candle is lit at all Masses through the Easter Season and at Baptisms and funerals throughout the year.

The priest or deacon, carrying the Easter candle, then leads the people into the darkened church. They light their own small candles from the Easter candle. After the presider has taken his place at the altar and the people have found their own places, he, the deacon, or a cantor sings a traditional song known as the Easter Proclamation. Those gathered hear how Christ has conquered the darkness of sin and death forever. The lights of the church are turned on, and the small candles are extinguished.

- **The Liturgy of the Word.** Those gathered hear and respond to a number of readings from the Old Testament and New Testament, recounting a brief history of God's plan of salvation. The history of salvation begins with creation, reaches its highest point in Christ, and lasts until the end of time. It is the story told in the Bible—the story of God's saving actions for humans. Important events of salvation history in the Old Testament include God's promise to Abraham, the Exodus, the covenant given to Moses, the Israelites' entering the land of Canaan, and the establishment of the kingdom of Israel under David. In the New Testament, salvation history is seen as coming together in the life, death, and Resurrection of Jesus. It continues today in the life of the Church.

- **The Liturgy of Baptism.** The priest blesses the water in the baptismal font or pool. The assembly prays a litany of the saints, a prayer for the intercession of the saints. Then the catechumens—those who have been preparing for entrance into the Christian community—come forward to be baptized and confirmed. On this night, those gathered rejoice in faith in the Resurrection and remember their calling to imitate Christ.

- **The Liturgy of the Eucharist.** As at every Mass, gifts of bread and wine are offered by the people through the priest to God. We give God thanks and praise for the tremendous gift of salvation. We pray that our reception of Holy Communion may make us stronger in faith and may enable us to live as Christians in daily life. At the end of Mass, the priest tells us, "Go in peace to love and serve the Lord, alleluia, alleluia." We answer, "Thanks be to God, alleluia, alleluia."

The light of the Easter candle is shared throughout the church.

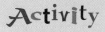

Activity

Read one of the following Old Testament passages for the Easter Vigil. Then, with a skit, dance, mime, painting, slide show, or some other creative rendering, express how you think this passage relates to salvation history and the Paschal mystery. Be prepared to share and explain your "creation" with the class.

- Creation—Genesis 1:1—2:2
- Abraham's sacrifice of Isaac—Genesis 22:1–18
- The crossing of the Red Sea—Exodus 14:15—15:1
- God's covenant with Israel—Isaiah 54:5–14
- God's invitation to an everlasting covenant—Isaiah 55:1–11
- How to walk in God's way—Baruch 3:9–15, 32—4:4
- God's promise of forgiveness—Ezekiel 36:16–28

Catholics have two traditional devotional practices that include reflection on the Paschal mystery. One of these practices is called the Rosary. The word *rosary* means "rose garden." Each individual prayer in the Rosary is like a rose in a rose garden. It is beautiful in itself, but it also contributes to the whole.

Many people believe that the Rosary originated with Saint Dominic, the thirteenth-century founder of a religious order that became known as the Dominicans. Actually, the Rosary predates that time, but the Dominican friars played an important part in making the Rosary a popular devotional prayer. Also, the Dominican, Pope Pius V (1566–1572), fostered the use of the Rosary and added a new feast for Our Lady of the Rosary to the Church year. That feast is celebrated on October 7.

The Rosary is a **sacramental**. Sacramentals are holy signs used by Catholics that have certain similarities to the Sacraments. They help us pray and remember God's love for us. These sacred signs are used by the faithful to show their identification with God.

The complete Rosary traditionally consisted of fifteen decades (groups of ten) of Hail Marys, each beginning with the Lord's Prayer and ending with a Glory to the Father. The focus of each decade is meditation on an event in the life of Jesus or his mother, Mary. Each event is recognized as a mystery—something that cannot be fully understood, but is accepted by faith.

The first group, known as the Joyful Mysteries, consists of five events related to the Incarnation: the Annunciation, the visitation of Mary to Elizabeth, the Nativity of Jesus, the presentation of Jesus in the temple, and the finding of the twelve-year-old Jesus in the temple. The second group, known as the Sorrowful Mysteries, consists of five events of the Passion—Jesus' agony in the garden, Jesus' scourging at the pillar, Jesus being crowned with thorns, Jesus' carrying of his cross through the streets of Jerusalem, and the crucifixion and death of Jesus. The third group, known as the Glorious Mysteries, consists of five events related to the glorification of Christ: the Resurrection, the Ascension, the descent of the Holy Spirit on Pentecost, the Assumption of Mary into heaven, and the coronation of Mary as queen of heaven and mother of the Church.

In 2002 Pope John Paul II introduced a change into this centuries-old prayer form when he added a new set of mysteries: the Mysteries of Light, or the Luminous Mysteries. These mysteries emphasize the divine nature and mission of Jesus and are drawn from his life. They are: the baptism of Christ in the Jordan, his self-manifestation at the wedding feast of Cana, the announcement of the kingdom along with the call to conversion, the Transfiguration, and the institution of the Eucharist as the sacramental expression of the Paschal mystery. The pope wrote "Each of these mysteries is a revelation of the kingdom now present in the very person of Jesus." (See the Catholic Source Book to learn about praying the Rosary.)

The Stations of the Cross

Another traditional Catholic devotion that incorporates events from the Paschal mystery is the Stations of the Cross. This prayer focuses on fourteen scenes from the passion of Christ.

As Christianity spread to all parts of the world, Christians began to make pilgrimages to the Holy Land to retrace the steps of Jesus. They wanted to see and pray in the places where Jesus himself had been. Many pilgrims to Jerusalem particularly wanted to retrace the steps of Jesus as he carried his cross to his death on Calvary (Golgotha). This route became known as the *Via Dolorosa,* or Way of Sorrows. The pilgrims stopped at fourteen places along the way to pray and meditate on one aspect of Christ's passion.

These teens have gathered to walk an outdoor Way of the Cross.

During the thirteenth century, the fighting of the crusades prevented people from making a pilgrimage to Jerusalem. So the Franciscans decided to bring the Stations of the Cross to the people. They introduced to local churches a series of fourteen paintings, woodcuttings, or ceramic pieces that represented each station. People could symbolically visit the Way of Sorrows, by stopping at each station in their own church and meditating on the passion.

Some modern churches—citing the fact that the Paschal mystery includes the Resurrection in addition to the passion and death of Jesus—have a fifteenth station: the Resurrection. Today in Jerusalem, the Franciscan friars lead a procession along the *Via Dolorosa* at 3:00 P.M. each Friday. The Stations of the Cross are especially popular during Lent. At each station, people pause and often say a version of this short prayer:

> " We adore you, O Christ, and we bless you,
> because by your holy cross you have redeemed the world. "

What is most important about the Stations of the Cross is not their number or their geographical location. What is most important is that we continue to walk in faith even in times of suffering (see the Catholic Source Book for the Stations of the Cross.)

Activities

1. Write a meditation for teens based on one of the Stations of the Cross. Be prepared to share your meditation with the class.
2. Do modern-day Stations of the Cross in a booklet, electronic slide form presentation, or dramatic presentation. Include a short reflection for each station.

A PERSON OF FAITH
ELIZABETH ANN SETON

Elizabeth Bayley was born in New York City on August 26, 1774. She was the daughter of an important Episcopal family. After Elizabeth's mother died when she was less than three, her father remarried. In 1791 Elizabeth met William Seton, the heir of a New York shipping firm: Seton, Maitland, and Company. They were married in 1794, and set up their home in New York City. Elizabeth had five children. The family had servants and traveled often. Elizabeth had many responsibilities as wife and mother, but she also gathered several friends to form the Society for the Relief of Poor Widows with Children.

Unfortunately, a continuing undeclared war between England and France negatively affected the shipping business, and William lost his family's wealth. At the same time, he came down with tuberculosis, a frequently incurable illness at the time. Elizabeth devoted herself to William's physical and spiritual care, encouraging him in his conversion from a nominal Christian to a man of deep faith. In 1803 Elizabeth traveled with William to Italy for his convalescence. After a seven-week sea voyage and quarantine for another month because of a recent yellow fever outbreak in New York, they reached the house of their friends, the Filicchi family. But the cold, damp confinement in a dungeon-like building during the quarantine proved too much for William's health and he soon died.

For about six months Elizabeth stayed on with the Filicchis, who were Catholic. There she learned about the Catholic faith. Upon returning to New York, Elizabeth studied Catholicism for a year and then was received into the Catholic Church. Elizabeth was ostracized by her family and by Protestant New York society. Elizabeth was also financially strapped because of the bankrupt family business. To support her family, she opened a school and boarding house for young children, but the school failed. Then, in 1808, Elizabeth moved to Baltimore and opened a school for young girls.

In 1809 Samuel Cooper, a wealthy convert and seminarian, purchased property in Emmitsburg, Maryland, for Elizabeth. There she began a religious community and a school for girls. She made her religious profession before Bishop John Carroll and, as founder of a religious community, the American Sisters of Charity, received the title, "Mother." By July of 1809 the community included Elizabeth and four sisters; daughters Anna, Catherine, and Rebecca; and two young students. Elizabeth's two sons attended St. Mary's College.

The community expanded rapidly and operated a free day school for young girls and a boarding school for girls. Mother Seton observed classes, taught, supervised textbook writing, led religious retreats and conferences, translated religious books from French to English, and wrote spiritual articles. The women also cared for people who were sick, taught religion to children and adults, and worked as nurses at the Emmitsburg Mount St. Mary's College and Seminary. In 1814 in Philadelphia, the sisters opened the first North American Catholic orphanage. A second orphanage was opened in New York in 1817. Elizabeth and her Sisters are considered the founders of the Catholic parochial school system in the United States.

In 1811 Elizabeth contracted tuberculosis. Her daughter Anna died of tuberculosis in 1812 and Rebecca in 1816. Elizabeth died in Emmitsburg at the age of forty-six. On Dec. 18, 1959, she was declared "Venerable." On March 17, 1963, she was declared "Blessed." On September 14, 1975, she was canonized as the first native-born saint of the United States. Her feast day is January 4.

Let's Talk!

1. Why was Elizabeth declared a saint?

2. What are some practical ways that teens today can imitate her?

Celebrating Faith

Opening Song:	"Follow the Light"
Leader:	Lord Jesus, thank you for always being with us, especially in times of hardship and suffering. Help us follow in your footsteps as did Saint Elizabeth Ann Seton, whom we now ask to intercede to God for us.
Reader 1:	Elizabeth, Loving Daughter,
All:	**Encourage in all children obedience and love.**
Reader 2:	Elizabeth, Searching Teenager,
All:	**Speak to today's confused, sometimes abused, young people.**
Reader 3:	Elizabeth, Faithful Wife,
All:	**Grant gifts of love and generosity to all spouses.**
Reader 4:	Elizabeth, Caring Mother,
All:	**Share your mother's heart with all parents.**
Reader 5:	Elizabeth, Grieving Widow,
All:	**Look with compassion on all bereaved wives.**
Reader 6:	Elizabeth, Loyal Friend,
All:	**Teach us to share friendship generously.**
Reader 7:	Elizabeth, Heroic Searcher of Truth,
All:	**Guide all who, with fear and doubt, seek the way.**
Reader 8:	Elizabeth, Courageous Convert,
All:	**Strengthen the newly baptized as they embrace the faith.**
Reader 9:	Elizabeth, Steadfast Religious,
All:	**Inspire young women to follow in your path.**
Reader 10:	Elizabeth, a Woman for All Women,
All:	**Bestow your charism of love and service on all women today.**
Leader:	Let us now offer spontaneous intercessions for people we know who are suffering. *(Spontaneous prayers)*
Leader:	Let us pray:
All:	**Our Father, you would not willingly call on us to suffer. You say all things work together for our good if we are faithful to you. Therefore, if you ordain it: through disappointment and poverty, sickness and pain, even shame and contempt and calumny, you will support us with the consolation of your grace and compensate us for any temporal suffering by the possession of that peace which the world can neither give nor take away.**

M. Irene Fugazy, SC, "Litany of St. Elizabeth Seton," (Sisters of Charity, Mount St. Vincent, New York); prayer by Saint Elizabeth Ann Seton, from the National Shrine of Saint Elizabeth Ann Seton.

Review

1. How was Jesus a different messiah from what many people were expecting?

2. Why did certain people want Jesus to be put to death?

3. How does each passion narrative present Jesus?

4. What is the Christian attitude toward suffering?

5. What happened at the Last Supper of Jesus?

6. What does Jesus' agony in the garden of Gethsemane tell us about the faith of the Apostles?

7. Who is to blame for the death of Jesus? Why does the death of Jesus not justify anti-Semitism?

8. What does the Apostles' Creed mean when it says that Jesus was buried and descended into hell?

9. How do the Gospels try to show us that the Resurrection of Jesus was a historical event and not just something the Apostles made up?

10. What is the Ascension of Jesus? What does the Church believe about this event?

11. What are the capital sins? What do these sins tell about human morality?

12. What are the four main events of Holy Week? What does the Church celebrate at these liturgies?

WORDS OF FAITH

Ascension—the taking up of the Risen Christ to heaven

blasphemy—the serious sin of showing contempt or lack of reverence for God and his name

capital sins—grave offenses, sometimes called "deadly sins" because they turn people completely away from God; called "capital" because they are the sources of other sins

crucifixion—a form of capital punishment by which a person was tied or nailed to a cross; the death of Jesus on the cross

Easter Vigil—the opening liturgy of the Easter celebration, held after sundown on Holy Saturday, during which salvation history is recounted and adults are initiated into the Catholic Church

Good Friday—the Friday before Easter; the day Jesus died on the cross for our redemption

Holy Thursday—the Thursday before Easter. On this night, the Church celebrates the institution of the Eucharist at the Last Supper of Jesus.

mortal sin—a very serious wrong that is contrary to God's law. The effect of mortal sin—if not repented—is eternal separation from God.

Enrichment

Choose one of the following.

1. Invite a local Jewish rabbi or leader to class to discuss Jewish customs and rituals, especially those surrounding Passover. As a class, walk through the Passover Seder meal.

2. Create a booklet of pictures, drawings or sketches that depict the Seven Last Words of Jesus as found in the Gospels. Place each of his last words on its own page so that it could be used as a kind of prayer book.

3. Dramatize the passion of Jesus in a class production of the Passion Play. Use the Gospel accounts of Jesus' passion, death, and Resurrection as the source for the script. Perform your class play for people in other classes in the school, students in grade school, or those in care centers.

4. Write a description of Jesus' trial and crucifixion from the viewpoint of one of the witnesses of these events, for example, Mary, his mother; Pontius Pilate; one of the Apostles; the chief priest; a member of the Sanhedrin; the people along the way to Calvary; a Roman soldier; or one of Jesus' disciples, such as Mary Magdalene.

5. Look through newspapers and magazine ads for examples and apparent illustrations of the capital sins. Prepare a short pictorial report that shows how advertisements seem to depict or promote these sins.

Paschal mystery—the events involved in our redemption: the passion, death, Resurrection, and Ascension of Jesus

passion—intense suffering for another, out of love for that person. The passion of Christ refers to the suffering and death of Jesus Christ out of love for humanity.

Redemption—God's saving activity in Jesus in freeing humankind from the bonds of sin and eternal death; the word means buying back or ransoming.

Resurrection—God's raising of Jesus from death to new life

sacramental—a holy sign used by Catholics that helps us to pray and remember God's love for us

second coming—the return of Jesus Christ as King and Judge at the end of time

sin—an offense against God that causes a rupture of communion with him, wounds our human nature, and injures solidarity with others

suffering servant—according to Isaiah, the one who would unjustly, but willingly, suffer and die for others

venial sin—a less serious wrong that weakens, but does not destroy, our relationship with God and other people, or a serious wrong done without full knowledge or free will

Children of Light

"For once you were darkness, but now in the Lord you are light. Live as children of light—for the fruit of the light is found in all that is good and right and true."

EPHESIANS 5:8–9

In this chapter, you will:

- explore how the Holy Spirit works in daily life and helps people make life-giving choices.

- identify the gifts of the Holy Spirit and learn how to live as one, holy, catholic, and apostolic Church.

- distinguish between the letter and the spirit of the Law.

- describe the help that sanctifying grace gives us to live as children of light.

- recognize that the Holy Spirit enables people to pray and that there are different types of prayer.

- learn to become better at listening to the Holy Spirit.

WORDS OF FAITH

actual grace	gifts of the Holy Spirit	marks of the Church
Church	Holy Orders	Pentecost
Confirmation	Holy Spirit	sanctifying grace
fruit of the Holy Spirit		

MAKING CHOICES

Have you ever stopped to think about all the decisions you make each day? Some of these decisions may not be very important—like what color socks to put on or what cap to wear. Other decisions may be very important, affecting not only your present well being but also your future. Some decisions have far-reaching consequences; many also affect the lives of others.

One of the most important moral decisions teens make each week concerns whether to drink alcohol. Even though it is illegal in the United States for anyone under the age of twenty-one to buy or possess alcohol, many young people are, in fact, drinking. In the United States, alcohol-related motor vehicle crashes are the second leading cause of teen death.

Teenagers and Alcohol

A survey conducted by the National Center for Social Research in 2001 revealed that, of the 20 million junior and senior high school students in the United States, about 50 percent drink alcohol every month. Consider these additional statistics:

- Twenty-four percent of eighth graders say they have used alcohol in the last thirty days.
- More than 100,000 twelve- to thirteen-year-olds binge drink every month. Binge drinking is defined as consuming four or more drinks in a row, three or more times in a two-week period.
- Three million teens ages fourteen to seventeen are regular alcohol drinkers who already have a confirmed alcohol problem.
- Forty percent of children and teens who begin drinking before the age of fifteen will become alcoholics at some point in their lives.

National Council on Alcoholism and Drug Dependence

Underage drinking can have serious negative consequences. A study of ninth-grade students in four urban high schools shows that alcohol and drug use are the best predictors for "regretted" sex, unwanted pregnancies, and sexually transmitted diseases—including AIDS. Alcohol poisoning kills brain cells and produces permanent brain damage; it can even lead to coma and death. And, as one study shows, teens who drink are almost twice as likely to attempt suicide as those who don't. Because alcohol can be so deadly in children and teens, the Church teaches that underage drinking and irresponsible drinking by adults are both morally wrong. These actions are sins against the Fifth Commandment: "You shall not kill."

If drinking is so dangerous and morally wrong, why do so many teens choose to drink? Some are bored; they have nothing better to do. Others are pressured by peers to drink. But the greatest number—79 percent—say that alcohol helps them forget their problems; they drink because "it feels good."

Reflection

What are your attitudes and behaviors toward alcohol?

Let's Talk!

1. During the era of Prohibition, alcohol became more desirable to many people simply because it was illegal. Do you think teens are tempted to drink because it is illegal? Do you think the legal age for drinking should be lowered? Justify your opinion.

2. Do you think there is a drinking problem among the students at your school? Why do you think that?

The Spirit of Life

Each Person of the Trinity conveys God's eternal love. Each Person invites us to enter into a covenant of friendship with him. God always sends the Holy Spirit when he sends his Son. Their mission is one and inseparable.

Though the ancient Israelites were unaware of the Holy Spirit as a distinct Person in God, they associated the Holy Spirit with being alive, with the principle of life itself. For them, the Holy Spirit, associated with God's life, was the power that helped them live by his commandments. In referring to receiving life, God said to Moses:

> " See, I have set before you today life and prosperity, death and adversity. If you obey the commandments of the LORD your God that I am commanding you today, by loving the LORD your God, walking in his ways, and observing his commandments, decrees, and ordinances, then you shall live and become numerous, and the LORD your God will bless you in the land that you are entering to possess. . . . I have set before you life and death, blessings and curses. Choose life so that you and your descendants may live, loving the LORD your God, obeying him, and holding fast to him; for that means life to you and length of days, so that you may live in the land that the LORD swore to give to your ancestors, to Abraham, to Isaac, and to Jacob. "
>
> DEUTERONOMY 30:15–16, 19–20

Reflection

Using the handout your teacher will provide, rate how easy or difficult it is for you to make life-giving choices regarding certain behaviors. In your journal explore why you gave yourself these ratings.

Apostles' Creed: I believe in the Holy Spirit,
Nicene Creed: We believe in the Holy Spirit, the Lord, the giver of life, who proceeds from the Father and the Son. With the Father and the Son he is worshiped and glorified. He has spoken through the Prophets.

What we are discussing in this chapter deals specifically with this part of the creed. We will discuss the coming of the **Holy Spirit** at Pentecost, as well as his role in Christian life. Specifically, we will explore how he works in our daily lives and helps us make life-giving choices.

Activity

Compile a list of ten choices for teens to make that would be life giving. Compile a second list of ten choices for teens to make that would be deadly. Discuss and compare the lists. Then compile a class list of the top ten life-giving and deadly choices of teens today.

The Power of the Holy Spirit

The Old Testament describes the Holy Spirit not as a divine Person but in terms of divine power. He is the power of God that rests on favored prophets, judges, and kings. Israel's prophets are called "men and women of the spirit" because he is with them in a special way. The Holy Spirit also rests on certain judges, allowing them to make good judgments. "The spirit of the LORD came upon him [Othniel], and he judged Israel" (Judges 3:10). "[T]he spirit of the LORD took possession of Gideon" (Judges 6:34). God's chosen leaders receive their special authority through the Holy Spirit. As the First Book of Samuel tells us, "the Spirit of God came upon [King] Saul in power" (1 Samuel 11:6) and, later, upon King David (see 1 Samuel 16:13).

In the following passage from the prophet Isaiah, the "stump of Jesse" refers to the messiah being a descendent of Jesse, the father of King David. While Isaiah focused on an earthly king who would usher in a golden age, Jesus fulfilled this in unexpected ways.

"The Tree of Jesse" from the Psalter of Ingeburg of Denmark, thirteenth century.

" A shoot shall come out from the stump of Jesse,
    and a branch shall grow out of his roots.
  And the spirit of the LORD shall rest on him,
        the spirit of wisdom and understanding,
    the spirit of counsel and might,
    the spirit of knowledge and the fear of the LORD. "

ISAIAH 11:1–2

" Here is my servant, whom I uphold,
    my chosen, in whom my soul delights;
  I have put my spirit upon him;
    he will bring forth justice to the nations. "

ISAIAH 42:1

The Gospel according to Luke describes the conception of Jesus by the power of the Holy Spirit (see Luke 1:35). Through the action of the Holy Spirit, the Father gives his Son to Mary and, through her, to the whole world. Jesus is Emmanuel, "God with us." The Holy Spirit also came upon Jesus at his Baptism by John (see Luke 3:21-22).

Activity

The Jesse Tree is a traditional Advent symbol, showing the family tree of Jesus. Using the handout your teacher will provide, select one person from the Jesse Tree. Read the corresponding Scripture passage(s) and find out more about the person. Then, in a brief report, tell how the Holy Spirit empowered this person.

TITLES FOR THE HOLY SPIRIT

Various titles for the Holy Spirit can be found in the New Testament. Some translations of the Gospel according to John, for example, call the Holy Spirit the *Advocate* or *Paraclete*. An advocate is a person who is called to be at our side, and paraclete is often translated as "consoler." Thus the Holy Spirit will be at our side forever, consoling us in times of trouble, helping us to pray, and reminding us all that Jesus has taught us.

An advocate takes on the cause of another person.

The Holy Spirit is called the Spirit of adoption. By believing in Christ, we are given a new life in the Holy Spirit. We become God's children and are given the ability to follow Jesus. Empowered by grace, we will lead lives worthy of God's sons and daughters and find fulfillment in our heavenly home.

The Holy Spirit is like the breath God gives. As the Catechism says, "The Word of God and his Breath are at the origin of the being and life of every creature" (CCC, #703). In Ezekiel's vision of the dry bones, it is the Holy Spirit that makes the bones come alive (see Ezekiel 37:1–14). In short, he is the creative and life-giving person who animates people of faith. When the Holy Spirit is absent from our lives, we are like Ezekiel's dry bones—lifeless and unenthused. When the he fills us, we are vibrant and spirited.

It is important to remember that the Holy Spirit never forces or coerces us to do something we do not wish to do. "Now the Lord is the Spirit, and where the Spirit of the Lord is, there is freedom" (2 Corinthians 3:17). He always *invites* us to enter into God's life and love. And he *enables* us to respond in a positive way, if we so choose.

Activities

1. Using the handout your teacher will provide, look up the New Testament passages describing the Holy Spirit. Identify the title used or implied in each passage. Then choose which title is your favorite. Give reasons for your choice.

2. Make a collage of pictures or words, or draw or paint a picture that expresses who the Holy Spirit is for you and how he works in people's lives. Recall some of the titles for the Holy Spirit to help you.

The Promise of the Holy Spirit

At the Last Supper, Jesus promised to ask the Father to send the Holy Spirit to his followers.

> " If you love me, you will keep my commandments. And I will ask the Father, and he will give you another Advocate, to be with you forever. This is the Spirit of truth, whom the world cannot receive, because it neither sees him nor knows him. You know him, because he abides with you, and he will be in you. "
>
> JOHN 14:15–17

> " [T]he Advocate, the Holy Spirit, whom the Father will send in my name, will teach you everything, and remind you of all that I have said to you. "
>
> JOHN 14:26

> " When the Advocate comes, whom I will send to you from the Father, the Spirit of truth who comes from the Father, he will testify on my behalf. "
>
> JOHN 15:26

> " I tell you the truth: it is to your advantage that I go away, for if I do not go away, the Advocate will not come to you; but if I go, I will send him to you. . . . I still have many things to say to you, but you cannot bear them now. When the Spirit of truth comes, he will guide you into all the truth; for he will not speak on his own, but will speak whatever he hears, and he will declare to you the things that are to come. He will glorify me, because he will take what is mine and declare it to you. "
>
> JOHN 16:7, 12–14

Reflection

Recount a time in your life when the Holy Spirit helped you accomplish something. How was he present in your life? How did you come to really experience his presence and in turn know what Jesus wanted you to do?

Notice in these sayings of Jesus, the Holy Spirit is a divine Person. As Jesus explains, the Holy Spirit—who is one with the Father and the Son—will continue Jesus' earthly ministry through the Apostles and the Christian community. In these passages, Jesus makes it clear that the Holy Spirit will not reveal something new to the Apostles and their successors. Instead, he will help them understand what Jesus has already revealed to them.

Pentecost

The Holy Spirit promised by Jesus came to Mary and the disciples fifty days after Easter, on **Pentecost.** This day was a Jewish feast celebrated fifty days after Passover. For Christians it is the birthday of the Church.

The believers' sorrow, fear, and uncertainty were suddenly vanquished as the Holy Spirit came to them and empowered them to proclaim the gospel. The change in them was immediate. They began preaching to the crowds in Jerusalem and baptized "about three thousand persons" that same day (see Acts 2:41).

Just as the Holy Spirit filled the hearts of Mary and the Apostles on Pentecost, so he continued to animate the early Christian communities. The Acts of the Apostles describes the first deacons as "full of the Spirit and of wisdom" (Acts 6:3). The Holy Spirit helped these men make wise and prudent decisions on behalf of the community. Paul, in his Second Letter to the Corinthians, describes the Holy Spirit as the "spirit of faith" helping community members to believe in the gospel. He enabled the community members to live in peace, bringing them consolation and encouragement. He also filled the faithful with great joy. The Holy Spirit who came on Pentecost continues to be present in the Church today.

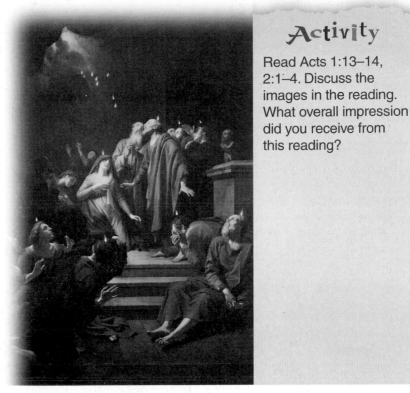

A depiction of the Holy Spirit descending on the Apostles in the form of tongues of fire. "The Pentecost," by Adriaen Van Der Werff.

Activity

Read Acts 1:13–14, 2:1–4. Discuss the images in the reading. What overall impression did you receive from this reading?

" And as for me, this is my covenant with them, says the LORD: my spirit that is upon you, and my words that I have put in your mouth, shall not depart out of your mouth, or out of the mouths of your children, or out of the mouths of your children's children, says the LORD, from now on and forever. "

ISAIAH 59:21

Activity

The Pentecost liturgy calls for a special hymn to be sung after the second reading and before the gospel acclamation at Mass. This hymn is called "Come, Holy Spirit." Using the handout your teacher will provide, read the words to this hymn. Then, in modern language if you prefer, present all or part of the hymn as a song, poem, rap, choral reading, dance, slide show, painting, drawing, or banner.

THE HOLY SPIRIT IN ACTION

The Holy Spirit inspired, enabled, and empowered the biblical authors to write all that he intended them to communicate. The Holy Spirit moves us, too, and brings us surprising new experiences of life. Consider this story:

I was only in high school when a spiritual director taught me this fundamental rule of the spiritual life. I had just had a wonderful experience in prayer and wanted to share it. If I had to guess, it probably had something to do with candles, a beanbag chair, and a record album like *Jonathon Livingston Seagull* or John Denver's "Sunshine on my Shoulders." (It was the '70s, after all.) The question I remember asking my spiritual director was this: Is it OK to listen to a record while trying to pray? Do I need to be on my knees? What about just staring out the window? Is it possible to pray the Rosary while listening to a song from another band I like?

"If it works, do it," he said. "Don't argue or struggle with the Holy Spirit."

The advice is as sound today as the first day I heard it. It's based upon a profound insight into the human person. The Holy Spirit intends to use every aspect of that which makes us human in order to communicate himself to us. Memories, understanding, intellect, will, sensations, emotions: there is no part of the human person that is foreign ground to the Holy Spirit. It is all God's creation, and its greatest purpose and meaning is expressed in communion with God. This means that God can—and will—seek communion with us in

every area of human life. Nothing is foreign to him. In fact, a lot of frustration in the spiritual life is due to resisting the pull of the Holy Spirit, often simply because the Spirit is claiming an area of human life that we didn't anticipate.

Suggestions:

"I simply pray better when I kneel." Then get on your knees. "I find that I pray better in the early morning." Then get yourself up. "Strange, but I actually feel close to God when I drive home from work in the evening." Then give yourself as completely as possible to the God of the homeward-bound drive.

Abraham has an experience of God and builds an altar (Genesis 12:7-8). Jacob sees a ladder of angels and erects a pillar to God on the spot (Genesis 28:10-22). The Old Testament is full of references to places being esteemed as holy because a revelation of God's love occurred there. One erects an altar because he or she plans to return, because one hopes to recreate the original experience. If it works, do it!

Shortened from Fr. Terrance Wayne Klein, "10 ways to improve your prayer life," *US Catholic* (March 1999)

Symbols for the Holy Spirit

The Holy Spirit is not visible to the human eye. Instead of using words to describe him, the following symbols are often used. (See the Catechism, #s 694–701.)

- **Water.** Throughout history, people have used water for cleansing and for drinking; water is a symbol for the action of the Holy Spirit in Baptism.

- **Anointing with oil.** Oil is used as food, for healing, and to produce light. To anoint a person is to make him or her sacred, set apart for God. Anointing with oil is a symbol for the action of the Holy Spirit in Baptism, Confirmation, and Holy Orders.

- **Fire.** Fire was used in traditional religious sacrifice to God. Throughout the centuries, fire has also been a source of warmth and light. Fire is a symbol for the transforming energy of the action of the Holy Spirit.

- **Cloud and light.** Cloud and light are symbols of God's guidance and protection. They often occur together in biblical manifestations of the Holy Spirit.

- **Seal.** In ancient times, a seal was a stamp that took the place of a person's signature. It was a legal sign of identity. It was also a sign of a covenant between two people. The seal as symbol of the Holy Spirit signifies "the indelible effect of the anointing with the Holy Spirit" in Baptism, Confirmation, and Holy Orders.

- **Hand.** The laying on of hands is a sign of the giving or conferring of power. When the Apostles laid hands on new converts, the Holy Spirit was given to them.

- **Finger.** In the Bible, the image of the finger of God refers to his power and action. The finger of God is also a symbol of the Holy Spirit who wrote God's law on tablets of stone (see Exodus 31:18).

- **Dove.** The dove is a traditional biblical symbol of God's presence and faithful love. "And when Jesus had been baptized, just as he came up from the water, suddenly the heavens were opened to him and he saw the Spirit of God descending like a dove and alighting on him" (Matthew 3:16).

Remember, human words can never adequately describe God. Likewise, these symbols cannot adequately describe the Holy Spirit. But they do point us in the right direction; they give us a place to start when we are trying to describe who the Spirit is and how he works.

Let's Talk!

1. Which symbol for the Holy Spirit is your favorite? Why?
2. What additional symbols for the Holy Spirit could be added to the list? Why?

The Gifts of the Holy Spirit

Even though we cannot see the Holy Spirit, we can know that he is present with us by what he does. We believe that he works in many ways. For example, he gives us seven spiritual gifts at Baptism. These **gifts of the Holy Spirit** are wisdom, knowledge, reverence, courage, understanding, right judgment, and wonder/awe.

To better understand the presence of the Holy Spirit in our lives today, we need to consider each of these gifts.

- **Wisdom.** Wisdom means "to see clearly." Wisdom refines common sense. It helps us see the "whole picture" regarding life and its meaning. It helps us see ourselves and others as God does.

- **Knowledge.** This spiritual gift is not about book knowledge or memorizing facts. Instead, it is the kind of knowing that comes from intimacy, from having a personal relationship with someone. Knowledge helps us know God and thus grow in friendship with him.

- **Reverence.** This spiritual gift helps us honor God, ourselves, and other people in appropriate ways. Reverence is described as respect—giving everyone and all things God has made their just due. It is also described as piety—responding to God's goodness in prayer and worship.

- **Courage.** This spiritual gift is also called fortitude. Spiritual courage helps us give witness to our faith and stand up for what we know is right. It helps us act on our beliefs and show love for others. It also helps us persevere in faith, even in times of discouragement and persecution.

- **Understanding.** To understand literally means to "stand under something." It means that we grasp the truth or bigger picture about a person or a situation. Understanding helps us see the world from the perspective of God and of other people. It leads us to reconciliation and peace in times of conflict.

- **Right judgment.** This spiritual gift helps us make decisions that are consistent with the gospel of Jesus. It helps us act in morally good ways— ways that are consistent with our friendship with God. Right judgment is also called counsel. This term reminds us that right judgment often involves asking others for help and offering good advice to others.

- **Wonder or awe.** Traditionally called *fear of the Lord*, this spiritual gift helps us remain open to the sometimes surprising, always loving presence of God. Wonder helps us appreciate the mystery of the Trinity and respond to God's initiative with love and goodness.

Essentially, when we are open to the gifts of the Holy Spirit working within us, we live and act in union with the **Church.** The word *church* (with a lowercase *c*) is the Lord's house, God's dwelling. A *church* is a building, an actual architectural structure. The word *Church* (with an uppercase *C*) refers to the people that God has gathered together through the entire world to form the Church, the Body of Christ and the Temple of the Holy Spirit. When we live and follow the teachings of Jesus and our Catholic Church we become a sign of communion with God.

Reflection

1. Which gift of the Holy Spirit has been most prominent in your life up to now? Cite examples when this gift helped you.

2. Which gift of the Holy Spirit do you think needs the most strengthening in you? Why?

Activity

Make a mobile, collage, or booklet depicting each of the gifts of the Holy Spirit.

THE MARKS OF THE CHURCH

The indwelling Spirit helps us cooperate with one another to form true community in Christ and to fulfill our role in the Church. The Holy Spirit gives the Church life and makes the Church holy. There are four distinguishing characteristics or **marks of the Church.** The Church, is one, holy, catholic, and apostolic.

The Church Is One

The word *one* means "united together." The Church is one because of

- its one founder, Jesus Christ
- the one Holy Spirit who forms and unites the Church with all of its many gifts of diversity
- the one faith proclaimed and celebrated through the sacraments
- the leadership of the bishops united with the bishop of Rome, the pope.

There are many gifts, but only one Spirit (see 1 Corinthians 12:1–11). The Church is one: she acknowledges one Lord and proclaims one faith. She celebrates one Baptism and is united in one Body. She is led by one Spirit.

Let us consider the Holy Spirit's action as unifier within the structure of the Catholic Church. The worldwide Catholic Church consists of twenty-two smaller Churches. These Churches are organized into five main Traditions— the Antiochene Tradition (West Syrian and East Syrian), the Byzantine Tradition, the Alexandrian Tradition, the Armenian Tradition, and the Roman Tradition. A Tradition is a particular religious family that has its own liturgy, spirituality, and laws. (See the chart in the Catholic Source Book.)

The twenty-two Churches are united as one Church in several ways. First, through the action of the Holy Spirit, all Catholic Churches accept the same faith received from the Apostles of Jesus. All profess the same creed. Second, all Catholic Churches celebrate the same seven sacraments. In addition, all Catholic Churches share the same apostolic succession of ordained ministers through the Sacrament of **Holy Orders.** And finally, all Catholic Churches recognize the bishop of Rome as the successor of Peter and head of the universal Catholic Church.

The universal Catholic Church encourages each of the smaller Churches to follow its own traditions and culture. Diversity brings great richness to the Church, but it also contributes to, rather than weakens, the unity of the worldwide Catholic Church.

Let's Talk!

Engraved on U.S. coins is the Latin phrase, *E Pluribus Unum*—in English, "one from many"—which implies unity in diversity.

- How does this saying characterize the United States?
- How does this same saying characterize the Church?
- How is diversity a "richness" rather than a "weakness"?

Research

Using the library or Internet, find out more about one of the Churches in the universal Catholic Church. Where is this Church located primarily? How does it celebrate the Mass?

Reflection

Write about a time when you found yourself standing up for what was true and right. Describe the event and what you said and did. This was a time you were a virtuous person—a time when you were holy, too.

The Church Is Holy

The word *holy* means "sacred, pure, like God." The Holy Spirit continually sanctifies the members of the Church, helping them become more and more like God. The Church is God's holy temple because the Holy Spirit dwells within it (see 1 Corinthians 3:16–17).

The Church is holy because its founder Jesus Christ is holy, and the Church is where the special presence of Christ can be found. The Church is also the way to holiness. This way to holiness can be found in hearing and reflecting on the Scriptures, celebrating the liturgy—especially the Eucharist and the other sacraments—and joining in the entire prayer life of the Church.

The Church is constantly striving for holiness, even though she is made up of people and leaders who, by human nature, are inclined to sin. The Church witnesses to holiness in that, over the centuries, it has raised up countless examples of heroic and holy men and women who have shown the world what it means to be virtuous and to follow in the footsteps of Jesus. In every age the Church has been and will continue to be an example of holy living in a sometimes broken, sin-filled world.

The Church Is Catholic

The word *catholic* means "universal." The Church is catholic because its unity comes from the unity of the Father, the Son, and the Holy Spirit. The Church is catholic because Christ is present in the Church. Christ is the head uniting his body, the Church. Because of Christ's presence in the Church, the Church has the means of salvation for all people. Furthermore, the Church is catholic because Christ gave the Church the mission to share his good news with all people. The Church has a missionary nature that Jesus himself defined when he said, "Go therefore and make disciples of all nations, baptizing them in the name of the Father and of the Son and of the Holy Spirit" (Matthew 28:19). In short, the Church is to be universal—to reach out and preach the coming of God's kingdom to all people. The Church therefore welcomes members of all races, countries, economic brackets, ages, and cultures.

After celebrating the Eucharist together, we are sent out to bring the message of Jesus to everyone we encounter.

The Church Is Apostolic

The word *apostolic* means "of the Apostles." The Church is apostolic because it is

- built on the foundation of the Apostles whom Christ chose to witness to his message and to lead his followers
- guided by the Holy Spirit, it continues to pass on the faith and teaching of the Apostles
- led by the successors of the Apostles, the bishops

The Church is built on the lasting foundation of the twelve Apostles. Our present-day bishops can trace their authority back to the Apostles through the Sacrament of Holy Orders. As the Catechism explains, "To proclaim the faith and to plant his reign, Christ sends his apostles and their successors. He gives them a share in his own mission" (#935). They receive from Jesus the power to act in his person.

Through Baptism, all Church members continue the mission of Jesus, first entrusted to the Apostles and their successors. The faith Christians have today is the same faith the first Apostles had and preached. They also share in the mission of the Apostles, namely, to share Jesus' good news with everyone, through words and actions. Like the Apostles, Christians have a responsibility to pass on the faith to future generations. The Holy Spirit calls everyone to witness to the good news in daily life and to reach out in love to all people.

Activity

Use the library or Internet to find the work of a missionary group, such as Maryknoll, Glenmary, Columban, or Divine Word, to find out what the group does. Explain how the community upholds and witnesses to the marks of the Church.

"Communion of the Apostles"
by Joos van Gent.

The Church as the People of God

Throughout the span of history, in every nation and culture, people who have honored God and attemptedto lead holy lives have been acceptable to him. But the reality of good individuals, not connected or linked to one another, was unacceptable to God. He willed a whole People of God who would honor and serve him by their holiness.

In the Old Testament, we see God carefully making a covenant with the Israelites and thus laying the foundation for his people. By sending his only begotten Son into the world, he established a new and eternal covenant. Jesus called together a race made up of all races. He acquired a people who previously were not united as a people. Through the power of the Holy Spirit, he established the Catholic Church as the People of God, "a chosen race, a royal priesthood, a holy nation, God's own people" (1 Peter 2:9).

When we profess "We believe in one holy catholic and apostolic Church" (Nicene Creed), we state our belief in the Catholic Church. We are stating the truth that Jesus, through the Holy Spirit, makes the Catholic Church one, holy, catholic, and apostolic. We believe that the Catholic Church is the Church founded by Jesus and handed on to the Apostles. We believe that the Catholic Church, governed by the pope, who is the successor of Peter, and by the bishops in communion with him, has the fullness of grace and truth entrusted to it by Christ.

The Church as the Body of Christ

By sending his Holy Spirit, Jesus spiritually assembles as his Body all those brothers and sisters who are called from around the globe. Through the Holy Spirit and the grace of the sacraments, especially the Eucharist, Jesus constitutes the Church as his Body. With Jesus as the head of the Body, the Church lives in and for Jesus, and he lives in and with the Church.

We become members of Christ's Body and are incorporated into the Church through faith and Baptism. Jesus said, "I tell you, no one can enter the kingdom of God without being born of water and Spirit" (John 3:5). Thus, Baptism is necessary for salvation just as the Church is necessary for salvation. "All salvation comes from Christ the Head through the Church which is his Body" (CCC, #846). But what happens to those who do not know Christ or his Church? If they do not know of Christ or the Church and yet sincerely seek God, and if they "try in their actions to do his will as they know it through the dictates of their conscience—those too may attain eternal salvation" (CCC, #847).

The Church as the Temple of the Holy Spirit

In many ways the Holy Spirit is the Church's soul, "the source of its life, of its unity in diversity, and of the riches of its gifts and charisms" (CCC, #809). The Spirit dwells with Christ as the Head of the Church and works throughout the Body of Christ. And as the ways of the Holy Spirit are a mystery, so too is the Church.

LETTER AND SPIRIT OF THE LAW ──

In the days of Jesus, the Pharisees and Sadducees taught that being a faithful Jew meant being faithful to the Law. Keeping the lesser laws was seen as a kind of fence around the greater laws; by keeping the lesser laws, a person was more likely to also keep the greater laws. The Sadducees especially believed this regarding purification laws and rules about the Sabbath.

For example, if a priest and a Sadducee encountered a bloodied man who seemed dead when they were on their way to the synagogue, those Sadducees who required strict adherence to the Law thought it was "most holy" to pass the man by without helping. According to a literal interpretation of the Law, the priest or Sadducee would be impure if he touched the man and would remain "unclean" for seven days. While he was "unclean," he would not be able to fulfill his obligations to worship God in the synagogue or temple. Another law required a good Jew not to do work on the Sabbath. Thus, it was thought to be "most holy" not to help a neighbor in need on this day.

Jesus, however, taught something different. Jesus pointed out that there are two aspects of the Law: its "letter," that is, what the Law actually says, "letter by letter," and its "spirit," that is, the purpose, or intent, of the Law. Jesus taught that while it is important to follow the law, it is most important to obey the spirit of the Law.

Once day Jesus told a story about a man beaten and bloodied and left by the side of the road. *(See Luke 10:29–37.)* A priest and a scribe pass him by, but a Samaritan man stops to help. Whom does Jesus praise for being holy? Not the priest nor the scribe, but the Samaritan! He alone obeyed the deeper, spiritual message of the Law: to love God and to love one's neighbor as oneself.

On numerous occasions, Jesus was criticized for doing work on the Sabbath. He let his Apostles gather the leftovers from the cornfields because they were hungry. He also cured sick people on the Sabbath. Jesus defended his actions by telling his critics that they had their priorities wrong. Loving one's neighbor is a *holy* way to obey the Law and to show love and reverence for God. In fact, when we love our neighbor, we are actually showing love for God.

The teachings of Jesus apply to Church members today when making decisions, especially moral decisions. If we are truly "holy," we will follow the law as the Holy Spirit directs us in our discernment of what is right and wrong. He helps us to keep our priorities straight. He helps us keep his laws and the laws of the Church. The Holy Spirit enables us to have a relationship of love with the Trinity and with others. He sanctifies us, or makes us holy.

"The Good Samaritan" by Vincent Van Gogh.

Reflection

Write about a time when you acted like the Good Samaritan described in the Gospel according to Luke. How did you show compassion toward another person when everyone else seemed to ignore or treat that person with contempt? How can you live each day in light of the Holy Spirit's call to justice and show love to your neighbors?

The Fruit of the Holy Spirit

Jesus once pointed out that we could know if a tree is good or not by the fruit it produces.

> " [E]very good tree bears good fruit, but the bad tree bears bad fruit. A good tree cannot bear bad fruit, nor can a bad tree bear good fruit. "
>
> MATTHEW 7:17–18

In a similar way, the Holy Spirit helps us to know whether or not we are living as "children of light." If we are truly living in the Holy Spirit, our actions will have good effects on other people and situations. We call these good effects the **fruit of the Holy Spirit.** These fruits, as listed in the New Testament, are "charity, joy, peace, patience, kindness, goodness, generosity, gentleness, faithfulness, modesty, self-control, and chastity" (CCC, #1832). The Church has also traditionally included goodness, modesty, and chastity among the fruits of the Holy Spirit. If we are not living in the Holy Spirit, our actions will have the opposite effects. "Children of darkness" produce hatred, sadness, turmoil, impatience, selfishness, evil, infidelity, oppression, and little concern for the rights of others.

We all know what happens when people are living in the Holy Spirit. The Church—a group that is one, holy, catholic, and apostolic—can truly be experienced. But what happens when there is scandal in the Church or among the Church's ministers? Has the Holy Spirit abandoned the Church? Should we, too, lose faith and leave the Church? The answer to these questions is "no." It is important to realize that the Church is both a human institution and a spiritual reality—the mystical Body of Christ. The human element of the Church is simply that—human. People are fallible; they can sin and make mistakes. Scandals, unfortunately, sometimes do occur, but the divine element of the Church is infallible. The Holy Spirit is always with us, helping us overcome our human temptations and limitations. God continues to bring salvation to people whom sin. Even in the midst of scandals, the Church is the best way God brings us to salvation. Instead of weakening our faith, scandals can strengthen our faith, reminding us to place our ultimate trust in God, rather than in people.

Although the Church is sanctified by the Holy Spirit and is the primary means of humanity's sanctification, the Church remains a pilgrim Church. As imperfect humans, we journey together toward holiness and perfection. In the Church, people are not yet completely holy.

The Catholic Church is the Church that Jesus founded and handed on to the apostles. The Pope and bishops ministering in union with him are the descendents of the first apostles in an unbroken line from St. Peter to today.

The Catholic Church contains the fullness of the means of salvation won for men by Jesus' passion, death and Resurrection. The Church that Jesus entrusted to Peter after the resurrection subsists in the Catholic Church. Many churches and ecclesial communities are not joined in full communion with the Catholic Church. The second Vatican council recognizes this lack of full unity but indicates that many elements of holiness and truth are found outside the visible structures of the Catholic church.

The seven flames represent the gifts of the Spirit.

Activity

Using pictures from magazines and newspapers, create a poster or collage that illustrates the fruits of the Holy Spirit.

—SEALED IN THE SACRAMENTS—

In the sacrament of Baptism, the Holy Spirit and his gifts are present. Christians are "sealed" and essentially changed. Christians enter into a new relationship with the Trinity through membership in the Church. So final is this "seal," that one may be baptized only once. The same is true of Confirmation and Holy Orders.

The sacraments of Baptism, Confirmation, and Holy Orders confer an indelible character or seal on the soul of the person. The seal stays as a permanent effect of these sacraments. Through this seal, the person is permanently configured with Christ.

In the sacraments, the symbol most associated with the Holy Spirit is the blessed oil known as *chrism*. Chrism is olive oil mixed with perfume. A person is anointed with holy chrism only at "life-changing" moments—immediately after Baptism, at Confirmation, and in Holy Orders for a priest or bishop.

Immediately after baptizing someone, the priest or deacon anoints the newly baptized person with chrism on the crown of the head, saying:

> " God, the Father of our Lord Jesus Christ,
>   has freed you from sin,
>   given you a new birth by water and the Holy Spirit,
>   and welcomed you into his holy people.
>   He now anoints you with the chrism of salvation.
>   As Christ was anointed Priest, Prophet, and King
>   so may you live always as a member of his body
>   sharing everlasting life. "
>
> THE RITE OF CHRISTIAN INITIATION OF ADULTS, #358.

"By Baptism, *all* sins are forgiven, original sin and all personal sins, as well as all punishment for sin" (CCC, #1263). In addition, the person is made a "new creature", an adopted son or daughter of God, a member of Christ's body, and a temple of the Holy Spirit (CCC, #1265). The baptized is given all the graces necessary for salvation—sanctifying and actual graces—and is incorporated into the Church, Christ's body.

Christian initiation is accomplished by three sacraments: Baptism which begins new life; Confirmation which strengthens that life; and the Eucharist which nourishes Christ's followers with his Body and Blood.

At **Confirmation,** the bishop (or his representative) lays his hands on the head of the person and prays that the Holy Spirit will come upon him or her as a Helper and Guide. Then, taking holy chrism, the bishop anoints the person on the forehead, saying: "N., be sealed with the Gift of the Holy Spirit" (The Rite of Confirmation, #27). At Confirmation, the person receives a special outpouring of the Holy Spirit. Baptismal graces are increased and deepened.

Let's Talk!

1. Have you been confirmed? If you have, what is something significant you remember about the celebration?

2. How do you think this sacrament has changed or will change you and your relationship with the Church?

At **Holy Orders,** the bishop lays his hands on a baptized man (whose suitability for this sacrament has been carefully examined) and says the consecratory prayer when the man is ordained. The consecratory prayer asks God for the outpouring of the Holy Spirit and his gifts proper to the priestly ministry. The Holy Spirit strengthens the new priest through his priestly consecration in his vocation and ministry. The bishop then anoints the hands of the new priest with chrism—a sign of his permanent consecration to God for service of the Church.

" The Father anointed our Lord Jesus Christ
   through the power of the Holy Spirit.
   May Jesus preserve you to sanctify the Christian people
   and to offer sacrifice to God. "

THE RITE OF ORDINATION OF A PRIEST, #24.

In the Sacrament of Orders, the recipient is configured to Christ to act as his representative as an ordained leader in the Church. He is configured to Christ as Priest, Pastor, and Teacher.

The Sacraments are intimately related to Jesus' Paschal Mystery. The graces won for men through Jesus' passion, death, and Resurrection flow through each sacrament. Christ continues to work in each of the sacraments thereby continuing the saving activity affected through his death and Resurrection.

It is important to remember that in each of these sacraments—Baptism, Confirmation, and Holy Orders—being anointed with chrism is not magic. The person does not automatically become perfect in holiness—never to sin again. Instead, the Holy Spirit strengthens one's Christian identity and helps one grow in holiness. Growing in true holiness is a lifelong process. It is a day-by-day challenge, something that affects all areas of one's life.

Sacramental People

Christians are "sacramental people." This expression means that the sacraments are a vital part of our lives. The sacraments help us grow in our spiritual life, our relationship with the Trinity. The term *sacramental people* also means that the whole community of the Church, united with Jesus, its Head, celebrates the liturgy.

All seven sacraments of the Church confer God's own life and help. This life and help called *grace* is not a "thing"; rather, it is a sharing in God's life and friendship. He freely gives us grace. When we are in his grace, we are in friendship with him. Grace helps us become more like him by making it possible for us to grow in holiness. Grace also helps us experience God's saving love, mercy, and forgiveness.

We cannot merit God's initial grace. We cooperate with his grace by living a good life and turning away from sin. As we cooperate with his grace, the merit for our good works "is to be attributed in the first place to the grace of God, then to the faithful" (CCC, #2008). We can merit only because God freely chose, "to associate man with the work of his grace" (CCC, #2025).

The Catholic Church distinguishes two types of grace. **Actual grace** is the assistance God gives us in a particular need, to perform a particular good action, or to avoid evil. **Sanctifying grace** is God's indwelling in us. Sanctifying grace makes us friends with God; it makes us holy. When we are in the state of sanctifying grace, we actually participate or share in the divine nature of God.

Through the Sacraments, one encounters the Holy Spirit and grows in holiness. That is why Catholics are encouraged to celebrate the Sacraments of Eucharist and Reconciliation frequently. The more we participate sincerely in the Church's sacraments, the more we grow in our relationship with God. We become stronger in resisting temptation and tend to sin less often. Living in the state of sanctifying grace helps us keep our focus on Christ as we strive to imitate him.

Actual graces given to us by God help us live in the state of sanctifying grace. But remember, one of his greatest gifts to humans is freedom. Humans are not perfect and thus sometimes choose to sin. Every sin has a negative effect on our friendship with God, realized through grace. Mortal sin completely destroys a person's relationship with him, effectively "killing" sanctifying grace within.

All is not lost, however. God continues to give us many actual graces, or helps, that move us to be sorry for our sins. If we cooperate with his supernatural helps, we can be restored to grace and our sins forgiven. This happens through the worthy reception of the Sacrament of Reconciliation or by making an act of perfect contrition with the resolve, or pledge, to confess any mortal sin in the Sacrament of Reconciliation. Perfect contrition is having true sorrow for sins primarily because they offend an all-good God.

Reflection

1. Write about a time that God gave you a special grace to avoid evil or do good. How did you respond to God's presence and love?

2. How do you think the Sacraments of Eucharist and Reconciliation have helped you grow in holiness?

3. How does "merit" relate to God's grace?

THE HOLY SPIRIT AND PRAYER

Christians are a prayerful people. Saint John Damascene defined prayer as "the raising of one's mind and heart to God." Prayer is a conversation, or dialogue, with the Holy Trinity or a particular Person of the Trinity. Sometimes we talk and God listens; other times, God talks and we listen.

Prayer, essentially, is one of the heartfelt ways we respond to God's invitation to friendship with him. Although it may seem that we are the authors of our own prayers, the Scriptures point out that it is actually the Holy Spirit within us who enables us to address God. Paul writes ". . . no one can say, 'Jesus is Lord,' except by the Holy Spirit" (1 Corinthians 12:3).

> " Likewise the Spirit helps us in our weakness; for we do not know how to pray as we ought, but that very Spirit intercedes with sighs too deep for words. "
>
> ROMANS 8:26

The Holy Spirit not only helps us pray, but is also *with* us as we pray.

- In a prayer of *adoration* we acknowledge that we are creatures before our Creator. We bless God who is the source of every blessing in life both now and forever.

- In a prayer of *petition,* we ask God to give us something we need. For example, we ask for patience in dealing with our parents. Or we ask for the ability to make the right choice in choosing a college.

- In a prayer of *intercession,* such as the general intercessions at Mass, we ask God to help other people, even our enemies. For example, we may ask him to make sick people better, or we may pray for world peace or an end to world hunger.

- In a prayer of *thanksgiving,* we express gratitude for something God has done. For example, we give thanks for the food we are about to eat. Or we give God thanks for the wisdom given to world leaders. We can face every joy and suffering with a prayer of thanksgiving.

- In a prayer of *praise,* we give God glory for his own sake, apart from what he does. For example, we praise God when we pray the prayer, "Glory to God" at Mass.

- In a prayer of *contrition* or *forgiveness* we express true sorrow for the sins we have committed. For example, we ask for forgiveness for the times we have missed Sunday Mass or did not show respect for ourselves or others.

Any of these types of prayers can be said alone (private prayer) or with others (communal prayer). They can be formal or informal.

The Church Unity Octave

Each year in January, the Church sets aside eight consecutive days to pray for Church unity. This time of prayer—which begins on January 18 (the Feast of Saint Peter's Chair) and ends on January 25 (the Feast of the Conversion of Saint Paul)—is called the Church Unity Octave. (The word *octave* means "eight.") The unity octave stems from Jesus' own prayer that his followers be united as one:

> " I ask not only on behalf of these, but also on behalf of those who will believe in me through their word, that they may all be one. As you, Father, are in me and I am in you, may they also be in us, so that the world may believe that you have sent me. "
>
> JOHN 17:20–21

During these eight days of prayer, we pray that the many Churches within the worldwide Catholic Church that are in union with Rome may grow closer together. We also pray for Orthodox Catholic Churches throughout the world and for the Anglican, Lutheran, Presbyterian, Methodist, Reformed, Baptist, Congregational, and other Christian denominations that are not presently in communion with the Catholic Church. At the present time, there are many historical, theological, cultural, and psychological obstacles that block the full union of all Christians. That is why the Catechism tells us that we as Church must pray and work for that unity.

During the Church Unity Octave, we are invited to reflect positively on the common source of life and light that we share as followers of Jesus. "To walk together, Christians need to be grounded in the Word of God, the revelation of God's face in Jesus, the renewing force of God's Holy Spirit, and the discovery of the love of God, Father, Son, and Holy Spirit" ("Week of Prayer 2002," *World Council of Churches*). Church unity is indeed the work of the Holy Spirit, helping us to overlook our differences and, instead, to look at the faith we share in common.

"St. Paul the Apostle."
Artist: Nicholas Markell.

This Eucharist celebration with the students of a Catholic school system took place on September 11, 2001.

Activities

1. Make a pie chart of your day, and divide the graph into sections to indicate how much time you spend doing different things. How much of the chart includes time with God? What can you do to strengthen that time?

2. If possible, attend an interfaith prayer service in your community. Share your experience with the class. What impressed you the most?

Ways to Listen to the Holy Spirit

The story of Pier (Peter) Giorgio Frassati is on the next page. He believed that listening to the Holy Spirit was always a matter of discernment involving the use of the seven gifts of the Holy Spirit. Here are some ways that you can increase your ability to listen to the Holy Spirit.

- **Listen to yourself:** Always remember that God loves you and made you the person you are. The Holy Spirit dwells within you and invites you to share in his own life and love. If you are truly listening to him within, you will have a healthy amount of self-esteem and confidence. You will keep trying to be the person God created you to be. You will also forgive yourself when you fall short or fail. You will learn to be gentle with yourself and to have patience when you are not perfect.

- **Listen to others, including the Church:** Always remember that God loves other people too and made them the persons they are. If they are living in his grace and friendship, the Holy Spirit dwells in them, even though it may not always seem like it. Have realistic expectations of your friends, your family, your teachers, and priests. Don't depend on them to make you happy or give you peace of mind. But learn from their experiences, both successes and mistakes. When conflicts occur between you and someone else, try to bring a sense of humility and humor to the situation. Ask the Holy Spirit to help you empathize, listen, and always be willing to forgive.

- **Listen to the circumstances in which you live:** The Holy Spirit also speaks to you in the situations in which you find yourself—if you are open to listening. For people of faith, no situation is entirely hopeless. There is always something to learn from every circumstance; each situation can be an opportunity for growth if your attitude is right. Don't fall into the trap of criticizing without being willing to work toward "fixing" the problem. Offer suggestions for workable solutions! Then join with others to make these solutions a reality.

- **Listen to God in prayer:** Develop an active prayer life. Pray in different ways, at different times or in different settings. Read the Bible frequently and learn how other people have grown stronger in their faith.

Reflection

What do you think the Holy Spirit is saying to you through the circumstances of life in which you presently find yourself?

A Person of Faith

Pier (Peter) Giorgio Frassati

Pope John Paul II has named more saints and blesseds (a stage toward canonization into sainthood) than any pope before him. Many of these new officially recognized holy ones of the Church are not monks and nuns or figures from the distant past. Some, like the Italian Pier Giorgio Frassati, lived lives similar to the way most young people today live their lives.

Pier was athletic and outgoing, an avid skier and mountain climber. He was known for being a person of joy and for spreading that joy to others. He also attended Mass daily and performed many acts of charity. Pier saw a natural connection between these two aspects of his spiritual life: "Jesus comes to visit me each morning in Holy Communion. I return his visit to him in the poor."

Alas, during one of his visits to a person sick with polio, he contracted the disease himself. He was only twenty-four years old. Nonetheless, he didn't let the fatal disease dampen his spirit of joy or his concern for others. In fact, the last thing he wrote was a request for medicine not for himself but for a friend who was ill but unable to afford it. Pier died in 1925.

During the beatification ceremony, the pope praised Pier for his embrace of "life's ordinariness," his devotion to the Blessed Sacrament, and the hope he spread through his simple expression of Christian joy to those around him. Pier lived out his faith and charity where he lived—in his family and school, in the university and society.

Pope John Paul called Pier "a living witness and courageous defender of this hope in the name of the Christian youth of the twentieth century which springs from the Gospel and to the grace of salvation which works in human hearts."

(See pp. 333–34 of *John Paul II's Book of Saints*, Matthew, Margaret, and Stephen Bunson, Huntingdon, IN: Our Sunday Visitor Publishing, 1999.)

Let's Talk!

1. What do you think Pope John Paul II meant by "life's ordinariness"? How would you describe the ordinary in your life? How different would that description be for someone who lived in another state, nation, or continent?

2. What connections do you see between the sacraments and works of charity?

Celebrating Faith

Leader: As we gather in prayer today, we remember that the Holy Spirit is here with us. He not only helps us pray, but also prays with us—helping us express what is in our hearts. And so we pray: Come, Holy Spirit, fill the hearts of your faithful,

All: **And kindle in them the fire of your love.**

Leader: Send forth your Holy Spirit and they shall be created.

All: **And you shall renew the face of the earth.**

Song: "His Eye Is on the Sparrow" (or "You Are Mine")

Reader 1: Most Holy Spirit, when we lose courage in the face of distress and daily problems, help us turn to you for consolation and solutions.

All: **For with you is the fountain of life, and in your light we see light.**

Reader 2: Divine Advocate, when we are enveloped by the darkness of doubt and indecision, walk with us and advise us.

All: **For with you is the fountain of life, and in your light we see light.**

Reader 3: Holy Spirit of truth, when we face the barriers we have erected between us as a result of jealousy, prejudice, or suspicion, send us the gift of community.

All: **For with you is the fountain of life, and in your light we see light.**

Reader 4: Holy Spirit of God, when we are discouraged by our own anxieties and fears, send us your wisdom and encouragement.

All: **For with you is the fountain of life, and in your light we see light.**

Reader 5: Holy Spirit of promise, when we feel isolated and alone, help us see what we share with other Christians.

All: **For with you is the fountain of life, and in your light we see light.**

Reader 6: Holy Spirit of Pentecost, when we are not at peace with ourselves or with others, teach us how to live and act as one Church.

All: **For with you is the fountain of life, and in your light we see light.**

(Pause for additional petitions and intercessions.)

Leader: Let us pray:

All: **Lord, by the light of the Holy Spirit**
you have taught the hearts of your faithful.
In the same Holy Spirit,
help us choose what is right
and always rejoice in your consolation.
We ask this through Christ our Lord. Amen.

Review

1. Who is the Holy Spirit? What is his relationship to God the Father and God the Son?

2. What was the role of the Holy Spirit in the Incarnation and in Redemption?

3. What happened on Pentecost after Jesus was raised from the dead?

4. What is the relationship between the Holy Spirit and the Church today?

5. What are the gifts of the Holy Spirit? Describe how each gift helps in one's life?

6. How is the universal Catholic Church organized?

7. How does the Holy Spirit help the Churches within the universal catholic Church be one?

8. How does the Holy Spirit help the Church be holy?

9. How does the Holy Spirit help the Church be catholic and apostolic?

10. Why does the Church teach that people can receive the Sacraments of Baptism, Confirmation, and Holy Orders only once?

11. How do the seven sacraments help growth in holiness?

12. What is the Church Unity Octave?

WORDS OF FAITH

actual grace—the assistance God gives us in a particular need or to perform a particular good action or to avoid evil

Church—the assembly of the faithful—those "whom God's word gathers together to form the People of God, and who themselves, nourished with the Body of Christ, become the Body of Christ" (CCC, #777). Through Baptism, "we are incorporated into the Church and made sharers in her mission" (CCC, #1213).

Confirmation—a Sacrament of Initiation that strengthens the spiritual life received in Baptism, sealing (or confirming) the person as being in union with Christ, making him or her ready to actively participate in the work and worship of the Church. The Holy Spirit is the prime agent in Confirmation. Through the powers of the Holy Spirit, divine filiation is deepened and an indelible character is imprinted on the soul of the recipient.

fruit of the Holy Spirit—the good effects that are a result of living in the Holy Spirit. The fruits of the Spirit are love, joy, peace, patience, kindness, generosity, faithfulness, gentleness, self-control, goodness, modesty, and chastity.

gifts of the Holy Spirit—spiritual gifts given by the Holy Spirit that help people live God's love: wisdom, knowledge, reverence, courage, understanding, right judgment, and wonder/awe

Enrichment

Choose one of the following.

1. Use the Internet or library to find out more about the Catholic charismatic movement. When did it originate? What are some of their practices? What is the importance of the Holy Spirit in their spirituality?

2. Read various parts of the Acts of the Apostles in the New Testament that relate to the workings of the Holy Spirit in the early Church. Draw a picture of one of these events.

3. At the advice of your teacher, arrange to attend a liturgy in a Catholic church of another Tradition. Do a report on your experience.

4. Plan a project to perform for the Make A Difference Day, such as helping those who are elderly maintain their homes or some other community-centered activity. If there is no local Make A Difference Day, decide and carry out as a class something that will show your Christian witness to your community, or plan to get involved in your school's service program, if there is one.

Holy Orders—the Sacrament of Service in which men promise to devote their lives to the Church as deacons, priests, or bishops

Holy Spirit—the third Person of the Holy Trinity

marks of the Church—the four essential or distinguishing characteristics of the Church: one, holy, Catholic, and apostolic

Pentecost—The day, "when the seven weeks of Easter had come to an end, Christ's Passover is fulfilled in the outpouring of the Holy Spirit, manifested, given, and communicated as a divine person: of his fullness, Christ, the Lord, pours out the Spirit in abundance" (CCC, #731). It occurs fifty days after the Resurrection of Jesus. We celebrate this day as the birthday of the Church.

sanctifying grace—God's divine life within us which makes us his friends

Your Light Must Shine

" You are the light of the world. A city built on a hill cannot be hid. No one after lighting a lamp puts it under the bushel basket, but on the lampstand, and it gives light to all in the house. In the same way, let your light shine before others, so that they may see your good works and give glory to your Father in heaven. "

MATTHEW 5:14–16

In this chapter, you will:

- explore the importance of group identity in relation to the development of personal identity.

- see that all Church members—laity and clergy—have a mission to build community within and outside the Church.

- realize that all are called to live the social gospel, just as Mary and the first Christians did.

- appreciate the Eucharist as the center of Church life and understand the parts of the Liturgy of the Eucharist at Mass.

- value prayers of blessing and see how veneration of Mary and the saints differs from worship of God.

WORDS OF FAITH

bishops	ecumenism	pope
canonization	Eucharist	priestly office
communion of saints	kingly office	prophetic office
	laity	religious vows
ecumenical council	magisterium	transubstantiation

— The Importance of Groups —

Some psychologists have defined *adolescence* as a time of rebellion and searching for independence from authority figures. Others have stated that the main task of adolescence is self-identity—finding out who you are and how you "fit in" with others. Searching for independence and searching for self-identity are really the same, involving one's understanding of, and relationship to, oneself *and* other people. Becoming an adult is not a solo adventure. It is a journey that involves other people as well as yourself.

The same can be said for spirituality. Relating to God is not a solo adventure. It is a journey that involves other people as well as yourself. Why? Because we are social beings. We don't function well in long-term isolation. We need others in order to grow as people and to experience genuine love. In fact, belonging to a group helps define our personal identity, just as belonging to the Church helps define our personal relationship with God.

Groups and Individuality

It is important to remember that discovering group identity, even Church identity, can be a confusing experience. Some people feel shy or awkward in group situations; they would much rather do things alone or with just one or two trusted friends. Other people blossom in the presence of lots of people; as far as they're concerned, "the more, the merrier." With so many different types of groups from which to choose, it's not always easy to figure out which ones are right for you and which ones are not. And even after you are in a certain group, you have to figure out how to belong to the group and still be your own person.

The following drawing illustrates the tension many people feel regarding groups. On the one hand is conformity; on the other, independence. You can lose yourself and conform completely to the group. Or you can be independent, be your own person. We need each other, and we need our *own selves*. So how do you balance conformity and independence?

Reflection

Where are you on the conformity-independence seesaw? Are you at one of the extremes or do you tend to be in the middle? Complete the handout from your teacher to find out. Then write a journal entry about whether you like your present attitudes regarding groups. Are there any changes you would like to make?

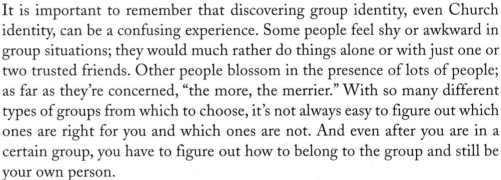

Group Conformity   Individual Independence

Conformity

First let's look at the conformity end of the seesaw. What is conformity? It's the pressure to do whatever the group does, whether you agree with it or not. Group conformity may express itself in seemingly trivial things, such as hairstyle, clothing, and shoes. Or it may express itself in more serious ways. For example, studies show that many teens are more likely to smoke, drink, and use drugs if their peer group smokes, drinks, and uses drugs. The same is true for shoplifting and committing other crimes. Many teens go along with things in order to fit in.

A certain amount of conformity is necessary in order to belong to a group, but extreme conformity is unhealthy. It can destroy a person's individuality. It can prevent people from ever finding out who they really are—and really being themselves.

Independence

Now let's look at the opposite: independence. Independence is being more or less free from peer pressure. It is having your own ideas about what is important, what is right, what is not right. It is being free to be who you are and say what you think—in a kind and gentle way. Can you be independent and still be in a group? Yes. As a matter of fact, the more you are yourself, the more group members will respect you. If they don't, it's not a good group to be in. Simple as that. So think about the groups you have belonged to so far in your life—family, friends, clubs, whatever.

One way to increase your sense of independence is to nurture your gifts and talents.

Let's Talk!

1. In what ways are you encouraged to conform at school? At home? In society? At church?

2. In what ways are you encouraged to be independent at school? At home? In society? At church?

Activities

1. Search through magazines for ads that try to sell something by using the human desire to conform and fit in. Bring several examples to class and be prepared to discuss why these ads are effective. Do the ads appeal to you? Why?

2. Search through magazines for ads that try to sell something by using the human desire to be independent, to be your own "boss." Bring several examples to class and be prepared to discuss why these ads are effective. Do the ads appeal to you? Why?

WHAT THE CHURCH IS

Activity

In a small group, make a list of five ways the Church has shaped and is shaping you as a person. When you have finished, compare your list to that of other groups in the class.

The word *church* (lowercase *c*) means "building used for worship." The word *Church* (uppercase *C*) means a convocation, the People of God called together, and a worshiping assembly. We come together, or assemble, because God's word has called us.

What we are discussing in this chapter deals with being active Church members. That is implied in the following part of the creed:
Apostles' Creed: I believe in . . . the holy catholic Church, the communion of saints . . . .
Nicene Creed: We believe in . . . one holy catholic and apostolic Church.

SIMPLE FAITH

As the woman walks up the driveway, Mary Larsen whispers her story: Recovering alcoholic. Five kids. Husband just got a job after a long time being unemployed. She's bringing a receipt, hoping for reimbursement for her son's school shoes.

Car accidents, surgeries, unemployment, mental illness, desperately sick children. Larsen soaks up hard-luck stories and reciprocates with kindness—and canned soup and cereal at the We Care Food Shelf, which she runs out of the four-car garage beside her southern Minnesota home.

"They're the most warm, caring people you'll ever meet," the woman, who didn't want to be identified, said of Mary Larsen and her family. "They're just like little angels to me. They're my angels."

Spurred by social-service agencies, church referrals, or word of mouth, people from 12 counties seek out Larsen. With her son, Joe; Sr. Magdalen Schwab, a Benedictine nun; and Sr. Gladys Meindl, a Franciscan nun, Larsen makes sure people leave her garage with boxes of groceries, sometimes a hug or gentle touch, and without prying questions or judgment. Larsen takes names for record-keeping purposes only, in a spiral notebook Schwab laughingly calls "Mary's computer."

This organization has no payroll. Every worker, starting with Larsen herself, volunteers the time to work with clients, solicit and organize donations, write out thank-yous to donors. They depend on donations, large and small, from individuals and corporations.

"It's a surprise every month when you open the mail," Meindl said.

Here, on the frontline of crisis, the impact of the dry growing season and the sputtering economy is apparent. In July, We Care gave 35,000 pounds of food, and quilts and cash to 212 families, up from 177 for the same month last year.

The stories are sometimes heartbreaking, but it is rewarding to be able to help, they say.

"Once, someone said we're the light at the end of the tunnel," Schwab said. "When they're so appreciative of anything they get, it kind of perks you up," Larsen said.

Larsen learned a tradition of giving on the farm with her parents, Frank and Clara Schwab, who often reached out to migrant workers on nearby farms. When Joe Larsen was in high school in the early 1970s, he brought home dented and surplus goods from his job at the Redwood Falls SuperValu. Sr. Magdalen sought out bargains in the grocery stores around Melrose, where she taught school. They gave away what they couldn't use. Pretty soon, people sought them out. Many food shelves have limitations on income, or on how often people can visit. Not We Care. Larsen has an 'as often as you need to' policy. "We don't have a limit as long as they don't waste anything," she said. And not only the poor need apply. Families from the Morgan area, experiencing hardship or illness, often find they need not ask for Larsen's help.

Dick Quast owns M&M Computers. He also served as mayor in the '80s and '90s. When he came home from the hospital after back surgery in 1999, he and his wife found a big box of groceries on their doorstep. "Our first reaction was, we don't need this; it should go to other people who are more desperate," he said. "We talked to her and she said, 'the project is We Care. We care about you, and this was something we wanted to do.'"

The Rev. Bob Wyffels, pastor at St. Michael's, holds up Larsen as someone who is living her faith.

She is an example, he said, of, "how much every person has to give of their time, of their care, of their willingness to say yes to God's call, of their willingness to be his instrument, to be his heart and his hands."

Visitors to Larsen's home come in by the driveway, but they might still see the little plaster angel praying by her front step, or the blue-draped Virgin Mary in her grotto at the corner of the house. Or maybe they'll see only Larsen, smiling and holding out her hands in welcome.

Larsen and Schwab say they do pray for the people they help. They'll pray with them, too, but only if asked. Each box of food also contains a slip of paper with a picture of a country angel, an encouraging poem, and the Larsen's, Schwab's and Meindl's home telephone numbers. Larsen spends hours on the phone, encouraging, offering resources, but more often just listening.

"It isn't always the money," Larsen said. "It's being cared about."

Shortened from Maria Elena Baca, "Pantry to the Prairie," Minneapolis Star Tribune *(September 6, 2003)*

Research

Find an example in a newspaper article, magazine story, or TV news coverage of a real-life story of people who accomplished something amazing or "miraculous" because they worked together. Be prepared to share and discuss your example in class.

The Church is always a community, the People of God.

The Importance of Church

The Bible tells us that when God called Abraham to have a covenant relationship with him, he did not call Abraham just as a single individual. He called Abraham as the patriarch or head of an entire family.

" God said to him, 'As for me, this is my covenant with you: You shall be the ancestor of a multitude of nations. . . . I will establish my covenant between me and you, and your offspring after you throughout their generations, for an everlasting covenant, to be God to you and to your offspring after you.' "

GENESIS 17:3–4, 7

In other words, God called *an entire people* to enter into friendship with him, to become the People of God. Three religions in today's world—Judaism, Christianity, and Islam—consider Abraham as their ancestor in faith. Likewise, when Jesus established the new covenant in his Body and Blood, he did not do so for his twelve Apostles only. Listen to what he said to them.

" Go therefore and make disciples of all nations, baptizing them in the name of the Father and of the Son and of the Holy Spirit, and teaching them to obey everything that I have commanded you. "

MATTHEW 28:19–20A

In other words, Jesus inaugurated the new covenant with the *Church*, the new People of God. From these actions of God—recorded both in the Old Testament and in the New Testament—we learn that faith is not just a private matter, something between God and the individual. Faith has a social dimension. Our religious nature involves our group identity as well as our personal identity.

Reflection

What is your attitude toward participating in the Sunday celebration of the Mass each week? Is it only an obligation or is it something to which you genuinely look forward? Why?

Teenagers and Church

All baptized Catholics regardless of age—are members of the Church. Anyone who is baptized, confirmed, and has received First Communion is a full participant of the Catholic Church. Over 65 million people in the United States are Catholic (USCCB). Forty percent of these Catholics are under the age of 38. More than half of these young people are teens or younger. You have a *major* part to play in the People of God. That is why, in his address to young people at the 2002 Youth Day in Toronto, Canada, Pope John Paul II said:

66 The world you are inheriting is a world . . . which needs to be touched and healed by the beauty and richness of God's love. It needs witnesses to that love. It needs you—to be the salt of the earth and the light of the world. . . . Even a tiny flame lifts the heavy lid of night. How much more light will you make, all together, if you bond as one in the communion of the church! 99

ORIGINS (VOL. 32. NO. 11), 183.

Without you, a large part of the Body of Christ would be missing. Without you, the Church's future would also be in trouble. That is why it is really important for you to understand what being Church is all about.

Let's Talk!

What are some ways that you and your friends can feel—and be—more involved in the Church and in shaping the Church, both in the present and in the future?

Pope John Paul II traveled to Toronto for the 2002 World Youth Day.

THE CHURCH'S MISSION

The mission of the Church is to continue the work of Christ in proclaiming and being a sign of the kingdom of God. The kingdom of God is his reign of justice, love, and peace. It is his presence expressed imperfectly in this world and fully in the kingdom to come and in heaven. The kingdom of God is another mystery of faith.

The kingdom of God that Christ will bring to perfection at the end of time has already begun. All members of the Church share in the mission of proclaiming and helping God bring about this kingdom. They have a responsibility to let their light shine and to be the salt of the earth. If this happens, people will be able to appreciate the kingdom of God here on earth.

Additionally, the mission of the Church is to build community, to let God's love shine through people. Members of the Church are called by God to enter into a communion of life, love, and truth with other believers. They are to share the light of Christ with one another. They are to build a community of faith, hope, and charity with others.

Reflection

1. How and when have other people been "salt of the earth" and "light of the world" to you?

2. How and when have you been "salt of the earth" and "light of the world" to other people?

Let's Talk!

1. When in your life have you experienced the kingdom of God? What was this experience like?

2. What are some everyday ways that teenagers can let their light shine and help build a community of faith, hope, and charity?

The Communion of Saints

Essentially, the whole Church consists of three groups of believers—those living on earth and still striving to follow the gospel, those who have already died and are in heaven, and those who have died and are in purgatory, being purified in preparation for entering heaven. We call the entire assembly of Church members the **communion of saints.**

According to the Catechism, the term *communion of saints* has two closely linked meanings: communion in holy things (*sancta*) and among holy persons (*sancti*). In one sense, all faithful members of the Church are called saints because Jesus has called us to be the holy People of God. In another sense, the term *saints* refers only to those deceased members of the Church, who have led lives of heroic virtue, have been **canonized** by the church, and are in heaven. Through an official statement declaring them a saint, the Church recognizes these persons' holiness throughout life. The Church applauds the witness of their lives and holds them up as role models for the way we should respond to God's grace. There are, however, many saints who have not been canonized, or officially recognized, by the Church. We celebrate these saints collectively on November 1, the feast of All Saints.

We believe that the greatest among the saints in heaven is the Virgin Mary. Mary is not only the Mother of God—being the mother of Jesus who is God incarnate—she is the Mother of the whole Church as well. By saying, "Be it done according to your will," "Mary was already collaborating with the whole work her Son was to accomplish" (Catechism, #973). This work continues—as Pope Paul VI, in his *Credo of the People of God,* said: "We believe that the Holy Mother of God, the new Eve, Mother of the Church, continues in heaven to exercise her maternal role on behalf of the members of Christ."

Indeed, all Church members on earth, in heaven, and in purgatory form a communion of love and concern for one another. The saints in heaven can intercede on behalf of the living and those who are in purgatory. Likewise, those on earth can pray for those in purgatory and can pray to the saints for help.

Reflection

Do you have a favorite saint? Is there a particular saint to whom you pray for help? Why do you have special devotion to this (these) saint(s)? Learn about your own Christian name and the saint from whom your name was taken.

Veneration or Worship?

Many Catholic churches contain statues of Mary, Joseph, or other saints. Some Church members like to pray before these statues and ask for God's blessings, either for themselves or for other people. What is important to realize is that praying with a saint is much different from praying to God. When someone prays to God, he or she gives adoration and praise to God, who alone is worthy of worship. When people pray with the saints, they are recognizing the saint's holiness and asking them to intercede with God on their behalf. In other words, they are asking them to ask God to bless them or someone for whom they are praying. This type of prayer is called intercession. They honor or venerate the saint, but they do not worship the saint.

Many Catholics have a special devotion to Mary, the mother of Jesus. They honor her holiness in following Jesus. They pray that she will help them follow him more closely. In many parishes throughout the United States, Mary is especially honored throughout the month of May. Children crown her statue with flowers and sing songs to honor her as the Church's mother and as their spiritual mother, too. Throughout the year, there are numerous other times that the Church honors Mary. Some of these special feasts of Mary can be found in the chart on this page.

In the Catholic Source Book, you will also find several traditional prayers to Mary. These prayers include the Hail Mary, the Hail, Holy Queen, and the *Memorare*. In addition, there is an ancient devotion prayed by the faithful when church bells ring at 6 A.M., 12 noon, and 6 P.M. each day. This prayer is called the *Angelus*, after its first words, "The angel." The prayer recalls Mary's role in the Incarnation of the Son of God. Many Catholics continue to say this prayer as a way of asking for God's blessing through Mary's intercession.

Research

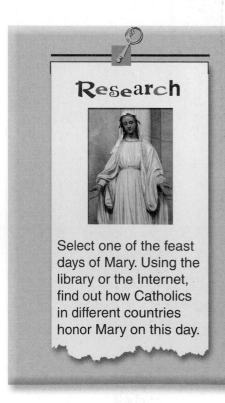

Select one of the feast days of Mary. Using the library or the Internet, find out how Catholics in different countries honor Mary on this day.

Feasts of Mary

Mary, Mother of God	January 1
Purification of Mary	February 2
Our Lady of Lourdes	February 11
The Annunciation	March 25
The Visitation	May 31
Immaculate Heart of Mary	Saturday following second Sunday after Pentecost
Our Lady of Mt. Carmel	July 16
The Assumption	August 15
Queenship of Mary	August 22
The Birthday of Mary	September 8
Holy Name of Mary	September 12
Our Lady of Sorrows	September 15
Our Lady of the Rosary	October 7
The Presentation of Mary	November 21
The Immaculate Conception	December 8
Our Lady of Guadalupe	December 12

THE CHURCH TODAY

Within the Church on earth there are two main groups of people, a smaller group of ordained members and a larger group of nonordained members. According to canon law, there are two classifications of the Christian faithful, clergy and laity. Clergy are those ordained men who have received the Sacrament of Holy Orders. They dedicate their lives to service in the Church as deacons, priests, and bishops. The **laity** are not ordained, but share in the common priesthood of *all* the faithful through their Baptism.

The people of God commonly understand three categories of the faithful: laity, religious, and clergy. Religious—those women and men members of institutes of consecrated life—may be either laity or clergy. Religious have a special commitment to God through their vows, but they remain either laity or clergy, depending upon whether they are ordained.

Although there are differences between ordained members and nonordained members in terms of ministry, one group is not "better than" or "holier than" the other. God calls all Church members to take part in the Church's mission. God calls everyone to holiness, to be a light to others. Further: ". . . all share a true equality with regard to the dignity and to the activity common to all the faithful for the building up of the Body of Christ" (*Documents of Vatican II,* "Dogmatic Constitution on the Church," #32).

The Ministerial or Hierarchical Priesthood

From among his disciples, Jesus chose twelve men to live and travel with him. They were his Apostles; their mission was to continue Jesus' work after he was gone. The Apostles became the first leaders of the Church. They were not kings or earthly rulers. Rather, they were ordinary men who worked hard and made many sacrifices to preach the gospel and to be servants to the People of God.

The successors of the Apostles today are the **bishops.** Members of the episcopate (bishops) have received the fullness of the Sacrament of Holy Orders, that is, all three orders, or degrees. The Sacrament of Holy Orders includes three degrees: diaconate (first degree), priesthood (second degree), and episcopate (third degree).

Bishops have the task of teaching, governing, and making holy in Jesus' name. The living teaching authority of the college of bishops in union with the **pope** (the Bishop of Rome) is known as the **magisterium.** The magisterium is responsible for faithfully handing on the teachings of Jesus and the Apostles in matters pertaining to faith and morals.

❝ For it is the duty of all the bishops to promote and to safeguard the unity of faith and the discipline common to the whole Church, to instruct the faithful in love for the whole Mystical Body of Christ, especially for its poor and suffering members and those who are suffering persecution for justice's sake (cf. Mt. 5:10). ❞

"DOGMATIC CONSTITUTION ON THE CHURCH," #23.

Reflection

How do you think God is calling you to serve the Church in the future—as an ordained minister, a layperson, or a member of a religious community? Why?

The bishops of the world gathered at the Second Vatican Council.

Research

Using the library or Internet, find out more about:

- One of the popes.
- A bishop who was a saint.
- A priest who was a saint.
- The present pope, an ordinary of the diocese (bishop), or a pastor.

Of the Apostles Jesus chose Peter to lead them. The pope, the bishop of Rome and thus the successor of Peter, is first among the world's bishops. He is leader of the bishops and the pastor of the whole Church. As part of his universal task of the "care of souls," the pope teaches the gospel through official pronouncements, encyclicals, homilies, and media broadcasts.

The college of bishops in union with the pope exercises its teaching authority in Church meetings known as **ecumenical councils.** Vatican I, the twentieth ecumenical council, met in Rome from December 1869 to October 1870. One of the most important teachings of this council concerned papal infallibility—that under the influence of the Holy Spirit, the pope is preserved from error when he speaks "ex cathedra" in matters pertaining to faith and morals. (*Ex cathedra* means "from the chair" of Saint Peter.) The most recent ecumenical council, Vatican II, met in Rome from October 1962 to December 1965. Its main purpose was to update and renew the Church, as well as to increase unity with other Christian Churches. The council also stressed the teaching that the bishops, gathered in an ecumenical council and in union with the pope, share in the infallibility of the Church.

Priests and deacons assist the bishops in their work. Priests receive two degrees of the Sacrament of Holy Orders, namely diaconate and priesthood. Secular (or diocesan) priests serve under the bishop in a particular diocese and promise obedience to him. In the Western Catholic Church, these priests make a solemn promise of celibacy; they do not marry. The Eastern Catholic Churches have had a long-standing practice of allowing married men to be ordained priests. This practice is still common today. Religious priests are members of religious orders, in addition to being ordained. They make the **religious vows** of poverty, chastity, and obedience, remain celibate (unmarried), and usually live in community.

Deacons receive the first degree of the Sacrament of Holy Orders, the diaconate. Transitional deacons are men who are ordained to the diaconate in preparation for the priesthood. Permanent deacons are men who do not intend to become priests but who wish to dedicate their lives in service to the Church. Permanent deacons may be single or married.

With the bishops, these ordained ministers have a responsibility to teach, govern, and help other Church members grow in holiness. The responsibilities of all ordained ministers include the following:

- They teach the true faith. This happens when they give homilies at Mass and teach in a variety of situations.
- They sanctify, or make holy, the Church by celebrating the sacraments with the people and praying the Liturgy of the Hours.
- They govern, or lead, the Church. Bishops and priests serve the people as true pastors. Most bishops head geographic areas in the Church known as dioceses.

The Laity

Just as the ministerial priesthood focuses on serving people's needs within the Church, so the lay faithful serve especially the needs of the world. Their sphere of service includes family life, cultural pursuits, economic interests, the trades and professions, political institutions, and international relations. As the bishops of Vatican II specify,

" [T]he laity, by their very vocation, seek the kingdom of God by engaging in temporal affairs and by ordering them according to the plan of God. . . . They are called there by God so that by exercising their proper function and being led by the spirit to the gospel they can work for the sanctification of the world from within, in the manner of leaven. In this way they can make Christ known to others, especially by the testimony of a life resplendent in faith, hope, and charity. "

"Dogmatic Constitution on the Church," #31.

Priest, Prophet, and King

In addition to the ministerial, or hierarchical, priesthood to which only some men are called, there exists the *common priesthood*, or priesthood of the faithful, in which all baptized Christians share. Hence, every Church member, by virtue of Baptism, shares in the mission of Christ, who is priest, prophet, and king.

" [Y]ou are a chosen race, a royal priesthood, a holy nation, God's own people, in order that you may proclaim the mighty acts of him who called you out of darkness into his marvelous light. "

1 Peter 2:9

How do laypeople participate in the **priestly office** of Christ? In essence, laypeople of faith offer everything in life as a spiritual sacrifice to God through Jesus Christ.

" For all their works, prayers, and apostolic endeavors, their ordinary married and family life, their daily labor, their mental and physical relaxation, if carried out in the Spirit, and even the hardships of life, if patiently borne—all of these become spiritual sacrifices acceptable to God through Jesus Christ (cf. 1 Pet. 2:5). "

"Dogmatic Constitution on the Church," #34.

Laypeople may also participate during the Eucharist in various liturgical ministries, such as:

- **Ushers or ministers of hospitality.** These laypeople greet others as they arrive for Mass. They help them find a seat and hand out worship aids. At the end of Mass, these ministers also distribute the parish bulletin.

- **Altar servers.** These laypeople can be either children or adults who assist the priest at the altar. They hold the Sacramentary, which is the book of prayers, and help in preparing the bread and wine.

- **Readers.** Readers proclaim the Scripture readings for the day's Mass. They also lead the general intercessions.

- **Extraordinary ministers of Holy Communion (or Eucharistic ministers).** These liturgical ministers help the presider distribute Communion during Mass. Some Eucharistic ministers also bring Communion to people confined at home or in care centers.

- **Music ministers.** These people lead the assembly in singing during Mass. Music ministers include vocalists (choir, cantors) and instrumentalists. The music selected, whether it is traditional or contemporary, is chosen to make the liturgy even more prayerful and meaningful.

Laypeople also participate in the **prophetic office** of Christ. A prophet is someone who speaks God's word. As prophet, Jesus continually reminded people of his Father's love and called people to faith and eternal life. Regardless of whether they are married or single, all lay members of the Church are called to speak God's word and to witness to Christ in everything they do. Each layperson is called to "stand before the world as a witness to the resurrection and life of the Lord Jesus and as a sign that God lives" ("Dogmatic Constitution on the Church," #38). In everything they do, laypeople look forward with hope to the coming of God's kingdom in its fullness. Laypeople teach others about God's kingdom through the example of their own lives and through involvement in catechetical formation, advising the clergy in temporal matters, and faithfully obeying the magisterium. Laypeople who have celebrated the Sacrament of Marriage have a special role in this prophetic office.

" [H]usband and wife find their proper vocation in being witnesses to one another and to their children of faith in Christ and love for Him. The Christian family loudly proclaims both the present virtues of the kingdom of God and the hope of a blessed life to come. Thus by its example and its witness it accuses the world of sin and enlightens those who seek the truth. "

"Dogmatic Constitution on the Church," #35.

Lay Church members also participate in the **kingly office** of Christ. Unlike earthly monarchs, Christ's kingship consisted of serving others rather than being served. As king, he inaugurates God's kingdom on earth and holds supreme authority over Church members. The laity share in this office by striving to bring justice to the world, by being involved in parish and diocesan councils, by serving on parish finance committees, by working with those who are poor and in need. In everything they do, lay members of the Church can help God spread his kingdom by working for truth, holiness, justice, love, and peace.

" They must assist one another to live holier lives even in their daily occupations. In this way the world is permeated by the spirit of Christ and more effectively achieves its purpose in justice, charity, and peace. . . . In this manner, through the members of the Church, Christ will progressively illumine the whole of human society with His saving light. "

"Dogmatic Constitution on the Church," #36.

Lay people are increasingly serving in a variety of ecclesial ministries. They serve as Church leaders in parishes, Catholic schools, and diocesan offices. These leadership positions include directors of religious education, pastoral ministers, financial officers, RCIA coordinators, superintendents of schools, and more.

Let's Talk!

What are some practical ways that teen Church members can exercise their priestly office? Their prophetic office? Their kingly office?

Research

Using the library or Internet, find out more about a layperson who was a saint. Some possibilities: Catherine of Siena, Perpetua and Felicity, Isidore the Farmer and his wife, Maria Torribia (Maria de la Cabeza), Mary Magdalen, and Thomas More.

Some ordained and some nonordained Church members are called by God to consecrate their lives publicly through the vows of poverty, chastity, and obedience. We sometimes call these vows the "evangelical counsels," meaning following the guidance, the counseling, of the gospel of Christ (*evangelion* in Greek means "good news" or "gospel" in English). The Catechism makes it clear that Christ calls *all* of us to follow the counsel of the Holy Spirit. However, "It is the *profession* of these counsels, within a permanent state of life recognized by the Church, that characterizes the life consecrated to God" (#915).

• By professing the vow the **poverty,** religious women and men promise not to own private property or to seek financial gain in order to get rich. They identify with those in society who are poor and remind people to place their trust in God rather than in money.

• By professing the vow of **chastity,** religious men and women promise to practice chastity in a celibate way as they respond to God's call, instead of seeking married and family life. They remind us that only God, not other humans, can fully satisfy the spiritual hungers of the human heart.

• By professing the vow of **obedience,** religious men and women promise to serve where they are needed. By obeying their religious superiors, they witness to the fact that God's will is more important than their own. By their example, they live the prayer, "Thy will be done, on earth as it is in heaven."

Consecrated men (religious priests and brothers) and consecrated women (religious sisters) are part of Church-approved religious communities. There are many communities, including the Jesuits, the Sisters of Mercy, the Carmelites, and a variety of Franciscan and Dominican groups. Religious serve the Church in many ways—through prayer, teaching, healthcare professions, missionary work, social work, parish ministry, and so forth. A few consecrated religious live in solitude as hermits. Most, however, live with community members in houses called convents or monasteries. Some religious are contemplative; their main work is prayer. Others are active, giving apostolic service to people at home or in other countries.

Members of the clergy, the laity, and religious life need to work together. By cooperating with one another and by building community, each in its special way, shares in the one priesthood of Christ. All Church members are called to have a profound respect for one another, regardless of their function in the Body of Christ. All Church members share the duty of caring for one another and helping everyone in the Church grow in holiness.

Research

Using the library or Internet, find out more about a man or woman religious who is honored as a saint. Some possibilities: Thérèse of Lisieux, Francis of Assisi, Aloysius Gonzaga, Teresa of Ávila, Bridget, and Rose Philippine Duchesne.

Community with Other Christian Faiths

In addition to our call to build community within the Church, we also have a duty to build community with people outside the Catholic Church. **Ecumenism** is the effort to strive toward unity among all Christian peoples. This involves communication and cooperation with people of other Christian faiths. Protestants, Eastern Orthodox Church members, and Catholics are separated from one another due to theological differences and historical circumstances, and yet all are rightly called "Christians" because they follow and believe in Jesus Christ. The ultimate aim in building community with Eastern Orthodox members, Episcopalians, Lutherans, Methodists, Presbyterians, Baptists, United Church of Christ members, and other Protestants is to restore unity among separated Christians. Each year the Church prays for the unity of these Churches during the Church Unity Octave. As the bishops of Vatican II point out, "The Church established by Christ the Lord is, indeed, one and unique" ("Decree on Ecumenism," #1). The bishops continue:

> " Cooperation among all Christians vividly expresses that bond which already unites them, and it sets in clearer relief the features of Christ the Servant. Such cooperation . . . should contribute to a just appreciation of the dignity of the human person, the promotion of the blessings of peace, the application of gospel principles to social life, and the advancement of the arts and sciences in a truly Christian spirit. . . . Through such cooperation, all believers in Christ are able to learn easily how they can understand each other better and esteem each other more, and how the road to the unity of Christians may be made smooth. "
>
> "Decree on Ecumenism, "#12.

Pope John Paul II with Romanian Orthodox Patriarch Teoctist in Bucharest.

Activity

Interview a Protestant minister. Try to find out what the Catholic Church and his or her denomination have in common. Be prepared to report your findings to the class.

Community with Other World Religions

Furthermore, Church members are called to communicate and collaborate with people who are non-Christians, including Jews, Buddhists, Muslims, Hindus, and people of still other religions. Church members have a duty to teach non-Christians about Christ. God wishes all people to come to the knowledge of the truth about his love and his plan of redemption in Christ. All salvation comes from Christ through the Church. God has given the Church the missionary task of preaching the gospel to all nations. The Holy Spirit guides and motivates the Church in this task of continuing the mission of Christ in today's world.

However, people of non-Christian religions are also to be respected. There is a historical and spiritual relationship between Christians and many non-Christians—especially Jews and Muslims. In a special way, Christians are related to people of the Jewish faith, who are people of the covenant. Christians are also related to Muslims, who worship the same God and share the same faith of Abraham.

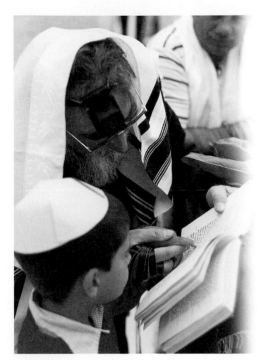

A Jewish rabbi with a young student.

Muslims gathered for prayer.

Let's Talk!

1. Why should Christians try to build community with Jews? What are some ways that young people in your town or city can do this?

2. Why should Christians try to build community with Muslims? What are some ways that young people in your town or city can do this?

THE SOCIAL GOSPEL

The call to community—both within and outside the Church—is part of what we call the "social gospel." The social gospel challenges us to put aside individual interests and, instead, work for the common good (see "The Church in the Modern World," #26). The common good requires that *all* people be treated with dignity, as beings made in God's image and thus entitled to certain rights.

The basic message of the social gospel is justice—treating everyone fairly, with equality and respect. Essentially, social justice means working to improve the lives of people in need in every aspect of society—family, economics, education, healthcare, and civil rights. Christian concern for the rights of everyone in society is based on a firm sense of human solidarity. We see everyone, regardless of race, gender, country of origin, religious preference, or anything else, as our brothers and sisters. We recognize all people as the daughters and sons of God. In short, we try to treat everyone as we ourselves would like to be treated.

Seven Themes of Modern Catholic Social Teaching

In 1996 the U.S. Catholic bishops identified seven themes underlying Catholic social teaching. These themes run through the many statements on justice made by Catholic leaders during more than a century. Through these statements, Catholic leaders hope that the Church and its members will serve as a beacon of justice in the world.

1. **Life and Dignity of the Human Person**
   In a world warped by materialism and declining respect for human life, the Catholic Church proclaims that human life is sacred and that the dignity of the human person is the foundation of a moral vision for society. . . . We believe that every person is precious, that people are more important than things, and that the measure of every institution is whether it threatens or enhances the life and dignity of the human person.

2. **Call to Family, Community, and Participation**
   In a global culture driven by excessive individualism, our tradition proclaims that the person is not only sacred but also social. How we organize our society—in economics and politics, in law and policy—directly affects human dignity and the capacity of individuals to grow in community. The family is the central social institution that must be supported and strengthened, not undermined. While our society often exalts individualism, the Catholic tradition teaches that human beings grow and achieve fulfillment in community.

3. **Rights and Responsibilities**
   In a world where some speak mostly of "rights" and others mostly of "responsibilities," the Catholic tradition teaches that human dignity can be protected and a healthy community can be achieved only if human rights are protected and responsibilities are met.

4. **Option for the Poor and Vulnerable**
   In a world characterized by growing prosperity for some and pervasive poverty for others, Catholic teaching proclaims that a basic moral test is how our most vulnerable members are faring.

5. **The Dignity of Work and the Rights of Workers**
   In a marketplace where too often the quarterly bottom line takes precedence over the rights of workers, we believe that the economy must serve

people, not the other way around. Work is more than a way to make a living; it is a form of continuing participation in God's creation. If the dignity of work is to be protected, then the basic rights of workers must be respected—the right to productive work, to decent and fair wages, to organize and join unions, to private property, and to economic initiative.

6. Solidarity

Our culture is tempted to turn inward, becoming indifferent and sometimes isolationist in the face of international responsibilities. Catholic social teaching proclaims that we are our brothers' and sisters' keepers, wherever they live. We are one family, whatever our national, racial, ethnic, economic, and ideological differences. Learning to practice the virtue of solidarity means learning that "loving our neighbor" has global dimensions in an interdependent world.

7. Care for God's Creation

On a planet conflicted over environmental issues, the Catholic tradition insists that we show our respect for the Creator by our stewardship of creation. Care for the earth is not just an Earth Day slogan, it is a requirement of our faith.

(Sharing Catholic Social Teaching: Challenges and Directions.)

Let's Talk!

How can young people show human solidarity with each of the following people?

- a teen in a juvenile detention center
- a family in Somalia who is starving
- a parish family who has recently lost a family member
- migrant workers who come to the United States illegally
- a teen who is pregnant but not married
- a worker who is on strike at his or her place of employment

Role Model of Social Justice

Mary, the mother of Jesus, has the distinction of being the first follower of Jesus and the first member of the Church. We can learn from her example, as well as the example of the first Christians, how we, too, can live the social gospel.

How did Mary live the social gospel? From the Gospels we learn that even as a young woman, Mary put the needs of others above her own needs.

- Although she herself was pregnant, Mary overlooked her own needs in order to travel to and help her cousin Elizabeth *(see Luke 1:39–40, 56).*

- When Jesus and Mary were guests at a wedding reception, Mary was concerned about the needs of the bride and groom and asked Jesus to help them *(see John 2).*

- After Jesus ascended into heaven, Mary remained with the Apostles, praying with them and encouraging them in their faith *(see Acts 1:14).*

Catholic missionaries respond to the spiritual and physical needs of people around the world.

Although the New Testament does not tell us what Mary did after Pentecost, we can assume she continued to be an active member of the early Church, showing the same love, compassion, and concern for others that she exhibited earlier in life.

The first Christians followed the example of Mary and Jesus. Their concern for the common good was an important part of their daily lives.

" All who believed were together and had all things in common; they would sell their possessions and goods and distribute the proceeds to all, as any had need. Day by day, as they spent much time together in the temple, they broke bread at home and ate their food with glad and generous hearts, praising God and having the goodwill of all the people. And day by day the Lord added to their number those who were being saved. "

ACTS 2:44–47

In addition to showing concern for those in need in their local communities, the early Christians showed solidarity with other Christians in distant locations. When the Church community in Jerusalem experienced famine, Church members in Antioch rallied to help them.

" The disciples determined that according to their ability, each would send relief to the believers living in Judea; this they did, sending it to the elders by Barnabas and Saul. "

ACTS 11:29–30

As Church members today, we are called to follow in the footsteps of Mary and the first Christians. We do so by embracing the principles of solidarity, friendship, social charity, and brotherhood. We follow Jesus by feeding the hungry, giving drink to the thirsty, giving clothing to those in need, providing shelter for the homeless, caring for those who are sick, visiting those in prison, and burying the dead. In short, we are to treat everyone as we would treat Christ himself *(see Matthew 25:31–46).*

Activity

As a class, select a local, national, or international charitable cause to which you would like to respond (a homeless family, an immigrant family that does not speak English, someone out of work, a victim of a natural or human-caused disaster, and so forth). Organize and carry out a project to help. (Perhaps hold a car wash, food drive, clothes drive, walkathon, or bake sale.) Send the proceeds to the charitable cause or person(s) you have decided to help.

THE CENTER OF CHURCH LIFE

As Church members, we must develop and sustain a meaningful relationship with the Trinity. How can we do this? One way is to have an active spiritual life, nourished by prayer and participation in the sacraments—especially the **Eucharist.** As the bishops of Vatican II asserted, the Eucharist is "the fount and apex of the whole Christian life" ("Dogmatic Constitution on the Church," #11).

The precepts or laws of the Church center on the importance of the Eucharist and other practices associated with the moral life. These positive laws are meant to help the faithful grow in a spirit of prayer and love of God and neighbor. The precepts of the Church can be found in the Catholic Source Book. The laws of the Church, including the precepts, are supported by the liturgical life of the Church.

This presentation of gifts took place at a Mass celebrating the Vietnamese New Year, Tet.

It is essential to remember that there can be no Church if there is no Eucharist. We cannot strive to build community with others unless we are continually nourished by the Eucharist. In an earlier chapter, we studied the first main part of Mass, which is known as the Liturgy of the Word. In this section, we will learn more about the second main part of Mass, the Liturgy of the Eucharist, and see how this liturgy unites followers more closely to Christ. The Sunday celebration of the Eucharist makes possible and strengthens the bonds of community between Church members, as well as encourages members of the Church to build community throughout the week with other Christians and non-Christians.

Precepts of the Church

The precepts of the Church are laws that name specific actions that all Catholics are obligated to carry out. According to the National Catechetical Directory, the following precepts apply to Catholics in the United States.

1. To keep holy the day of the Lord's resurrection: to worship God by participating in Mass every Sunday and holy day of obligation; to avoid those activities that would hinder renewal of soul and body on the Sabbath (e.g., needless work and business activities, unnecessary shopping, etc.).

2. To lead a sacramental life; to receive Holy Communion frequently and the Sacrament of Reconciliation regularly—minimally, to receive the Sacrament of Reconciliation at least once a year (annual confession is obligatory only if serious sin is involved); minimally also, to receive Holy Communion at least once a year, between the First Sunday of Lent and Trinity Sunday.

3. To study Catholic teaching in preparation for the Sacrament of Confirmation, to be confirmed, and then to continue to study and advance the cause of Christ.

4. To observe the marriage laws of the Church; to give religious training, by example and word, to one's children; to use parish schools and catechetical programs.

5. To strengthen and support the Church—one's own parish community and parish priests, the worldwide Church and the pope.

6. To do penance, including abstaining from meat and fasting from food on the appointed days.

7. To join in the missionary spirit and apostolate of the Church.

The Liturgy of the Eucharist

Following are the basic parts of the Liturgy of the Eucharist, the second main part of the Mass. Only validly ordained priests can preside at the Eucharist and consecrate the bread and wine to become the Body and Blood of Christ.

1. Presentation and Preparation of Gifts

At this time, members of the assembly bring the bread and wine to the altar table. They may also bring the financial collection, which is used to maintain the church and to help people in need. After receiving the gifts at the altar, the priest prays over the bread and wine, asking that our sacrifice may be acceptable to God, the almighty Father. He then washes his hands as an expression of his desire for inward purification.

2. The Eucharistic Prayer

This prayer is the Church's great prayer of thanks, praise, and consecration. It is the center and high point of the entire Mass. Eucharistic Prayers contain the same basic structure.

• They start with a **preface** in which the Church community joins with the angels and saints in heaven in giving thanks and praise to God for salvation history. Following the preface, the priest prays a prayer known as the **epiclesis.** In this prayer, the Church asks the Father to send his Holy Spirit on the bread and wine, so that by his power they may become the Body and Blood of Jesus Christ. The epiclesis also asks that all who share in the Eucharist may be one body and one spirit.

Activity

Using a missal or worship aid, work in a small group. Choose one of the approved Eucharistic Prayers for Mass and prepare a chart showing how it includes each of the parts listed in the text. When you have finished, compare your selected Eucharistic Prayer with that of other groups in the class.

- In the **institution narrative** the priest takes the wheat bread and grape wine and invokes the blessing of the Holy Spirit. The priest then speaks the words of consecration spoken by Jesus at the Last Supper: "This is my body which will be given for you....This is the cup of my blood." The priest, through the power of the Holy Spirit, consecrates the bread and wine to become the Body and Blood of Christ—just as Jesus did at the Last Supper. This change of the whole substance of the bread and wine into the whole substance of the Body and Blood of Christ our Lord is called **transubstantiation**. These actions are much more than a memorial of what happened in the past. They also make present Christ's sacrifice of himself to God; this is called the real presence of Christ in the Eucharist.

- The people then respond with a **memorial acclamation** in which they profess their belief in the passion, death, Resurrection, and glorious return of Jesus.

- This is followed by the **anamnesis,** or *remembering*, recalling Christ's sacrifice of love and presenting this sacrifice to God as reconciling us with him.

- **Prayers** for the entire Church community follow the anamnesis. These prayers include intercessions for all Church members, living and dead, in communion with the pope, the local bishop, and all pastors.

- The Eucharistic Prayer ends with the **Doxology:** "Through him, with him, in him, in the unity of the Holy Spirit, all glory and honor is yours, almighty Father, for ever and ever. Amen."

It is important to realize that the Eucharist is Jesus. He is really present, Body and Blood, Soul and Divinity, under the appearance of bread and wine. The real presence of Christ is achieved through the action of the priest.

The chalice and paten.

3. The Communion Rite

The Lord's Prayer begins the Communion rite. After the prayer, the priest invites us to give one another a sign of peace, a reminder of our oneness with other members of the liturgical assembly. If we are in a state of grace, we receive Communion. If we aware that we had sinned mortally, we must not receive Communion without first receiving the Sacrament of Reconciliation. After a prayer, the Communion rite ends, as does the Liturgy of the Eucharist.

What happens in Holy Communion? We really receive the Body and Blood of the Lord Jesus Christ. The Catechism explains this mystery with the following words:

" Communion with the Body and Blood of Christ increases the communicant's union with the Lord. . . . Since receiving this sacrament strengthens the bonds of charity between the communicant and Christ, it also reinforces the unity of the Church as the Mystical Body of Christ. "

CATECHISM, #1416.

We are united as believers. We form one body in Christ. "Truly partaking of the body of the Lord in the breaking of the Eucharistic bread, we are taken up into communion with Him and with one another" ("Dogmatic Constitution on the Church," #7). We both express and achieve our identity as Church.

4. The Concluding Rite

The last part of the Mass is a Concluding Rite, also known as the *Dismissal Rite.* In this rite, the priest blesses us and then commissions us to go out into the world to serve God in our relationships and our work. Strengthened by the grace of the Eucharist, all are empowered to build community with others, help those in need, and bring the light of Christ to all areas of modern life. That is why the Eucharist is sometimes called the Sacrament of Unity.

Activities

1. Write a prayer or poem that you can pray after you receive Communion. In your prayer, try to express what the Eucharist means to you. Be prepared to share all or part of your prayer with the class.

2. Search through liturgical songbooks, CDs, or worship aids to find a closing song for Mass that you think particularly expresses the purpose of the Dismissal Rite. Be prepared to talk about the lyrics of the song and how they inspire you to serve God throughout the week.

Prayers of Blessing

The Concluding Rite includes a prayer of blessing. "To bless" means "to grant one's favor or gifts." A prayer of blessing is really a request that God's gifts be given to certain people, objects, places, or occasions in human life. It also expresses acceptance of and thanks for these gifts. "[B]ecause God blesses, the human heart can in return bless the One who is the source of every blessing" (Catechism, #2626).

Prayers of blessing are often accompanied by the raising of the right hand or by the making of the Sign of the Cross. In many Catholic churches, blessed water is kept in fonts at the church entrance. Church members dip their hands in the blessed water and then bless themselves by making the Sign of the Cross, saying, "In the name of the Father and of the Son and of the Holy Spirit."

There are many times in daily life when we can bless ourselves, that is, ask God to bless us. We can say a prayer of blessing upon waking, before and after meals, at school or work, and before going to bed at night.

Many families pray a blessing prayer before meals.

There are also many times when we can ask for God's blessing for other people. For example, we can bless a bride and groom as they begin their married life together. We can bless family members, especially on their birthdays or anniversaries. We can bless people who are sick or who are dying. We can pray a blessing for classmates, co-workers, guests, travelers, or people who are making a new beginning.

Sometimes we ask God's blessing on certain places and objects. For example, the Church has special rites for blessing a new building or home, school, library, parish hall, hospital, business office, or gymnasium. There are also blessings for boats, cars, tools, and work equipment. Perhaps you have participated in a blessing of animals that takes place on or near the feast of Saint Francis of Assisi, October 4. There is the blessing of fields and flocks that takes place in agricultural areas both at planting time and at the time of harvest. Many people have religious objects that are blessed by priests. Such objects include crucifixes; rosaries; statues of Jesus, Mary, or other saints; medals; scapulars; and holy cards. Asking God to bless certain things is really a reminder to us to use these things with reverence and devotion, as instruments for deepening our relationship with the Trinity.

Activity

Write a prayer of blessing for someone (or a group) you know who especially needs God's favor and gifts. Be prepared to share your prayer with the class. You need not share the name of the person or group.

Seven Secrets of Successful Catholics

Who are successful Catholics? They are Church members whose faith is the framework for their lives and their actions. Their faith helps them navigate their way through life—giving them inspiration and honest reflection. While there are many "secrets" to being a successful Catholic, here are seven that one author identifies.

1. Stay close to the Eucharist.

2. Be an active member of a faith community.

3. Rely on your conscience and good judgment, but never alone.

4. Regularly do things that call you out of yourself in service to others.

5. Always remember that God is merciful and forgiving.

6. Live in the moment, recognizing daily opportunities for holiness.

7. Believe in prayer and pray regularly.

Paul Wilkes, The Seven Secrets of Successful Catholics
(Mahwah, NJ: Paulist Press, 1998).

Reflection

Over the next month, keep a diary of your efforts in following the seven secrets of successful Catholics. Tell how these actions have helped to make the Church more meaningful to you, and why.

A PERSON OF FAITH
Henriette Delille

Henriette Delille, the youngest child of a Catholic white Creole and his mistress (a free black), was born in 1813 in New Orleans. Henriette was a "quadroon," someone who was one-fourth black. Although her skin was light enough for her to pass as white, Henriette preferred to call herself "a free woman of color." According to the social customs at the time, Henriette studied music, dance, and French literature. In essence, she was trained to be a mistress for a wealthy white man.

At age eleven, Henriette was enrolled in a school run by French nuns. There Henriette learned how faith could change the course of one's life. She learned how to pray, and she began to minister to people who were sick and aged. By the time she was fourteen, she was a lay catechist, teaching religion to poor black slaves. Before long, Henriette's Catholic faith meant more to her than formal dances and living life as a white man's mistress. She believed that women of color had a right to get married. Furthermore,

she believed that blacks, just as whites, could serve the Church.

So, with courage and resolve, Henriette gave up her privileged life to help black slaves, orphans, and other poor people in New Orleans. She was determined to devote her life to improving the lives of the racially mixed underclass. She also encouraged black men and women to have their marriages ratified by the Church, even though such ceremonies were not valid according to civil law.

In 1837, with two other free women of color, Henriette founded the Sisters of the Holy Family. In 1842, she used part of her inheritance to buy a house where she could teach religion to nonwhites, even though educating nonwhites was illegal. The religious sisters built a hospice in 1849 to better serve those who were sick, aged, and poor. They ministered to the victims of the yellow fever, cholera, and malaria epidemics that swept through pre-Civil War New Orleans. In 1850, they opened a school for pay for free black girls. In 1852, Delille and her companions officially made vows as religious.

Henriette died on November 16, 1862. There were only twelve religious sisters in her order at the time of her death, all of them Creole free women of color. After the Civil War, the sisters began to admit former black slaves. They received permission to wear religious habits and became known as the Sisters of the Holy Family. Through evangelization, education, housing, and healthcare, they ministered to people on the margins of society. Today the sisters also work in Texas, Washington, DC, and Belize.

In 1989, the Vatican began the canonization process for Henriette Delille. If she is canonized, she will be the first African American–Creole saint. Canonization efforts are also underway for two other women of color—Sister Thea Bowman of the Franciscan Sisters of Perpetual Adoration in LaCrosse, WI, and Mother Mary Elizabeth Lange, a black Latina who founded the Oblate Sisters of Providence in 1828.

Today black women are welcome in religious communities. In the United States there are three predominately African American communities of religious women— the Oblate Sisters of Providence in Baltimore, the Sisters of the Holy Family in New Orleans, and the Franciscan Handmaids of Mary in New York.

Let's Talk!

1. What forms of racism exist in your school? In your parish? In your community?

2. How can you work to improve the racial tensions found in your school, parish, and community?

Activity

Design a poster that promotes racial equality. Include a motto that emphasizes unity and respects the beauty of diversity as well. Be prepared to explain your poster to the class.

Celebrating Faith

Opening Song: "One in His Name"

Leader: Lord, we thank you for calling us to be members of your Church. We ask you to bless us and to bless all Church members as we pray together.

Leader: The angel spoke God's message to Mary,

All: and she conceived of the Holy Spirit. Hail Mary . . .

Leader: "I am the lowly servant of the Lord:

All: let it be done to me according to your word." Hail Mary . . .

Leader: And the Word became flesh

All: and lived among us. Hail Mary . . .

Leader: Pray for us, holy Mother of God,

All: that we may become worthy of the promises of Christ.

First part of the Angelus, from Catholic Household Blessings and Prayers (Washington, DC: Bishops' Committee on the Liturgy, USCCB, 1998), 363.

Leader: Let us pray:

All: O Lord Jesus Christ, keep us always in your love. Let us hear your voice and believe what you say, for you alone have the words of life.

Teach us how to profess our faith, bestow our love, and impart our hope to others. Make us convincing witnesses to your gospel in a world so much in need of your saving grace.

Make us the new people of the Beatitudes, that we may be the salt of the earth and the light of the world in these early years of the third Christian millennium.

Mary, mother of us all, protect and guide the Church. Keep us all close to your maternal heart. Amen.

Based on the prayer of Pope John Paul II at the 2002 Youth Day in Toronto, Canada.

Review

1. What are healthy attitudes to have regarding groups?

2. What is the Church? Why do we need the Church?

3. How is the Church an example of unity? How is it an example of diversity? Is diversity in the Church something positive or is it something negative? Explain.

4. What is the highest teaching authority in the Church?

5. Who makes up the ordained members of the Church? Who makes up the nonordained members of the Church?

6. What are the responsibilities of the Church's bishops?

7. How does the laity participate in the priestly, prophetic, and kingly offices of Christ?

8. What are the ministries that laypeople can participate in during Mass?

9. What are the meanings of the religious vows of poverty, chastity, and obedience?

10. What is ecumenism? Why is the Church concerned about building community with Protestants and Eastern Orthodox Churches?

11. What are the parts of the Liturgy of the Eucharist? What happens in each?

12. How does veneration of Mary and the saints differ from the worship we give to God?

WORDS OF FAITH

bishops—Church leaders who are the successors of the Apostles. Bishops receive all three degrees of the Sacrament of Holy Orders.

canonization—an official Church statement by which a person is declared to have lived a holy life of heroic virtue. In the last stage of the process of canonization, the person is named a saint.

communion of saints—all faithful Church members on earth, in heaven, and in purgatory; communion in holy things (*sancta*) and among holy persons (*sancti*)

ecumenical council—a meeting of the world's bishops, gathered by the pope to exercise their "collegial authority over the universal Church" (CCC, Glossary). Their decisions must be ratified by the pope.

ecumenism—the effort to strive toward unity among all Christian peoples. This involves communication and cooperation with people of other Christian faiths.

Eucharist—the Sacrament of the Body and Blood of Christ. The Eucharist is both a sacrifice and a sacrament. During the Mass, the bread and wine are changed into the Body and Blood of Christ.

Holy Orders—a Sacrament at Service of Communion, in which men promise to devote their lives to the Church as deacons, priests, or bishop

kingly office—part of the saving mission of Christ, in which he inaugurates God's kingdom on earth and holds supreme authority over Church members. All baptized Church members share in the kingly office of Christ.

Enrichment

Choose one of the following.

1. Find an example from written or visual literature (novels, short stories, children's books, videos) that demonstrates how individuals are shaped (for better or worse) by involvement in a group. Be prepared to share and discuss your example in class.

2. With several other people, make a mural that shows how the Church is a community of faith, hope, and love. Display the mural where people in your school can see it.

3. As a class, invite a leader or active member of the Jewish or the Muslim faith to be a guest speaker. Try to find out what Jews and Catholics or Muslims and Catholics have in common. Write a report summarizing your findings.

4. Attend a Mass of another cultural group (for example, Mexican American, Asian American, African American). Write a report of how the Mass differed from the liturgy you usually attend. Tell how the cultural influences added to the meaning and beauty of the Eucharist.

5. With a partner or small group, make a banner that reminds young people of their call to be active members of the Church, using a theme from this chapter. Display the banner in the prayer corner or somewhere in your school where others will see it.

laity—baptized members of the Church, including women and men in consecrated life, who are not ordained

magisterium—"The living teaching office of the Church, whose task it is to give as authentic interpretation of the word of God, whether in its written form (Sacred Scripture), or in the form of Tradition" (CCC, Glossary). It guarantees that the Church remains faithful to the teaching of the Apostles in matters of faith and morals.

pope—the bishop of Rome and leader of the entire Catholic Church. As the successor of Peter, the pope is the head of the college of bishops.

priestly office—the mission of Christ as priest, who offered everything in his life as a sacrifice to God. All baptized Church members share in the priestly office of Christ.

prophetic office—part of the saving mission of Christ, in which he proclaimed the kingdom of God. All baptized Church members share in the prophetic office of Christ.

religious vows—simple or solemn promises of poverty, chastity, and obedience made by members of religious communities so that they may more completely devote themselves to God and to service of the Church

transubstantiation— "…The change of the whole substance of the Eucharistic bread and wine into the whole substance of the Body and Blood of Christ our Lord." (CCC, # 1376)

Walking in the Light

" This is the message we have heard from him and proclaim to you, that God is light and in him there is no darkness at all. If we say that we have fellowship with him while we are walking in darkness, we lie and do not do what is true; but if we walk in the light as he himself is in the light, we have fellowship with one another, and the blood of Jesus his Son cleanses us from all sin. "

1 JOHN 1:5–7

In this chapter, you will:

- discover the meaning and importance of forgiveness in Christian life.

- explore the connection between accepting God's forgiveness and being called to forgive others.

- appreciate various prayers of contrition in Catholic life.

- see how God's forgiveness is received in the Sacraments of Baptism, Reconciliation, Eucharist, and Anointing of the Sick.

- understand the Church's stance toward peace and the moral principles needed before war may be waged justly.

- learn how Dorothy Day changed her life as a result of God's forgiveness and how to forgive yourself and others.

WORDS OF FAITH

absolution	conscience	forgiveness
Anointing of the Sick	contrition	Reconciliation
	conversion	

— UNDERSTANDING FORGIVENESS —

In a world where hurt is an everyday burden and sin an everyday reality, getting even seems to be the way many people want to go. There seems to be no room for forgiving. And yet that is what Jesus calls us to do—to forgive those who hurt us—not just seven times but seventy-seven times, meaning without end (see Matthew 18:12–22).

What Forgiveness Is Not

To understand what Jesus is asking us to do, we must first realize what forgiveness is not.

- **Forgiveness does not mean excusing a hurtful action or a sinful action** or saying that what happened didn't matter or was really okay. When we excuse people, we are actually overlooking or tolerating the hurt or the sin. When we say the person really couldn't help it, we condone the wrong that was done. We say he or she wasn't to blame. For example, with regard to crime, we may say there were overwhelming environmental disadvantages or family dysfunctions that led the person to do what he or she did. Such understanding can lead to mercy, but we need to realize that people are still responsible for their decisions and actions.

- **Forgiveness does not mean exempting a criminal from punishment.** A legal pardon means that the person is free to return to society. However, a legal pardon is not the same as forgiveness. A court may legally pardon an offender although the family members of the victim still feel hatred and resentment toward the offender. On the other hand, the families of the victim may forgive the murderer and have no ill will against him, but still want him to be punished. The punishment is a just consequence of the person's action. In society, we have a responsibility to see that criminals are arrested and brought to justice. To let criminals continue in crime is to endanger even more innocent people.

- **Forgiveness does not mean that we roll over and play dead.** In our own lives, we can forgive someone without trying to be that person's best friend, or acting as if nothing wrong has happened, or naïvely letting ourselves be victimized by the person again.

Let's Talk!

1. Do you think juveniles who commit adult crimes should be tried as adults? Why?
2. Are there any crimes, or sins, that are "too big" to be forgiven? Explain.

Reflection

What are your feelings toward someone who has betrayed or hurt you? What do you think your future relationship with this person will be like?

Activity

Read about the crucifixion of Jesus in Luke 23:26–34a. In a small group, discuss why Jesus was acting in a courageous way. Then think of three situations today when young people could follow Jesus' example. Be prepared to share your ideas with the class.

What Forgiveness Is

So what is **forgiveness?** There are three separate Greek words that mean "to forgive."

- The first Greek word defines forgiveness simply as a legal transaction, a cancellation of an owed debt. The person is set free and does not have to pay back the debt.

- The second Greek word defines forgiveness as a duty of mercy or love toward the offender. Forgiveness means dealing mercifully with a sinner because that is the Christian thing to do. It means treating the offender with the dignity owed to him or her as a person made in God's image. It means treating the offender the same way we would like to be treated if we were in that person's situation.

- The third Greek word defines forgiveness in terms of freeing the *victim*. The victim—the one who has been sinned against or mistreated—releases resentment, lets it go, thus freeing himself or herself from the "prison" of anger. C. S. Lewis, a Christian writer, explains it in this way: "Real forgiveness means looking steadily at the sin, the sin that is left over without any excuse, after all allowances have been made, and seeing it in all its horror, dirt, meanness and malice, and nevertheless being wholly reconciled to the man who has done it."

Robert Enright, a developmental psychologist at the University of Wisconsin, defines this same type of forgiveness with these words: "giving up the resentment to which you are entitled and offering to the persons who hurt you friendlier attitudes to which they are not entitled." Some people make the mistake of thinking that it is more "macho" or "manly" to get even for wrongs rather than to forgive them. That's just not true. Forgiveness is not a sign of weakness or cowardice. It is a sign of courage.

Allen C. Guelzo. "Fear of Forgiving," Christianity Today (8 February 1993): 42+; Elizabeth Dreyer in "The importance of being sorry," U.S. Catholic. (August 1998): 18+.

Research

Look up the following Scripture passages: Mark 11:25, Luke 6:37, Ephesians 4:32. In a small group, discuss which meaning of forgiveness is meant in each passage.

Forgiving others sets us free.

THE FORGIVENESS OF SINS

What we are discussing in this chapter deals specifically with the following part of the creed:

Apostles' Creed: I believe in . . . the forgiveness of sins . . . .

Nicene Creed: We acknowledge one baptism for the forgiveness of sins.

Although we often say that God calls us to forgive those who have sinned against us, it is important to realize that only he has the power and authority to forgive sin. Although God forgives the sin, we too are called to forgive. By forgiving someone, we show his grace working through us.

We have discussed the belief that sin is an offense against God and that it damages communion with the Church. It interrupts or destroys the community we are to have with others. Most of us know when we have sinned. An "inner voice" informs us. We feel guilty. We call this inner voice **conscience.** It is a gift from God that helps us know right from wrong. Remember the seesaw analogy we used in the last chapter? A healthy conscience can be described as a seesaw. It is balanced in the middle between two extremes. On one side is a lax, or lazy, conscience. This conscience fails to tell us when we have done wrong. It allows us to persist in self-righteousness and pride, to think that we are good and everyone else is bad. On the other side of the seesaw is a scrupulous, or overactive, conscience. This conscience falsely tells us that everything we do is wrong. We are overly self-conscious, and we may be tempted to give up in despair.

A healthy conscience, on the other hand, is an essential tool to genuine self-knowledge. It reminds us that we are not perfect or all good. At the same time, a healthy conscience does not demean or belittle us. It does not lead to self-hate or depression. Rather, it motivates us to try harder and to be more compassionate toward others who also are not perfect. In short, a healthy conscience leads to solidarity and friendship—and right decisions.

Let's Talk!

1. Some people use the argument "everyone else is doing it" as the means to justify their behavior. Do you believe that this idea makes something all right to do?

2. How can you be sure that you are developing a healthy conscience?

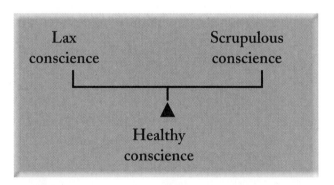

We form a healthy conscience by following the teachings of Jesus found in the Bible and the moral teachings of the Church. Followers of Jesus have an obligation to follow their conscience at all times. Such decision making presumes that we have honestly searched for the truth, prayed about the possible choices and their consequences, and tried to understand what God is asking us to do in the present situation.

Forgiveness and Conversion

God's forgiveness is closely connected to a heartfelt process of change known as **conversion.** In conversion, we turn away from sin and turn toward the way of God. Instead of walking in the darkness of sin, we "lay aside the works of darkness and put on the armor of light" (Romans 13:12). Our lives truly change, just as the day is different from night. For this reason, light and darkness are sometimes symbols that describe stories of true conversion. Consider the account of the conversion of Saul.

Reflection

Describe a time when you experienced a "conversion" in the way you saw someone or something. How did your life change as a result of this experience?

" Now as he [Saul] was going along and approaching Damascus, suddenly a light from heaven flashed around him. He fell to the ground and heard a voice saying to him, "Saul, Saul, why do you persecute me?" He asked, "Who are you, Lord?" The reply came, "I am Jesus, whom you are persecuting. "

ACTS 9:3–5

After Saul experienced the vision of the Risen Christ, he listened to his conscience and realized that he was seriously wrong in persecuting the Christians. Then he began to feel contrition—sorrow for what he had done. The awful truth blinded him. He could no longer deny the darkness in which he was really living. For three days Saul was without sight. During that time he decided to change his life in a radical way and dedicate it to Christ. When a disciple named Ananias came to him, Saul was baptized, and "something like scales fell from his eyes, and his sight was restored" (Acts 9:18).

The conversion of Saul, who is also known as Paul, was sincere and genuine. Instead of continuing to walk in darkness, he began to walk in the light of faith and repentance. In response to God's forgiveness for his many sins, Paul became God's beacon of light to others in darkness, bringing "salvation to the ends of the earth" (Acts 13:47).

"The Conversion of Saint Paul" by Parmigianino; Kunsthistorisches Museum, Vienna, Austria.

Activity

Using a Bible and the handout your teacher will give you, read the Scripture passages and prayers for Mass on the Feast of the Conversion of Saint Paul, which the Church celebrates on January 25. Write a short essay explaining what the readings and prayers tell you about the nature of religious conversion.

Let's Talk!

Reflect on the story of Jesus and the paralyzed man. Why did Jesus first forgive the man's sins and then heal him of his paralysis? What reason did Jesus give for doing it this way?

Jesus and the Forgiveness of Sin

Forgiving sinners was an important part of the ministry of Jesus. It is also what got him into trouble with some of the Jewish leaders. Judaism teaches that only God can forgive sin. So when Jesus publicly forgave the sins of others, he was, in fact, implying that he himself was God. Jesus forgave sins, both to reveal God's love for people and to point out his identity as the Messiah and Son of God. Many of the Jewish leaders refused to accept this good news and, instead, regarded Jesus' actions as blasphemous.

" And just then some people were carrying a paralyzed man lying on a bed. When Jesus saw their faith, he said to the paralytic, 'Take heart, son; your sins are forgiven.' Then some of the scribes said to themselves, 'This man is blaspheming.' But Jesus, perceiving their thoughts, said, 'Why do you think evil in your hearts? For which is easier, to say, "Your sins are forgiven," or to say, "Stand up and walk"? But so that you may know that the Son of Man has authority on earth to forgive sins'—he then said to the paralytic—'Stand up, take your bed and go to your home.' And he stood up and went to his home. When the crowds saw it, they were filled with love, and they glorified God, who had given such authority to human beings. "

MATTHEW 9:2–8

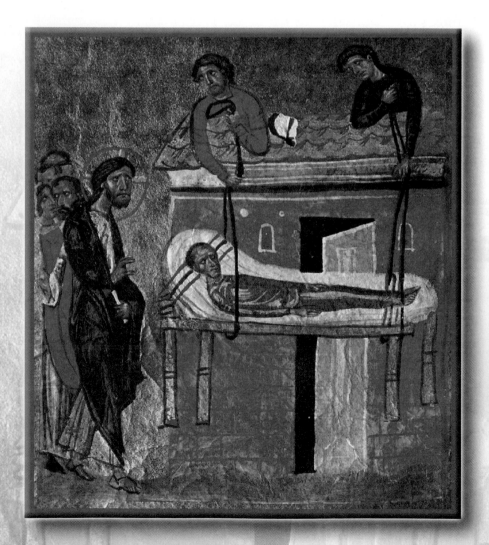

Twelfth-century Byzantine art in Mount Athos Monastery, Iberon, Greece.

JESUS CALLS US TO FORGIVENESS

Jesus makes it clear that all of us need forgiveness. Listen to this story from the Gospel according to Luke. What does Jesus say?

"A Woman Anoints Christ's Feet" by James J. Tissot.

Research

Read Luke 7:36–50: Jesus at Simon's house. What do you think Jesus meant when he said, "The one to whom little is forgiven, loves little"?

Jesus forgave the woman who came into Simon's house. She believed in him and was sincerely sorry for her sins. The story summarizes the call of Jesus to all people: ". . . repent, and believe in the good news" (Mark 1:15). Because we are human and imperfect, we are always in danger of sinning. That is why Jesus continually calls us to repentance and conversion. He calls us to an inner change, a change of heart. True repentance involves not only sorrow for sins but also a firm resolution to try not to sin again. Like the adulterous woman whom Jesus forgave, we are to go on our way and not sin again (see John 8:11). In short, forgiveness of sin involves sincere **contrition** or sorrow on our part. We must listen to the voice of conscience and be aware of our sins. We must admit that we were wrong and be truly sorry for having sinned.

Prayers of Contrition

Contrition is sorrow for sin. Contrition is a prayer in which a person accepts responsibility for wrong decisions and actions. In an act of contrition, there is an expressed sorrow for sin, as well as the desire to try not to sin again. A traditional Act of Contrition said during the Sacrament of Reconciliation may be found in the Catholic Source Book. In addition to this traditional Act of Contrition, there are other kinds of prayers of contrition. These include the penitential psalms, the penitential rite during Mass, and the Jesus Prayer.

Activity

Read about the following times Jesus forgave someone's sins: Zacchaeus, the tax collector (Luke 19: 1–10), the repentant thief who was crucified with Jesus (Luke: 23 39–43), the woman caught in adultery (John 8: 1–11). Discuss how each passage connects forgiveness with contrition. How do you think each passage applies to people today?

Penitential Psalms

Among the 150 psalms found in the Old Testament, the greatest number belongs to a literary type known as the "lamentation"; that means crying out or grieving. Some of the psalms of lament are individual expressions of contrition. Others are communal or national laments. Many psalms of lament talk about past situations, in which healing and forgiveness have already been given. Of the psalms of lament, seven are known as "the penitential psalms."

- Psalm 6 is a lament concerning grave illness that may be physical or moral. The psalmist asks God to deliver him and save him.

- Psalm 32 is a song about the joy of being forgiven.

  " Happy are those whose transgression is forgiven,
     whose sin is covered (Psalm 32:1). "

- Psalm 38 expresses contrition that sin has resulted in pain and alienation. The psalmist prays that God may come to his aid and heal him.

- Psalm 51 was supposedly written by King David to express sorrow for committing adultery with Bathsheba and then arranging her husband's death. The psalm is an ageless expression of sincere contrition and is sometimes referred to as the *Miserere,* from the Latin beginning of the poem.

- Psalm 102 is an individual lament that seems to be adapted for communal use. The psalmist is in great difficulty, perhaps dying from physical illness. He prays to God to hear his prayer and restore him to health.

- Psalm 130 is another individual lament in which the penitent seems to be drowning in his sins and their consequences. The psalmist begs God to rescue him from "the depths" and to forgive all his sins.

- Psalm 143 describes sin as the "enemy." Sin has led the psalmist into darkness, from which he prays for deliverance. The psalmist also prays that God will teach him how to change his life, to walk in God's ways.

The Penitential Rite During Mass

The penitential rite occurs at the beginning of Mass. It has three possible forms. One form includes the saying of a prayer known as the Confiteor. The Confiteor was once part of the prayers recited by the priest at the foot of the altar. The other two forms contain versions of the "Lord, have mercy," a litany of prayers in which we ask God to forgive our sins and show us mercy.

The Jesus Prayer

The Jesus Prayer is a short prayer that dates back to the early Church. "Lord Jesus Christ, Son of God, have mercy on me, a sinner." Many people consider it to be a type of prayer known as an "aspiration" because it is said repeatedly until it becomes as automatic as breathing. Some people have associated the prayer with meditation techniques involving controlling one's breathing, bowing one's head, and concentrating on one's heart.

Activity

Read one of the penitential psalms in your Bible. Then draw or paint a picture illustrating the psalm. The picture may be realistic or abstract. Be prepared to share your picture with the class.

Reflection

Write your own prayer of contrition to say each night before retiring.

FORGIVENESS AND THE CHURCH

After his Resurrection, Jesus conferred on his Apostles the power to forgive sins in God's name. "Receive the Holy Spirit. If you forgive the sins of any, they are forgiven them; if you retain the sins of any, they are retained" (John 20:22–23). The Catechism explains further:

Saint Peter holding keys— the symbol of authority in the Church.

“ In imparting to his apostles his own power to forgive sins the Lord also gives them the authority to reconcile sinners with the Church. This ecclesial dimension of their task is expressed most notably in Christ's solemn words to Simon Peter: 'I will give you the keys of the kingdom of heaven, and whatever you bind on earth shall be bound in heaven, and whatever you loose on earth shall be loosed in heaven' (*Mt* 16:19; cf. *Mt* 18:18; 28:16–20). 'The office of binding and loosing which was given to Peter was also assigned to the college of the apostles united to its head' (*LG* 22 § 2). ”

CATECHISM, #1444

The Church teaches that the power to forgive sins in God's name has been given to the Church. It is transmitted to bishops, the successors of the Apostles, and to priests through the Sacrament of Holy Orders. Just as Christ sent his Apostles to preach repentance and forgiveness of sins in his name to all people everywhere, so the Church continues this same ministry of reconciliation today.

Four Sacraments of Forgiveness

The Church has four sacraments that convey God's forgiveness. These sacraments are Baptism, Reconciliation (or Penance), Eucharist, and the Anointing of the Sick. Here is a brief overview of each one.

Baptism

The word *baptism* means, "to plunge or immerse in water." In Baptism, people are cleansed of sin and become members of the Church, God's family. The Church has baptized new members since the day of Pentecost when approximately three thousand people responded to Peter's challenge to "Repent, and be baptized every one of you in the name of Jesus Christ so that your sins may be forgiven; and you will receive the gift of the Holy Spirit" (Acts 2:38).

Baptism is the first and chief sacrament of the forgiveness of sins. It takes away original sin and any personal sins we may have committed up to that time. Baptism unites us to Christ who died and was raised to new life, and gives us the Holy Spirit. "Through Baptism we are freed from sin and reborn as sons of God; we become members of Christ, are incorporated into the Church and made sharers in her mission" (Catechism, #1213). In this sacrament, the new Christian professes his or her conversion to Christ, promising to turn away from evil and to walk in the light of Christ, and is welcomed into the Church.

Activity

In the Catholic Church, most adult Baptisms take place at the Easter Vigil service. Using a Bible and the handout your teacher will give you, read once more one of the Scripture passages for the Easter Vigil. Summarize the passage and tell in your own words what the passage says to us about conversion.

Reconciliation, or Penance

The Church celebrates God's forgiveness of sins committed after Baptism in the Sacrament of **Reconciliation,** which is a Sacrament of Healing. In this sacrament the person is also reconciled with the Church. At the present time there are three ways Catholics may celebrate the Sacrament of Reconciliation: individual confession to a priest, the communal rite with individual confession and absolution, and, on rare occasions, the communal rite with general absolution.

The communal rite with general absolution may be used when there is immanent danger of death—for example, when soldiers are going to war, and there is not enough time for a priest to hear the confession of each individual. The Vatican has declared that conditions for the use of general absolution do not exist, at present, in the United States. Individual confession of sins and absolution is the ordinary way we are reconciled with God and the Church.

The Sacrament of Reconciliation has four main parts: contrition, confession, penance, and absolution.

- **Contrition.** This involves the examination of conscience and the realization that one has sinned. There is a sincere sorrow for such sin and true intent to try to do better in the future.
- **Confession.** The telling of sins to a priest and the confession of all mortal sins is required.
- **Penance.** The priest may offer some brief spiritual advice before giving the penitent a penance to perform to show the sincerity of repentance and the willingness to repair the harm caused by sin. The main types of penance are fasting, prayer, and almsgiving. The penitent then prays an Act of Contrition.

- **Absolution.** The word *absolve* means "to clean" or "to take away a stain." In the Sacrament of Reconciliation, bishops and priests act in Christ's name to forgive sins. Any sins confessed in the Sacrament of Reconciliation are sealed with secrecy; this is called the *seal of the sacrament* or the *seal of confession.* This secrecy is absolute and admits no exceptions. Under no circumstances may the priest or bishop ever reveal what was confessed to him.

In the name of Christ, the priest absolves the penitent of his or her sins.

Activity

Using the handout your teacher gives you, reflect on the examination of conscience based on the Ten Commandments. To prepare for the Sacrament of Reconciliation, write your answers to the questions in your journal.

Eucharist

As you know, the word *Eucharist* means "thanksgiving." The Eucharist is both a meal and a sacrifice. At Mass, the Church joins with Jesus in offering his Body and Blood to God the Father. The Church commemorates Christ's sacrifice on the cross and makes this sacrifice present: "the sacrifice Christ offered once for all on the cross remains ever present" (Catechism, #1364). The sharing of the Body and Blood of Christ in Communion is a sign of oneness with God and other members of the Church.

The Church teaches that sincere participation in the Eucharist wipes away venial sins and helps preserve us from mortal sins. The formal forgiveness of mortal sins, however, belongs properly to the Sacrament of Reconciliation.

Anointing of the Sick

In the Sacrament of the **Anointing of the Sick,** God forgives sins and initiates spiritual and sometime physical healing; the ill person is strengthened. In the sacrament, the priest lays his hands on the head of the sick person. The priest and the people assembled pray that God might restore the person to health, both physically and spiritually. The priest says a prayer that the person may receive peace, courage, and the grace to accept whatever God wills. The priest anoints the person's forehead and hands with blessed oil.

The Anointing of the Sick is celebrated for people who are elderly, seriously ill, or dying. People facing serious surgery may also be anointed.

The grace of the sacrament has several effects. It unites the sick person to the suffering of Christ, for the person's own good and for the good of the Church. It strengthens the person to endure suffering in a Christian manner. It forgives venial sins and mortal sins as well, if the person is sorry and unable to confess them. It may restore the person to physical health, if that is God's will. And it prepares the person for death and the passage to everlasting life. Anyone in danger of death from sickness or old age may receive the sacrament. The Sacrament of Anointing was once called *Extreme Unction* (anointing). It was celebrated only when the person was dying or in grave danger of dying. The name change reflects the true purpose of the sacrament: to confer strength and healing on those who are sick. The term *Last Rites* refers to the Sacraments of Reconciliation, Anointing of the Sick, and Eucharist received by a dying person.

OUR CALL TO FORGIVENESS

Reflection

When in your life have you experienced God's forgiveness? How do you think this forgiveness has helped you to be more compassionate and forgiving of other people?

People who live in any kind of community will always have opportunities to forgive and to ask for forgiveness.

In addition to turning away from sin and accepting God's forgiveness of sins, Christians have a further obligation—to forgive themselves and to forgive others for wrongs committed. Forgiving others is a way to show our gratitude to God who has first forgiven us.

Another reason we should forgive others is found in the Lord's Prayer. When Jesus taught his disciples to pray, he wanted them to understand what forgiveness is and what it demands. He taught them to pray, "forgive us our debts, as we also have forgiven our debtors" (Matthew 6:12). We, too, should be merciful to others just as God has been merciful to us. Indeed, this is the meaning of the Beatitude, "Blessed are the merciful, for they will receive mercy" (Matthew 5:7). While our actions don't control God, it is only fair to expect him to judge us with the same mercy and forgiveness we have shown others.

Activity

The message of mercy is strong in Jesus' parable of the unforgiving servant found in Matthew 18:23–35. Read this parable. Then, in small groups, discuss how the message of the parable applies to young people today.

The Process of Forgiveness

Forgiving others from one's heart is not easy. It usually does not happen automatically or quickly. True forgiveness is itself a form of conversion. It can sometimes be a long, painful process. Ethicist Lewis Smedes defines four distinct psychological stages in the process of forgiveness.

- **Stage 1: We feel the hurt.** Acknowledging that we have been hurt is an important first step toward forgiveness. We have to feel the pain before we can be healed of it.

- **Stage 2: We are filled with hatred, anger, and revulsion toward the offender.** We feel active resentment toward the person who has hurt us. Many people in this stage withdraw from the offender. Other people lash out with angry words or fists. The natural tendency is to want to "get even," to inflict the same hurt on the one who hurt us.

- **Stage 3: We gradually heal.** A wise person once said, "Time changes everything." As we move further and further away from a hurtful event, it tends to hurt less. We start to heal. Healing means that we gradually—little by little—let go of the pain.

- **Stage 4: We open ourselves to love again.** Gradually, we let go of our anger, hatred, and resentment. We no longer allow our resentment to judge the trespasser. We stop thinking about ways to get revenge. We learn to trust again, to try to love again. That does not mean we will necessarily be friends with the offender. It means that we genuinely want what is morally good for the offender—that he or she will attain a true change of heart in the future.

Mark Rafenstine. "Forgiveness: A Path to a Better You,"
Current Health 2, *a* Weekly Reader *publication (December 2000): 13.*

Healing can be a difficult process. It doesn't always follow these four stages exactly. And sometimes we have to repeat a step or two in the process. For example, we may think we have forgiven a certain person's offense, but then something happens that makes the hurt come back even more strongly. Once again we have to deal with the pain and the feelings of resentment. Once again we struggle to show mercy as God has shown mercy to us.

Reflection

On a scale of 1 to 10 (with 1 being very easy and 10 being very difficult):

- How hard is it for you to forgive others most of the time? Why?

Activity

Using a fiction or nonfiction book, movie, or article, write a summary of someone's journey of healing and forgiveness. What stages or steps did the person have to go through?

Forgiving Everyone

Forgiving people we love who have hurt us is hard enough, but Jesus challenges us to go even further than that. He calls us to forgive everyone, including our enemies.

" You have heard that it was said, 'You shall love your neighbor and hate your enemy.' But I say to you, Love your enemies and pray for those who persecute you, so that you may be children of your Father in heaven; for he makes his sun rise on the evil and on the good, and sends rain on the righteous and on the unrighteous. For if you love those who love you, what reward do you have? Do not even the tax collectors do the same? And if you greet only your brothers and sisters, what more are you doing than others? Do not even the Gentiles do the same? Be perfect, therefore, as your heavenly Father is perfect. "

MATTHEW 5:43–48

When Jesus forgave the soldiers who crucified him, he showed us how to love our enemies (see Luke 23:34). When we love our enemies, we are truly walking in the light of faith. We are witnessing to our belief that love is more powerful than sin. With God, nothing is impossible.

Jesus taught his followers that those who show mercy will receive mercy.

"Christ and the Adulteress" by Rocco Marconi.

Activity

In a small group, compare each of the following Scripture passages to Matthew 5:43–48. Discuss what you think each passage tells us about loving everyone.

- The weeds and the wheat—Matthew 13:24–30
- The banquet—Luke 14:16–24
- Marks of the true Christian—Romans 12:14–21
- Imitating God—1 John 4:16b–21

LOVE YOUR ENEMY

Throughout history, many Christians have shown us that loving one's enemies, although sometimes very difficult, is not impossible for people of faith. Let us explore four examples of people who have loved their enemies.

POPE JOHN PAUL II

In 1980, Pope John Paul II wrote about forgiveness in the encyclical *Rich in Mercy*. The pope reminded Catholics that "Christ teaches us to forgive always" (#14). Less than six months later, Pope John Paul II was challenged to take those words to heart. On May 13, 1981, a twenty-three-year-old Turkish national, Mehmet Ali Agca, fired a gun at the pope as the pope entered St. Peter's Square. Although the would-be assassin failed to kill the pope, the physical damage was extensive.

The pope was rushed to a hospital, where he underwent surgery. For the next three days, he remained in critical condition with a high fever. On the fourth day he got out of bed and, despite great pain, forgave Agca. The pope was released from the hospital on June 3, but the doctors readmitted him to the hospital on June 20 for additional intestinal surgery.

Agca, in the meantime, was arrested and imprisoned. He went to trial on July 19, was found guilty, and was sentenced to life in prison. Agca expressed sorrow at shooting two innocent bystanders in the crowd at St. Peter's Square, but he expressed no remorse for shooting the pope. He said he acted alone, but later said he received instructions to kill the pope from three Bulgarian secret service agents and three Turkish members of the KGB to protest the pope's

Pope John Paul II and Mehmet Ali Agca on December 27, 1983.

support of the Solidarity Trade Union in Poland. The six men Agca accused were found and brought to trial, but they were acquitted for lack of evidence.

Two years later Turkish terrorists, to protest Agca's imprisonment, kidnapped the fifteen-year-old daughter of a Vatican employee. They offered the girl's life in exchange for Agca's release. Pope John Paul II spent two months trying to negotiate with the kidnappers until they finally dropped their demand for Agca's release. The girl was never seen again. Despite these tragic developments, Pope John Paul II met with Mehmet Ali Agca in prison on December 27, 1983. The men talked for twenty minutes, and again the pope extended his forgiveness.

In 2000, Pope John Paul II declared a jubilee year, a time when debts should be forgiven. The pope encouraged the Italian government to grant clemency to prisoners during this time. With the pope's

approval, Italian President Carlo Ciampi signed a clemency order for Agca on June 13. Agca was released from prison and extradited to Turkey to serve a sentence for the 1979 killing of a journalist.

Let's Talk!

1. If someone shot you in an attempt to kill you, would you try to gain clemency for that person? How would you feel if the person were released from jail?

2. Do you think Christians have an obligation to forgive people who express no remorse and don't want to be forgiven? Explain.

CHILDREN'S MOVEMENT FOR PEACE

After Mayerly Sanchez's closest friend, fifteen-year-old Milton Piraguata, was stabbed to death in a gang fight, Mayerly vowed to find a way to stop street killings in Colombia. She had just turned twelve. In a country where homicide by gunshot is the leading cause of death, Sanchez says Christ's presence helps her lead 100,000 children in a campaign that has been nominated three times (in 1998, 1999, and 2000) for the Nobel Peace Prize.

While still twelve, Sanchez joined the leadership of the Columbia Children's Movement for Peace. This movement provides young people with the tools to promote nonviolence to their peers and to their elected officials. Through the program, Sanchez and her preteen teams present neighborhood kids with alternatives to gangs—education, skills training, and recreation. Activities and games reinforce the message of nonviolence, as do the movement's rallies, marches, media campaigns, and art contests.

The teams of children go into schools with projects and drama. Sanchez says that this children-to-children approach is more effective than adults speaking to children. The message of peace also goes from child to adult, from the school dramas that parents attend to a visit some of the children had with Colombian President Andres Pastrana.

Through their art and drama, the children teach parents to affirm them and, when necessary, to discipline them in love rather than in uncontrolled anger. This helps create a nonviolent culture, Sanchez says.

The second of three daughters of a Bogota bus driver, Sanchez grew up in a town of blood and dust. Cazuca, her mountainside hometown outside of Bogota, began as squatter's territory for war refugees. The village now has electricity and running water, and most of the roads are paved. The drive-by shootings of her preteen years have abated, but if she stays late at a friend's house, she usually spends the night rather than risk assault or robbery.

"It's sad; it discourages you when you find out somebody has been killed," Sanchez says. "Until my last breath, I'll keep working for peace. There are highs and lows, but you have to go on."

Shortened from Jeff M. Sellers, "A child shall lead them: in strife-torn Colombia, a teenage girl guides 100,000 kids in the search for peace—and adults aren't far behind," Christianity Today *(3 December 2001): 46+.*

Research

On the Internet or in the library, find information on another person or group that forgave an enemy. Prepare a presentation for the class and include questions for a follow-up discussion.

Activity

In a small group, write and perform a skit for younger children, showing them how to resolve neighborhood or school conflicts.

Mayerly Sanchez leads a children's march for peace.

Photo by Jon Warren/World Vision.

JOSEPH CARDINAL BERNARDIN

Joseph Cardinal Bernardin, Archbishop of Chicago, was both startled and devastated. It was November 11, 1993, and he had just learned that Steven Cook, a man he did not know, was accusing him of sexual abuse. He recorded his reaction in his final book, *The Gift of Peace*.

" Who, in God's name, was this person, and why was he accusing me of something that he must have known, as I did, never took place? I then recalled hearing that this same person had already brought complaints to the Archdiocese of Cincinnati against a priest who was on the faculty of St. Gregory's seminary there. I began to surmise that because, in Steven's judgment, he had not received a satisfactory response from Cincinnati, his lawyer had decided to bring me into the case since I was Archbishop at the time. . . . The truth, I decided, was the only defense I had. . . . The truth will set you free. I believed that, and I trusted the Lord who, for reasons I could not yet fathom, had permitted this trial to enter my life (21, 23). "

It took one hundred days for the false charges against Cardinal Bernardin to be resolved. Meanwhile, almost daily his name was "dragged through the mud" of national media headlines and news stories. Instead of being angry about what had happened,

Bernardin was filled with concern for his accuser. Steven, he learned, was gravely ill with AIDS.

Bernardin arranged to meet with Steven and flew to Philadelphia to talk with him. At the meeting a great sense of peace and reconciliation took place. Steven apologized for lying, and the cardinal forgave him. Bernardin celebrated Mass for Steven and administered the Sacrament of the Anointing of the Sick to him.

" Steven and I kept in touch after that and, six months later, when I received a diagnosis of pancreatic cancer, his was one of the first letters I received. He had only a few months to live when he wrote it, filled with sympathy and encouragement for me. He planned to visit me in Chicago at the end of August, but he was too ill. Steven died at his mother's home on September 22, 1995, fully reconciled with the Church (40–41). "

Fourteen months later, the cardinal himself died of cancer. At his funeral, many Church members remembered him as a man who took hard stands for justice and who through his example gave many people the gift of forgiveness and peace.

Selections from Joseph Cardinal Bernardin,
"The Gift of Peace: Personal Reflections,"
(Chicago: Loyola Press, 1997).

Joseph Cardinal Bernardin willingly forgave the man who falsely accused him.

Activity

Using the handout your teacher will give you, read the final words of Cardinal Bernardin in his book *The Gift of Peace*. After reflecting on these words, write a prayer asking God for the ability to forgive and to be a peacemaker in your own life.

THE TRUTH AND RECONCILIATION COMMISSION

Until late in the twentieth century there existed in South Africa a political system known as apartheid. Basically, apartheid segregated the black majority from the white minority and denied blacks many human rights—including voting privileges. During the struggle for human rights and equality in South Africa, many people were tear-gassed, bitten by police dogs, beaten by police, detained, tortured, killed, imprisoned, and exiled. Apartheid did not end until 1994, when the first bi-racial elections were held and Nelson Mandela was elected as the nation's first black president.

Although apartheid ended, a major problem remained: How were the black and white races going to cooperate with one another and coexist in peace? How were the hatreds that had grown throughout the years going to come to an end? And how were people going to heal from their many years of mistreatment, oppression, and human rights violations?

In 1995 the South African government passed the Promotion of National Unity and Reconciliation Act, a law that established the Truth and Reconciliation Commission. The purpose of the commission was to highlight the deep damage to human relationships inflicted by past gross human rights violations in South Africa. The commission consisted of three committees—the Human Rights Violations Committee, the Reparation and Rehabilitation Committee, and the Amnesty Committee.

- **Human Rights Violations Committee.** This group investigated human rights abuses that took place between 1960 and 1994. This established the identity of the victims and the nature and extent of the harm they had suffered.
- **Reparation and Rehabilitation Committee.** This group provided support for victims in an effort to acknowledge their dignity and heal their families and communities.
- **Amnesty Committee.** This group allowed human rights violators to "confess" their sins and apologize in public. In exchange for their honesty, the violators would receive amnesty; they would be free from prosecution for the confessed crimes.

Public hearings between the victims and the offenders proved to be highly emotional and dramatic. Many victims succumbed to tears or expressed anger as they retold their experiences. Of the 21,000 statements on human rights violations, it was discovered that the greatest proportion of victims were youth, many under the age of eighteen.

The commission presented its final report to President Nelson Mandela on October 29, 1998. Although everyone appearing before the commission did not experience healing and reconciliation, it was clear that a significant number of people made giant steps forward in the process of forgiveness. Rights violators who confessed were given the opportunity to become human again. Some even expressed contrition, although this was not required. Victims finally knew the truth about what had happened to their loved ones, as well as the identities of those to forgive.

Among the conclusions of the commission were some important reflections on the meaning and importance of reconciliation— among individuals, between racial communities, and within whole countries. All Christians would do well to meditate on these findings.

Nelson Mandela spent 27½ years in prison because of his activities promoting human rights for blacks in South Africa. After apartheid ended, he was elected president of the country.

- Reconciliation is not easy. It takes persistence and time.

- Respect for our common humanity is the foundation for reconciliation.

- Reconciliation brings with it a form of restorative justice, in which the guilty party is restored to society. It avoids revenge and does not look for punishment. This requires a new kind of society where the one reconciling can contribute to that society and the culture promotes human rights and political stability.

- When there is full disclosure of what happened and the reasons behind violations, forgiveness is more possible.

- People must be ready to accept responsibility for human rights violations of the past.

- Reconciliation doesn't mean people can erase their memories. In fact, memories are important if we are to learn from the past and make right its violations so that the present and the future may be secure.

- Everyone must accept moral and political responsibility for promoting human rights and democracy and for addressing conflicts nonviolently.

- People, especially those who have benefited from discrimination, must be committed to changing situations of inequality and poverty.

See Truth and Reconciliation Commission. Final Report, Volume 5, chapter 9 (29 October 1998).

Let's Talk!

1. Why do you think honesty and knowledge of what happened are so important to the process of healing and forgiveness?

2. What moral responsibility do you have to nurture a culture of human rights and democracy in your neighborhood? Your school? Your town or city? Your country?

Activity

The chairman of the Truth and Reconciliation Commission was Anglican Bishop Desmond Tutu from Capetown, South Africa. The now-retired bishop received the Nobel Peace Prize in 1984. Using the handout your teacher will give you, read some of Bishop Desmond Tutu's reflections on the work of the Truth and Reconciliation Commission. Then, in a small group, discuss practical ways your generation might go about building racial harmony in the United States.

"PEACE BE WITH YOU"

Every time the Risen Lord visited his Apostles, he wished them peace. This wish included all meanings of the word *peace:* peace of mind, peace with one another, and peace with God. We might say that in his wish, Jesus was urging the Apostles to get beyond their fear, anger, and hatred about the events surrounding his crucifixion and death. We might say he was urging them to heal and to move on—to bring God's forgiveness to people in all countries. Indeed, with true forgiveness comes peace—both exterior and interior. Peace is an important gift that Christ won for us when he forgave sin and reconciled the human race with God his Father.

In his Sermon on the Mount, Jesus presented the Beatitudes—ways of living that lead to holiness. One of these Beatitudes is "Blessed are the peacemakers, for they will be called children of God" (Matthew 5:9). As Christians, we are to live in harmony with others, settle arguments, and be ministers of reconciliation.

> " I say to you that if you are angry with a brother or sister, you will be liable to judgment; and if you insult a brother or sister, you will be liable to the council; and if you say, 'You fool,' you will be liable to the hell of fire. So when you are offering your gift at the altar, if you remember that your brother or sister has something against you, leave your gift there before the altar and go; first be reconciled to your brother or sister, and then come and offer your gift. "

MATTHEW 5:22–24

"Sermon on the Mount" by Jean-Baptiste de Champaigne; Musée Magnin, Dijon, France.

Let's Talk!

1. What do you think the Catechism means when it says that peace is a requirement of respect for and development of human life?

2. In a war, which side does God favor? Explain.

3. What are some ways you can be a peacemaker?

In short, our responsibility to work for peace in the world comes from the Fifth Commandment: "You shall not murder" (Deuteronomy 5:17).

The morality of living in peace with others stems from the new commandment: "Just as I have loved you, you also should love one another" (John 13:34), as well as the ancient law, "[Y]ou shall love your neighbor as yourself" (Leviticus 19:18). It is also based on respect for all human life, which is made in God's image. The Catechism explains,

> " Respect for and development of human life require peace. Peace is not merely the absence of war, and it is not limited to maintaining a balance of powers between adversaries. Peace cannot be attained on earth without safeguarding the goods of persons, free communication among men, respect for the dignity of persons and peoples, and the assiduous practice of fraternity (#2304). "

As Christians, we are to renounce violence, bloodshed, and terrorism, and—wherever possible—to avoid war.

The Church's Stand on War

Although the gospel calls us to peace, the Church has had a varied history regarding war. In some centuries, the pope actually called Christians to battle for a religious cause, or crusade. Even today, religious differences are the cause of continued bloodshed in and between various countries—Muslims and Jews in the Middle East, Catholics and Protestants in Northern Ireland, and so on. In conflicts between countries, chaplains accompany the troops to the battlefield.

So what is the Church's policy regarding war? Actually, the Church's policy is quite broad. On the one hand, it supports *pacifists* who are against all wars and *conscientious objectors* who are against specific wars they believe are being waged for immoral reasons. On the other hand, the Church supports the rights of individuals and countries to defend themselves and their land from aggressors. The Church also supports the obligation of people to aid their neighbors who are being threatened with force. War may be waged if certain strict moral conditions are met. These conditions make up what is known as the "just-war doctrine."

Reflection

How would you describe yourself: a complete pacifist, a conscientious objector, or a militant? Explain.

The Just-War Doctrine

Basically, the just-war doctrine includes the following moral principles:

There must be a just cause for going to war.
For example, one nation cannot go to war against another simply because it wants to exploit that nation's resources for itself. However, a nation can go to war to protect itself or another nation from the serious, certain, and permanent damage of an unjust aggressor.

The war must be declared by competent authority.
In the United States, for example, it takes an act of Congress to declare war.

There must be a right intention for going to war.
A wrong intention would be revenge or hatred. A right intention would be self-defense or prevention of further violence from the aggressor in the future.

War must be the last resort after all other means to keep the peace have failed.

There must be a serious possibility of success.
No country should risk the lives of its citizens by entering into a hopeless conflict.

An excessive amount of force (weapons) cannot be used.

Civilians must not be the targets of war actions, directly or indirectly.

The war must not produce worse suffering.

If all these conditions are met, then the Church deems that it may be morally acceptable to wage war. However, discussion of what is allowed in times of war or threats of war continues within the Church and between nations.

Let's Talk!

1. Do you think the just-war doctrine could be applied to a long-standing family feud? Why?

2. Would you volunteer for the armed services if it seemed that a war was about to happen? Under what conditions? Why?

3. Do you think pacifists and conscientious objectors are being sincere or are they just cowards? Explain.

Research

Work with a small group to do research on one of the following wars or international conflicts (undeclared wars) in U.S. history: the Civil War, World War I, World War II, the Korean War, the Vietnam Conflict, or the Persian Gulf Conflict. Apply the principles of the just-war theory to this war and decide, to the best of your understanding, whether the United States was justified in fighting this war. Be prepared to share your thoughts with the class.

Activity

Write a poem, rap, song, or essay about the need for forgiveness in a real-life conflict in today's world. Be prepared to share your work with the class.

Learning to Forgive Others

Forgiveness takes practice. Here are some actions you can take to help yourself learn how to forgive others:

1. Make a decision to get through the hurt and heal. Detach yourself, as much as possible, from your anger. Try to think, rather than just react. Remind yourself that peace is more important than revenge.

2. Define for yourself what the hurt was and how it was inflicted. Be as truthful as possible. Don't deny the situation or the hurt feelings you have experienced.

3. Strive to understand the person who has hurt you. Don't try to excuse the hurtful behavior, but try to understand it.

4. Determine what part you may have played in what happened. Consider what you have learned from the experience. What changes need to be made in the future?

5. Initiate a forgiveness discussion, if possible. Even if the other person doesn't apologize, let go of your anger. Get back in control of your own life and emotions. Be willing to put the bad experience behind you and move on.

! Let's Talk!

After reading about Dorothy Day on page 202, discuss these questions:

1. Do you think Dorothy Day is truly a saint? Why?

2. In what ways could young people today follow Dorothy Day's example of being a peacemaker?

3. In what ways can young people today follow Dorothy Day's example of helping people who are poor?

A Person of Faith

Dorothy Day

Dorothy Day was born on November 8, 1897, in Brooklyn. Her family soon moved to San Francisco, where they survived the 1906 earthquake. The family then moved to Chicago, where Dorothy's father was sports editor for a newspaper. During high school, Dorothy declared herself to be an atheist. After two years of college, she moved to New York to work as a reporter for *The Call,* the city's only socialist daily. Day's interest in social reform grew as she covered rallies and demonstrations led by labor organizers and revolutionaries.

During World War I, Dorothy worked for *The Masses,* a magazine that opposed U.S. involvement in the war. In 1917 she was arrested for protesting in front of the White House. Her issue was women's right to vote. She was convicted and sent to prison, where she began to read the Bible.

In 1918, during a terrible flu epidemic, Dorothy worked as a nurses' aide at Kings County

Hospital in Brooklyn. There she met Lionel Moise, a newspaper reporter. In 1919 she became pregnant, and Moise said he would leave her unless she had an abortion. Dorothy relented and had the abortion. Moise soon deserted her anyway, and her decision haunted her for the rest of her life. In 1920 Day married Barkeley Tobey, a literary promoter who had been married eight times before. After a year Barkeley left her.

Around 1925 Dorothy began to live with Forster Batterham, a botanist and heavy drinker. Dorothy got pregnant again, and this time the experience transformed her. After giving birth to a girl whom she named Tamar, Dorothy turned to the Catholic Church for the forgiveness she sought. She had Tamar baptized, and in 1927 Dorothy herself was baptized. Batterham, who detested the Catholic Church and refused to get married, left her.

To support herself and her child, Dorothy worked as a writer for various Catholic magazines. In 1932 she covered the Hunger March in Washington, DC. It was during the Depression, and people were marching to draw attention to the need for jobs, unemployment insurance, old-age pensions, healthcare, and housing. Day was greatly impressed and prayed to live her Catholic faith in a way that truly helped people who were poor. The next day she met Peter Maurin, who persuaded her to join him in founding *The Catholic Worker,* a newspaper that raised people's awareness of the plight of people who were poor.

Soon Day and Maurin founded a series of homeless shelters; they and several friends lived in the shelters with the people who came to them for help. The Catholic Worker became a national movement; soup kitchens and houses of hospitality were established in other cities. Dorothy never tried to reform the alcoholics, drug addicts, or marginalized people who lived with her. Instead, she concentrated on being Christ to them, letting them know about God's forgiveness.

Day became actively involved in the pacifism movement. She wrote against the Spanish Civil War (1936), World War II, the Korean War, the Vietnam Conflict, and nuclear weapons. She frequently joined in protests, which landed her in jail eight times. Her civil disobedience and commitment to gospel nonviolence gained international attention. Eventually, her actions had a direct effect on the Second Vatican Council's document, "The Church in the Modern World," which upheld the rights of conscientious objectors.

The last time Day appeared in public was at the International Eucharistic Congress in 1976. She begged for God's forgiveness for the atomic bombing of Hiroshima. Dorothy died of congestive heart failure on November 29, 1980. On March 16, 2000, the Vatican gave its approval to start the process by which Day might be canonized a saint. Meanwhile, the Catholic Worker Movement continues to grow. There are now over 125 houses and farming communes in the United States and in seven other countries.

Celebrating Faith

Opening Song:	"Give Us Your Peace"
Leader:	Gracious and loving Father, you know that we sometimes lose our way. We make wrong decisions. We sometimes seem to prefer sin to your friendship. Hear us as we pray, that we may turn away from sin and walk in your light.

Side 1: Have mercy on me, O God,
according to your steadfast love;
according to your abundant mercy
blot out my transgressions.

Side 2: Wash me thoroughly from my iniquity,
and cleanse me from my sin.

Side 1: For I know my transgressions,
and my sin is ever before me.

Side 2: Against you, you alone, have I sinned,
and done what is evil in your sight,
so that you are justified in your sentence
and blameless when you pass judgment.

Side 1: You desire truth in the inward being;
therefore teach me wisdom in my secret heart.

Side 2: Purge me with hyssop, and I shall be clean;
wash me, and I shall be whiter than snow.

Side 1: Let me hear joy and gladness;
let the bones that you have crushed rejoice.

Side 2: Hide your face from my sins,
and blot out all my iniquities.

Side 1: Create in me a clean heart, O God,
and put a new and right spirit within me.

Side 2: Do not cast me away from your presence,
and do not take your holy spirit from me.

Side 1: Restore to me the joy of your salvation,
and sustain in me a willing spirit.

Side 2: Then I will teach transgressors your ways.
and sinners will return to you.

Side 1: Deliver me from bloodshed, O God,
O God of my salvation,
and my tongue will sing aloud of your deliverance.

Side 2: O Lord, open my lips,
and my mouth will declare your praise.

Side 1: For you have no delight in sacrifice;
if I were to give a burnt offering, you would not be pleased.

Side 2: The sacrifice acceptable to God is a broken spirit;
a broken and contrite heart, O God, you will not despise.

Psalm 51:1–4, 6–17

Review

1. Define *forgiveness* in terms of what it is and is not.

2. What is the difference between a lax conscience, a scrupulous conscience, and a healthy conscience?

3. What is the connection between forgiveness and contrition?

4. What is the connection between forgiveness and conversion?

5. What are the penitential psalms?

6. What is the first Sacrament of Forgiveness in the Church? What are the effects of this sacrament?

7. What is the Eucharist? How is it a Sacrament of Forgiveness?

8. What are the four main parts of the Sacrament of Reconciliation? What are the effects of this sacrament?

9. What are the four main parts of the Sacrament of the Anointing of the Sick? Who may receive the sacrament? Who are the ministers of this sacrament?

10. What are the effects of the Sacrament of the Anointing of the Sick?

11. What is the Church's stance, in general, toward war and peace?

12. What are the conditions needed before war can be waged justly?

WORDS OF FAITH

absolution—the forgiveness of sin, by a bishop or a priest who acts in God's name in the Sacrament of Reconciliation, or Penance

Anointing of the Sick—the Sacrament of Healing and Forgiveness for people who are seriously ill, elderly, or in danger of dying. In the sacrament, the person's forehead and hands are anointed with the blessed oil of the sick.

conscience—the internal voice that helps individuals know right from wrong

contrition—sincere sorrow for the sins one has committed, coupled with the resolution to do better in the future

conversion—a sincere change of mind, will, and heart—away from sin and toward God

forgiveness—pardon for one's actions; being reconciled with God and others. The act of forgiveness includes the effort to let go of feelings of resentment, hatred, and hurt.

Reconciliation—one of the Church's Sacraments of Healing and Forgiveness; the sacrament through which the sinner is reconciled with God and the Church

Enrichment

Choose one of the following.

1. View and discuss a movie that deals with the decision to seek revenge or to forgive. Do you think the right decision was made? Why?

2. Rewrite the story of the conversion of Saint Paul, using a modern-day teenager as the main character of a skit. With one or two others, perform your skit for the class.

3. Read one of the penitential psalms in your Bible. Then write a modern version of the psalm, in the form of a poem, song, or rap. Be prepared to share what you have written with the class.

4. With a partner or small group, make a banner or poster about one of the themes in this chapter—forgiveness, peace, reconciliation, nonviolence. Display the banner in the prayer corner or somewhere in your school where others will see it.

Eternal Light

" Arise, shine; for your light has come,
and the glory of the LORD has risen
upon you.
For darkness shall cover the earth,
and thick darkness the peoples;
but the LORD will arise upon you,
and his glory will appear over you. "

ISAIAH 60:1–2

In this chapter, you will:

- come to value the Christian view of death and afterlife.
- explore the Church's teachings on particular judgment at death and the general judgment of both the living and the dead at Christ's second coming.
- reflect on love, rather than desire for reward or fear of punishment, as the motivation behind true Christian morality.
- study the structure and meaning of the Order of Christian Funerals.
- appreciate ways that Catholics pray for the dead, including the Office of the Dead, Masses for the Dead, and All Souls' Day observances.
- learn how to live with integrity by being faithful to oneself and one's values.

WORDS OF FAITH

death	heaven	particular judgment
eschatology	hell	purgatory
eternal life	immortal	resurrection of the body
general judgment	parousia	

—Looking Back, Going Forward-

Throughout this book, we have talked about what we believe, what our faith is. There are many things that we cannot fully understand because we are not God. Life is a great mystery, and we find deeper and deeper meaning in life. We also find meaning in the end of life, which is perhaps the greatest mystery of all.

What is **death**? From the medical point of view, it is the permanent cessation of all vital bodily functions, total brain function as well as function of the respiratory and circulatory systems. From the viewpoint of Catholic Tradition, death is the separation of the soul from the body. In short, death is the end of human life as we know it. It is faith that gives us the answer of what happens to us at the end of life. Every person receives a judgment by God at the moment of death. At this **particular judgment**, when we give our life to Christ, we will either enter into "the blessedness of heaven—through a purification or immediately—or immediate and everlasting damnation" (CCC, #1022).

Reflection

1. Did you know anyone who died? What was that person's relationship to you? How did this person's death affect you?

2. What is your closest personal experience with death? Were you ever in danger of dying? What were your feelings at the time? What were your feelings afterward?

3. What are your feelings about death, especially knowing that someday you will die?

The Unexpected

Many young people do not like to talk about or think about death. In fact, many young people think they are invulnerable, that is, that death will never happen to them. They see death as something so far off in the future that it doesn't really exist—until death comes knocking close to home. Consider the following story of an aunt passing on articles of faith and spiritual knowledge to her two young nieces.

PASSING ON FAITH

Years ago, I learned a lesson about passing on religious faith during a golden summer while my family was on vacation. My daughters were young, about ages 3 and 6, and we were staying with my wife's extended family in a spacious summer home just a short walk from Lake Michigan's beautiful shoreline.

One sunny afternoon I went to get my daughters up from their naps so we could head down for a day at the beach, but they weren't in their beds. And they weren't in the living room or the kitchen or on the deck. I began to worry, knowing that the lake was just a half block away. I was about to call out for them when I heard familiar whispering in Aunt Marie's room.

Sitting on the edge of the bed was Aunt Marie, with Judy and Patti plopped on either side of her. Marie was holding a well-worn prayer book jammed full of holy cards. The girls' eyes were wide with curiosity. I listened in on their hushed whisperings. "Now, this is your great-great-grandmother's," said Aunt Marie, holding a prayer card in her hand. "She died just a few days before Dennis was married. She baked the best bread and cakes and was always one for helping a sick neighbor or someone down on their luck.

"And this one's from old Mrs. Clancy. She was a great help to our mother after Father passed away. And here's a prayer card for Father Sheehy. He was a wonderful priest. He went off to the missions in Bolivia. He always spoke so lovingly about the people there."

As she talked, she'd hand off a card to the girls. They'd hold them reverently in their tiny hands, looking at them front and back. "And now let's pray for the people I promised to pray for," said Aunt Marie. The three of them bowed their heads as she began a litany that included neighbors, troubled relatives, poor souls in purgatory, shopkeepers, the congregation of nuns who taught her years ago, and deceased family members. As always, she ended her prayer with, "God help the sick."

I left them to their prayers and stood out on the deck appreciating the fine day. In a few minutes the girls came dashing out, towels in hand, eager to go to the beach. We were a motley caravan traipsing down to the shoreline with plastic rafts, inner tubes, beach chairs, and blankets.

The waves were high that day, and I watched as Aunt Marie and Uncle Johnny walked the girls into the surf, hand in hand, laughing as the waves crashed into them. Clinging together, they stood, holding one another up as the currents pushed and pulled them. They were safe, hanging on together.

Shortened from Tom McGrath, "How to pass on the articles of faith," *US Catholic* (June 2000)

Let's Talk!

1. Who hands on their faith to you? In what ways do they do this?

2. How can you share your hopes and beliefs with others? With whom can you share them?

BELIEF IN AN AFTERLIFE

If a person dies in God's grace, that person will be with him after death—and with all their loved ones. The Catechism teaches that "through Baptism, the Christian has already 'died with Christ' sacramentally, in order to live a new life; and if we die in Christ's grace, physical death completes this 'dying with Christ' and so completes our incorporation into him [becoming one with him] . . ." (#1010).

In the days of Jesus, belief in the afterlife was a topic that was hotly debated among Jewish scholars. **Eternal life** was thought to be the face-to-face vision of God, sometimes referred to as *resurrection*. The religious group known as the Pharisees, in particular, believed in resurrection, in other words that God would grant eternal life to good people who had been faithful to the Law in life. The Sadducees, another religious group of the time did not believe in resurrection, angels, or spirits. For the Sadducees, life "continued" only through one's children and grandchildren. Thus when some of the Sadducees posed the following question to Jesus, they were more or less making fun of the idea of life after death.

" Teacher, Moses said, 'If a man dies childless, his brother shall marry the widow, and raise up children for his brother.' Now there were seven brothers among us; the first married, and died childless, leaving the widow to his brother. The second did the same, so also the third, down to the seventh. Last of all, the woman herself died. In the resurrection, then, whose wife of the seven will she be? For all of them had married her."

Jesus answered them, "You are wrong, because you know neither the scriptures nor the power of God. For in the resurrection they neither marry nor are given in marriage, but are like angels in heaven. "

MATTHEW 22:24–30

Basically, Jesus saw that the Sadducees' question was not sincere since they do not believe in the resurrection or in life after death. Jesus' answer tells us two important things about the afterlife. First, it really exists. Second, life after death is different from life on earth.

Let's Talk!

1. Do you want to live forever? Why?

2. What do you think happens after death? What has influenced you to think this way?

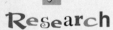

Research

Using the library or the Internet, find out something about another faith's beliefs concerning life after death. In a class discussion, share your findings.

The Sadducees believed that life continued only through one's children.

Reasons for Believing

There are important reasons for believing in an afterlife. The first reason involves the fact that Jesus showed that God has power over life and death. He indicated this by raising people from the dead. We learn from the Gospels that Jesus raised Jairus's daughter and a widow's son at Nain. Furthermore, many people were present when Jesus raised his friend Lazarus to life.

A second reason to believe in the afterlife is the Resurrection of Jesus himself. Many passages in the New Testament testify that God the Father raised Jesus from the dead. Many disciples, in addition to the Apostles, saw him alive: Jesus "appeared to [Peter], then to the twelve. Then he appeared to more than five hundred brothers and sisters at one time, most of whom are still alive, though some have died. Then he appeared to James, then to all the apostles" (1 Corinthians 15:5–7). We also read that ". . . he presented himself alive to them by many convincing proofs, appearing to them during forty days and speaking about the kingdom of God" (Acts 1:3).

A third reason to believe in the afterlife is what Jesus himself said:

> " Do not let your hearts be troubled. Believe in God, believe also in me. In my Father's house there are many dwelling places. If it were not so, would I have told you that I go to prepare a place for you? And if I go and prepare a place for you, I will come again and will take you to myself, so that where I am, there you may be also. "

JOHN 14:1–3

"Raising of Lazarus" by Sebastiano del Piombo; National Gallery, London.

Activity

Read John 11:17–27, 38–44. Then reenact the story of Lazarus from the point of view of one of the following people—his sister Martha, Lazarus himself, a witnessing Pharisee, or a witnessing Sadducee. Be prepared to share with the class your reenactment of how this person responded to the raising of Lazarus.

THE CHURCH AND ETERNAL LIFE

In this chapter we are discussing the following part of the creed:

Apostles' Creed: I believe in . . . the resurrection of the body, and the life everlasting. Amen.

Nicene Creed: We look for the resurrection of the dead, and the life of the world to come. Amen.

The Church was founded on faith in the Resurrection of Jesus. From the day of Pentecost, the Apostles preached fearlessly about Jesus, the Messiah and Son of God, who conquered death. "God raised him up, having freed him from death, because it was impossible for him to be held in its power" (Acts 2:24). After his own vision of the Risen Christ, Paul began to preach the same message.

> " Christ has been raised from the dead, the first fruits of those who have died. For since death came through a human being, the resurrection of the dead has also come through a human being; for as all die in Adam, so all will be made alive in Christ. "
>
> 1 CORINTHIANS 15:20–22

Furthermore, Paul preached that all who believe in Jesus would experience a similar resurrection.

> " Do you not know that all of us who have been baptized into Christ Jesus were baptized into his death? Therefore we have been buried with him by baptism into death, so that, just as Christ was raised from the dead by the glory of the Father, so we too might walk in newness of life.
>
> For if we have been united with him in a death like his, we will certainly be united with him in a resurrection like his. We know that our old self was crucified with him so that the body of sin might be destroyed, and we might no longer be enslaved to sin. For whoever has died is freed from sin. But if we have died with Christ, we believe that we will also live with him. We know that Christ, being raised from the dead, will never die again; death no longer has dominion over him. The death he died, he died to sin, once for all; but the life he lives, he lives to God. So you also must consider yourselves dead to sin and alive to God in Christ Jesus. "
>
> ROMANS 6:3–11

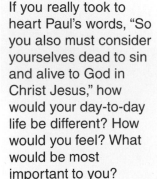

Reflection

If you really took to heart Paul's words, "So you also must consider yourselves dead to sin and alive to God in Christ Jesus," how would your day-to-day life be different? How would you feel? What would be most important to you?

Death is not the end of life. That is why we can say with Paul as he quotes the prophets,

> " Death has been swallowed up in victory."
> "Where, O death, is your victory?
> Where, O death, is your sting? "

1 CORINTHIANS 15:54–55

The Church teaches about "the four last things"—death, judgment, heaven, and hell. The Council of Florence in 1439 and the Council of Trent in 1563 approved "the four last things" as Church doctrines.

This area of theology that studies the four last things is called **eschatology.** The word *eschatology* means "last or farthest things." Eschatology is the study of the "last things"—the final coming of Jesus' kingdom at the end of time; the last or final judgment; our own death; the particular judgment; life after death in heaven, purgatory, or hell; and the eventual resurrection of the body.

Let's Talk!

What opinions do you have about the "last things"? Why?

Activity

In a small group, read Luke 14:16–24. Discuss what the parable says about the afterlife. Then, as a group, make a collage, sculpture, mobile, or mural that reflects the parable's description of the afterlife.

Particular Judgment

In this chapter, we have already dealt with the topic of death. Now we will explore the Church's teachings about judgment, heaven, and hell.

What happens to us spiritually at the moment of death? The Church teaches that people are judged on the basis of how they have lived. This individual experience at death is called the particular judgment. The idea of the particular judgment stems from belief in God's justice. He will reward the righteous, the people of faith who have tried their best to follow his law. He will punish the unrighteous, the people who have deliberately and persistently sinned against him and not repented, even at the point of death. This judgment is based not on a person's exterior actions alone but on a person's inner motives and values. The Lord "will bring to light the things now hidden in darkness and will disclose the purposes of the heart" (1 Corinthians 4:5).

Essentially, our new, eternal life begins at death:

> " [T]he souls of the righteous
> are in the hand of God,
> and no torment will ever touch them.
> In the eyes of the foolish they seemed to have died,
> and their departure was thought to be a disaster,
> and their going from us to be their destruction;
> but they are at peace. "
>
> WISDOM 3:1–3

According to the teachings of Pope Benedict XII in *Benedictus Deus* (1336), at death our souls are assigned either to heaven, purgatory, or hell. In one sense, God judges us on how well we have loved and kept his commandments throughout life. In another sense, we really judge ourselves. What happens in the particular judgment—the judgment of our own soul by God at the time of our death—is consistent with the way we have chosen to live our lives on earth. We will live forever—with God or without him—according to what we have chosen on earth—for or against him.

Reflection

If you were to die tonight, how do you think you would be judged? How would you judge yourself? Why?

"The Burial of Count Orgaz"
by El Greco; Toledo, Spain.

THE FOUR LAST THINGS

According to Church teaching, **heaven** is the perfect sharing of life and love with the Trinity. It is not a geographical place. Heaven is an eternal relationship of oneness with God, of communion with him. We receive the reward of heaven as the result of accepting his grace throughout life, or at least at the end of life, as repentance is always possible during life. In his or her final union with God, the person of faith experiences the eternal vision, or presence, of the all-loving God. Heaven is the ultimate fulfillment of the longings of the human person in a state of perfect happiness.

In the Old Testament, the Israelites believed that no one could look directly at the face of God and live. New Testament teaching leads to the Christian belief that heaven is the experience of God in the *beatific vision*, seeing God "face to face," "as he is." (See 1 Corinthians 13:12 and 1 John 3:2.)

Purgatory

Purgatory, too, is not a geographical place. Rather, it is a state of purification between death and heaven. Belief in purgatory is consistent with our belief in God's steadfast love and mercy. At the moment of death, selfishness may still exist in the soul of a basically good person. The person needs to experience further purification before entering into full union with God. Purgatory frees the person from the temporal punishment (being deprived of the entrance into heaven for a time) due to sin.

Essentially, the person "in" purgatory has made a choice for God during life or at least at the time of death, but needs further sanctification. Immediate obstacles to union with God include venial sins that were unrepented at the time of death and temporal punishment still due for venial sins as well for mortal sins previously forgiven.

Let's Talk!

1. What do you think it means to say that heaven is seeing God "face to face," seeing God "as he is"?

2. Do you think we should be afraid of the particular judgment at death? Why?

Activity

Read the following Scripture passages: Matthew 5:8, Revelation 22:4, 1 John 3:2, 1 Corinthians 13:12. Then draw or paint a picture or write a poem or essay describing what the passages tell you about heaven.

Let's Talk!

The Church designates the entire month of November as a month to remember in a special way those who have died. The month begins with the feasts of All Saints on November 1st and All Souls on November 2nd.

- What are your feelings toward those who have died? Are they still close to us?
- Do our prayers for them continue a kind of relationship with them? How do our prayers help both them and us?

Although purgatory is not mentioned in the Bible, the concept derives from the act of praying for the dead as found in the Second Book of Maccabees. The writer recounts that Judas Maccabeus and his army prayed for those who had died in battle and took up a collection so that they could offer sacrifice for them in Jerusalem:

" In doing this he acted very well and honorably, taking account of the resurrection. For if he were not expecting that those who had fallen would rise again, it would have been superfluous and foolish to pray for the dead. But if he was looking to the splendid reward that is laid up for those who fall asleep in godliness, it was a holy and pious thought. Therefore he made atonement for the dead, so that they might be delivered from their sin. "

2 MACCABEES 12:43–45

Intercessory prayers for the dead are important. With these prayers we can intercede on behalf of those who are "in" purgatory.

Hell

Like heaven and like purgatory, hell is not a geographical place. Rather, it is eternal life without God. **Hell** is eternal separation from God resulting from the choice to reject his love and grace even at the final moments of earthly existence. It is important to realize that hell is not God's getting even with sinners. Instead, hell is his ultimate respect for our free choice. Hell is *our* choice—our option during life to reject God's grace, to choose ultimately selfish desires over God, to prefer sin over goodness.

It is also important to realize that although the Catholic Church teaches that the soul of a person who dies in mortal sin goes directly to hell (chooses to be separated from God), the Church has never taught that any specific person has, in fact, died in the state of mortal sin. It is not our place to judge others for eternity, not even someone like Hitler or a terrorist who died in the act of killing thousands of innocent people. That is God's responsibility. We believe that his mercy and unconditional love are much greater than our sense of justice. We continue to hope that all people—even the worst criminals—will ultimately respond in a positive manner to his love and grace, even at the instant of death.

"Cerberus" by William Blake.

The General, or Last, Judgment—

At the end of the world, Christ will come again. This second coming of Christ, in Greek, is called the **parousia.** When this happens, there will be a collective judgment of both the living and the dead. This event is called the **general judgment,** or the last judgment. To understand the overall concept of general judgment, it is essential to take a look at each part of its definition.

The End of the World

Originally, the "day of the Lord" did not connote the notion of judgment. However, it developed into a day of judgment at the time of the prophets. References to such thinking may be found in the teaching of Jesus as he quoted from the Old Testament prophet Isaiah:

> " Immediately after the suffering of those days
>   the sun will be darkened,
>   and the moon will not give its light,
>   the stars will fall from heaven,
>   and the powers of heaven will be
>   shaken. "
>
> MATTHEW 24:29; SEE ALSO ISAIAH 13:10.

"The Last Judgment" by Michelangelo in the Sistine Chapel at the Vatican.

Activity

Using the handout your teacher will give you, look up the Old Testament passages that refer to the day of the Lord. Summarize each passage. Then, in a small group discuss what you think these passages mean.

Both the Living and the Dead

On the day of the Lord, Christ will return in glory to judge both the living and the dead. Christians refer to this day by using the words of the prophet Daniel: "Many of those who sleep in the dust of the earth shall awake, some to everlasting life, and some to shame and everlasting contempt" (Daniel 12:2). Christ will see what is in our hearts and judge us according to what we have done during life and whether we accepted God's grace. Then he will punish the wicked and reward the faithful.

Today the Church emphasizes not so much the catastrophic end of the world, but rather the triumphal second coming of Christ and the transformation of the world. Again the Church quotes the prophet Daniel:

" I saw one like a human being
    coming with the clouds of heaven.
And he came to the Ancient One
    and was presented before him.
To him was given dominion
    and glory and kingship,
that all peoples, nations, and languages
    should serve him.
His dominion is an everlasting dominion
    that shall not pass away,
and his kingship is one
    that shall never be destroyed. "

DANIEL 7:13–14

The day of the Lord is just that, the day of Christ's triumph. He will come as king of all the nations, announcing that God is the Lord of all history. On that day God's kingdom will be victorious over evil. Christ the King has absolute authority over everything in creation, including all forms of political governance.

In 1925, Pope Pius XI established a new feast in the Church year known as the Solemnity of Christ the King. This feast is celebrated each year on the last Sunday of the liturgical year, which is the last Sunday of Ordinary Time, the Sunday before the First Sunday of Advent. Catholics celebrate this day not in fear, but with joyful anticipation. Like the people of Jerusalem who waved palm branches to welcome Jesus' arrival, we yearn for the coming of God's kingdom in its fullness.

Activity

Using the handout your teacher will provide, read and summarize the Scripture readings for the Solemnity of Christ the King. Then, in a small group, discuss what you think this feast means to people of faith.

Resurrection of the Body

The soul is **immortal**—it does not die when it is separated from the body at death. At the end of time when Christ comes again in glory, the bodies of the dead will be raised and will be reunited with their souls. This is known as the **resurrection of the body**. This Christian belief affirms the goodness of all creation, the physical as well as the spiritual.

Belief in the resurrection of the body excludes the possibility of reincarnation, which is rebirth in new bodies or forms of life. Just as God the Father raised Jesus from the dead and gave him a glorified body, so on the last day God will raise up all the faithful to live forever with him. Resurrection is a miraculous gift from God. It is not the resuscitation of a corpse. It transforms human limitations; it surpasses the biological body, as we know it; it transcends death itself.

The Church celebrates the resurrection of the body at the funeral Mass of every Catholic. It also celebrates this belief in a special way on August 15, the feast of the Assumption of Mary into heaven. On this day, Church members celebrate Mary's participation in her son's Resurrection. We celebrate it in anticipation of our own resurrection at the second coming of Christ.

For centuries, the Church opposed cremation of the human body after death because the ordinary person believed that those who chose cremation were rejecting belief in the resurrection of the body. People did not understand that burning did not destroy the essence of the body. Today we understand that the atoms of the body continue in a different form when the body is burned; the essence of the "body" doesn't really disappear. The Church now teaches that cremation is acceptable, provided the person still believes in God's power to glorify the human body and raise it up on the last day.

"Mary Queen of Heaven," National Gallery of Art, Washington, DC.

Reflection

After death, do you want your body to be buried or cremated? Why?

Research

Using the library or Internet, research the burial customs of one culture, past or present. What religious beliefs are connected with the customs? Share your findings with the class.

"Peaceable Kingdom" by Edward Hicks.

Renewal of All Creation

At the second coming of Christ at the end of time, the Holy Spirit will renew the hearts of all people, engraving in them a new law. As the Catechism says, God will reconcile all peoples who are now divided, transform creation, and dwell in peace with people in the transformed creation. This belief is a source of great hope.

At the end of time, the kingdom of God will come in its fullness. This kingdom will be unequaled in human history. It will be a realm of justice, equality, and righteousness (see Psalm 99:4) where those who are oppressed and in need will be defended (see Psalm 146:5–10) and the faithful will be rescued from evil (see Psalm 97:10). All creation will be transformed into the new Jerusalem—a state of eternal peace, justice, and love in God's presence. The Book of Revelation describes this kingdom in beautiful, symbolic language:

> " Then I saw a new heaven and a new earth; for the first heaven and the first earth had passed away, and the sea was no more. And I saw the holy city, the new Jerusalem, coming down out of heaven from God, prepared as a bride adorned for her husband. And I heard a loud voice from the throne saying,
>
> "See, the home of God is among mortals.
> He will dwell with them as their God;
> they will be his peoples,
> and God himself will be with them;
> he will wipe every tear from their eyes.
> Death will be no more;
> mourning and crying and pain will be no more,
> for the first things have passed away. "

REVELATION 21:1–4

The new Jerusalem has "the glory of God and a radiance like a very rare jewel" (Revelation 21:11). It "has no need of sun or moon to shine on it, for the glory of God is its light, and its lamp is the Lamb" (Revelation 21:23). "And there will be no more night; they need no light of lamp or sun, for the Lord God will be their light, and they will reign forever and ever" (Revelation 22:5). In the end, all will be well. God will make "known to us the mystery of his will, according to his good pleasure that he set forth in Christ, as a plan for the fullness of time, to gather up all things in him, things in heaven and things on earth" (Ephesians 1:9–10). Somehow, God will elevate all created matter and bring it to perfection.

Activity

Read Matthew 25:31–46 in your Bible. In a small group describe how a Christian should view the second coming of Christ. Be prepared to share with the class what you have discussed.

SOME LAST WORDS

No one knows when or how the kingdom of God will come in its fullness. As Jesus tells us, only God knows this (see Mark 13:32). That is why Jesus advises us to stay alert at all times. "Blessed is that slave whom his master will find at work when he arrives. Truly I tell you, he will put that one in charge of all his possessions" (Matthew 24:46–47). We are to be like the wise bridesmaids in one of Jesus' parables who are prepared when the bridegroom arrives. We are to keep awake, for we know "neither the day nor the hour" (Matthew 25:13).

For people of faith, the details or time of "the end" are not the main issue. Instead, what is most important is living *now* as followers of Jesus in the daily light of God's friendship. When we live in his grace, Jesus lives within us: "The time is fulfilled, and the kingdom of God has come near . . ." (Mark 1:15). Indeed, his kingdom is among us.

The signs of God's kingdom will include catastrophe and universal destruction, as well as universal hope. In reference to the hope Jesus promised, we read: "[T]he blind receive their sight, the lame walk, the lepers are cleansed, the deaf hear, the dead are raised, the poor have good news brought to them" (Luke 7:22). When we continue the work of Christ in today's world, we are helping to further his kingdom. In doing so, his Lordship becomes real in the life of each disciple.

Throughout this course, you have learned a great deal about the Church's faith. Now it is your turn to put this faith into action each and every day. You do not necessarily have to do great things, just simple things with love.

Let's Talk!

1. How can you continue the work of Christ in today's world?

2. What positive steps can you take to do great things in simple ways?

Activity

In small groups, read Mark 13:1–31. Then discuss these questions:

- What images does Jesus use to describe the end times?

- What is Jesus saying about the end times?

Research

Search through recent newspapers and magazines for a story about a person or group doing something positive to help others. Share the story with the class and explain how it is a "sign" to you of God's kingdom.

Motives for Doing Good

There is more to life than the present world. We have a duty to proclaim the kingdom of God and to work toward its fulfillment. We are to help build this kingdom by cooperating with the Holy Spirit. We are to move beyond self-centeredness to real concern for others. Specifically, we are to perform the physical or Corporal Works of Mercy and the Spiritual Works of Mercy.

Doing everything with love means that we don't seek a reward or a pat on the back. We don't consider ourselves "righteous" because we have so many good deeds to our credit. Our focus is not on ourselves or what we might get from a certain action. Rather, our focus is on Christ, on trying to love and give of ourselves as he did. People who truly love never stop to count what it costs them. In fact, they never stop, period. There is always someone new to help, someone who needs others to bring them the light of Christ.

Corporal Works of Mercy

Feed the hungry.
Give drink to the thirsty.
Clothe the naked.
Shelter the homeless.
Visit the sick.
Visit the imprisoned.
Bury the dead.

Spiritual Works of Mercy

Warn the sinner.
Teach the ignorant.
Counsel the doubtful.
Comfort the sorrowful.
Bear wrongs patiently.
Forgive injuries.
Pray for the living and the dead.

FAITH IN ACTION

The following is a true story of one Christian who decided to help others. What he learned was a lesson about love.

"Come no later than May," our host had told us. "The summer in Calcutta is much too hot." So we came in May—and still Calcutta was sweltering. . . .

My team was assigned to the Home for the Dying, where Mother Teresa's work had begun. In my typical "can do" optimism, I thought, Great! This is the perfect place for a doctor. I can make a difference here.

Sister Pricilla greeted us graciously and began to assign us various tasks. I introduced myself as a physician from the United States. In this city where little or no medical care is available to the "untouchables." . . . My mind raced. Putting my medical training into practice in one of the neediest places on earth would be a way to shine for Jesus.

"Follow me, please," Sister Pricilla's soft British accent directed. We entered the men's ward, a large room with rows of cots cradling skeletal bodies. As a doctor, I instinctively wanted to stop and treat these men. But to my surprise, we walked quickly through the ward and on to the next.

Now we were in the women's ward, a similar room filled with emaciated women with vacant eyes. Again we passed through the ward without stopping. Can there be a needier place than even this? I wondered.

We entered a primitive kitchen where a simple lunch of rice would be prepared over an open fire. How odd, I thought. What do they want

with a doctor in the kitchen? Oh, yes, maybe they're going to feed me first. But once again Sister Pricilla led me through the kitchen, out the back door, and into a narrow alley.

There she pointed to an oversized pile of stinking, rotting garbage. "We need you to take this garbage down the street to the dump," she explained, handing me two buckets and a shovel. "The dump is several blocks down the street and on the right. You can't miss it."

Recovering from a moment of stunned silence, I began to react with silent indignation: Garbage! Don't they get it? I'm a doctor! Doctors don't haul garbage. They save lives!

With a vengeance I attacked the pile, filled the buckets, and headed down the street. With each trip I began to feel more and more sorry for myself. . . .

It was midafternoon when I finished, set down my buckets and shovel, and headed back through the kitchen, the women's ward, and the men's ward—where my gifts could have been so useful—to rejoin my team and say goodbye to Sister Pricilla.

Just before she appeared, I saw it. A small sign, crudely hand-painted with Mother Teresa's own words: "We can do no great things, only small things with great love." I fought back the tears. This proud doctor had needed to learn this lesson. Serving is not about how much you know, how many degrees you hold, or what your credentials are. Serving is about your availability and your attitude. . . . Jesus calls us to do the small things, because in his kingdom they count the most.

Gary Morsch, *"What I Did for Mother Teresa,"* Christian Reader *(May 2001): 77+.*

Let's Talk!

1. What lesson do you think the doctor learned about doing good and helping others?

2. How do you think young people can apply this same lesson to their lives today?

Reflection

What are your usual motives for choosing to do good and help others?

ORDER OF CHRISTIAN FUNERALS

In 1970 the Church revised its funeral rites according to the new Order of Christian Funerals. This new liturgy emphasizes the resurrection and the belief that people will rise with Christ on the last day. Instead of wearing black vestments at funerals, as had been done in the past, most priests now wear white—a color that symbolizes rejoicing and hope. The funeral rites praise and worship God, thanking him for the gift of the deceased person, commending that person to his mercy, and offering consolation to those who are mourning.

Basically, the Order of Christian Funerals consists of three main parts: the vigil for the deceased, the funeral liturgy, and the rite of committal. Here is an overview of each.

Vigil for the Deceased

This liturgy takes place after a person has died but before the funeral. It may be celebrated in the family's home, the funeral home, the church, or some other suitable place. Usually the vigil follows the structure of the Liturgy of the Word.

- **Introductory Rites.** These rites may consist of appropriate songs about the resurrection and prayers for the deceased. The body may be sprinkled with holy water, in remembrance of the person's Baptism in Christ.

- **Scripture Readings.** This section of the vigil consists of a first reading, a responsorial psalm, a gospel reading, and a homily by a priest or deacon. The readings remind the faithful that death is not the end of life for those who have faith. Christ calls all to join him in eternal union with God.

- **Prayer of Intercession.** This part of the vigil consists of a litany-style prayer of intercession, the Lord's Prayer, and a concluding prayer. A family member or friend may give a eulogy in remembrance of the deceased, or people may be invited to share their recollections of the person.

- **Concluding Rite.** The vigil ends with a blessing and perhaps another song.

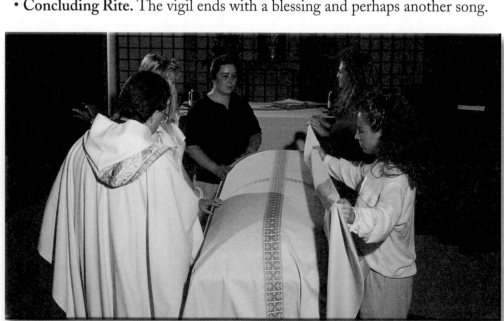

Let's Talk!

If you have ever been to a vigil service for someone who died, describe what it was like. Do you think the service comforted the mourners in any way? Explain.

Funeral Liturgy

The funeral liturgy is the main celebration of the Church for the deceased. The funeral may take place either at Mass or outside Mass. If the funeral takes place at Mass, the structure of the Mass is the same as usual with the following additions:

- **Reception at the Church.** The priest and ministers welcome the casket at the entrance of the Church. The priest greets the family and then sprinkles the coffin with holy water, a sign of Baptism and the person's membership in the Christian community. In many parishes across the United States, a white cloth called a pall is placed over the coffin as a further reminder of the white garment given at Baptism. The priest then leads the coffin and mourners into church while an entrance song is sung. Mourners take their places in the front pews, while the coffin is placed before the lit Easter candle, another symbol of Baptism and the light of Christ.

- **Final Commendation and Farewell.** At the end of Mass, the priest and people pray especially for the deceased. The priest may sprinkle the casket with holy water again and then incense it. The incensing shows respect for the human body as the temple of the Holy Spirit. There is a song of farewell and a prayer of commendation that calls upon God's mercy. The funeral liturgy concludes with singing and a procession out of the church.

Funeral liturgies outside Mass consist of four basic parts:

1. The introductory rites (the greeting, the placing of Christian symbols, an entrance procession and a prayer)

2. The Liturgy of the Word (readings, homily), the general intercessions, and the Lord's Prayer

3. A final commendation (the same as at the end of a funeral Mass)

4. The procession to the place of committal

Let's Talk!

Why do you think the revised rite of funerals has so many references to Baptism?

Rite of Committal

This rite is celebrated at the grave or mausoleum, depending on the selected resting place of the deceased's body, or the crematorium if cremation follows the funeral. The rite may also be celebrated when burial occurs at sea. As the *Order of Christian Funerals* explains:

> In committing the body to its resting place, the community expresses the hope that, with all those who have gone before marked with the sign of faith, the deceased awaits the glory of the resurrection. The rite of committal is an expression of the communion that exists between the Church on earth and the Church in heaven: the deceased passes with the farewell prayers of the community of believers into the welcoming company of those who need faith no longer but see God face to face (#206).

Mausoleums are "resting places" for bodies and cremated remains.

Activity

In a small group, select five songs that would be appropriate to sing at a vigil service, funeral, or committal service. The songs should deal with resurrection and everlasting life. The songs should also give mourners consolation and hope. Be prepared to share with the class the words of these songs.

The structure of the rite of committal is as follows:

- **Invitation.** The priest invites us to pray for the deceased, as well as for the mourners.

- **Scripture verse.** This short verse reminds us that our true home is with God in heaven.

- **Prayer over the place of committal.** The priest blesses the open grave, the mausoleum, or the place of cremation.

- **Committal.** The priest asks God to bless the deceased, to be gracious to him or her, and to give the person eternal peace.

- **Intercessions.** Prayers for the deceased and for the mourners, that they may be comforted in their sorrow, are offered.

- **The Lord's Prayer.** Everyone prays the Lord's Prayer together, asking that God's kingdom may come.

- **Concluding prayer.** In this prayer, the priest asks that God will show mercy to the deceased and raise him or her to new life.

- **Prayer over the people.** The priest blesses everyone and then bids all who have gathered to "Go in the peace of Christ."

PRAYERS FOR THE DEAD

Christians have a moral obligation to bury the dead and a moral obligation to pray for the dead. Prayers can help those in purgatory and shorten their time of purification. At every Mass, a prayer for the dead is offered in the general intercessions and during the Eucharistic Prayer. As Eucharistic Prayer II says, "Remember our brothers and sisters who have gone to their rest in the hope of rising again; bring them and all the departed into the light of your presence." There are a number of other times to pray for the dead. These times include Masses for the Dead, the Office of the Dead, and the feast of All Souls.

Masses for the Dead

The Church celebrates Masses for the Dead apart from the funeral liturgy. Traditionally, such Masses have been known as "requiem" Masses, *requiem* being a Latin word meaning "rest": "Give them eternal rest, O Lord, and may perpetual light shine on them forever." Masses for the Dead have their own prayers, Scripture readings, and preface. These prayers and readings emphasize the Resurrection of Christ as well as the resurrection of all the faithful.

> " Father, all-powerful and ever-living God,
> we do well always and everywhere to give you thanks
> through Jesus Christ our Lord.
> In him, who rose from the dead,
> our hope of resurrection dawned.
> The sadness of death gives way
> to the bright promise of immortality.
> Lord, for your faithful people life is changed, not ended.
> When the body of our earthly dwelling lies in death
> we gain an everlasting dwelling place in heaven.
> And so, with all the choirs of angels in heaven
> we proclaim your glory
> and join in their unending hymn or praise: "

PREFACE FOR CHRISTIAN DEATH I, ORDER OF MASS.

Often, the family of the deceased asks a priest to say a Mass on the anniversary of the person's death. In the West, the usual times for these Masses have been on the third, seventh, and thirtieth days after death. Today, many people celebrate a Mass for the Dead on the yearly anniversary of the death of a loved one. It has long been the custom of Christians to mark the date of death as the time of a person's entrance into eternal life and light.

Activity

Using the handout your teacher will provide, plan the Liturgy of the Word for a Mass for the Dead. Be prepared to explain why you selected the readings you did.

Office of the Dead

In the Church's Liturgy of the Hours, there are special prayers for the faithful departed, known as the Office of the Dead. This prayer dates back at least to the seventh century. Religious sisters and brothers were required to pray the Office of the Dead whenever one of their members died.

Today the Church encourages all Church members to pray part of the Office of the Dead at the vigil for the deceased. At morning prayer, the Office of the Dead recalls the Resurrection of Jesus Christ, "the true light, which enlightens everyone" (John 1:9). At evening prayer, the Office of the Dead calls upon the Risen Christ, the source of all hope.

All Souls' Day (November 2)

Throughout the Church's history, there has been the custom of praying for the dead, especially the souls in purgatory. In the eleventh century, Saint Odilo, abbot of Cluny, introduced November 2 as a day to remember and pray for all the faithful departed. On this day, the monks prayed the Office of the Dead that is part of the Liturgy of the Hours and celebrated Masses for the Dead. Slowly the practice spread throughout the Church. During the fifteenth century, Dominicans in Spain began the tradition of having each priest say three Masses on this day for the souls in purgatory. During World War I, Pope Benedict XV extended to all priests the privilege of saying three Masses on November 2.

There are many traditions that accompany the celebration of All Souls' Day. For example, in many parishes there is a Book of the Dead in which people can write the names of those who have died. The parish then prays especially for these deceased people on November 2. Some parishes have a procession to the cemetery on this day. People visit the graves of their loved ones, leaving flowers and candles on the graves.

In some Hispanic countries, All Souls' Day is celebrated as *Día de los Muertos,* the day of the dead. In addition to participating in Masses, many people celebrate the day with special foods and family rituals. Among the most popular foods for this day are the "bread of the dead" (a rich coffee cake decorated with meringues that look like bones), sugar skulls, marzipan death figures, tamales, enchiladas, and chalupas. The purpose of the cultural celebrations is to mock the power of death and reinforce belief in resurrection.

Jesus' Resurrection is a pledge of our own resurrection.

Activity

Using the library or the Internet, research various cultural customs regarding Halloween, All Saints' Day, and All Souls' Day. If possible, find out why these customs developed.

Being Faithful

Every day is a preparation for death and life forever with God. Here are some steps you can take to be faithful to yourself and your values day by day.

Reflection

Make a plan for this next year or the summer that will help you live faithfully. Make your plan as practical as possible, so that you can really put it into practice.

1. Know who you are. Know what values are important to you and why.

2. Listen to your conscience. Don't "cut corners" with honesty. If you think something is wrong, admit it. If you think something is right, act on it.

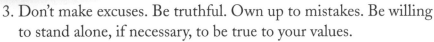

3. Don't make excuses. Be truthful. Own up to mistakes. Be willing to stand alone, if necessary, to be true to your values.

4. Get advice from trusted others, such as parents, teachers, counselors, Church ministers.

5. Pray.

6. Be willing to put your beliefs into action. If you truly believe that Christians should serve the poor, make sure your actions reflect that.

7. Never give up on yourself. Start over, if you have to. Realize that it's never too late to try again to become the kind of person you want to be.

Black Elk

Having faith in the resurrection is not always easy, especially when one's life is filled with wars, massacres, and great suffering. That is what makes the faith of Black Elk, a semi-blind Oglala Sioux (1866–1950), so remarkable.

At ten years of age, Black Elk witnessed "Custer's last stand" at the battle of Little Big Horn. He was also a participant in the Ghost Dance movement that ended tragically with the massacre of Indian women and children at Wounded Knee, South Dakota, in 1890.

Then, in 1904, Black Elk experienced a conversion. While he was acting as medicine man at the bedside of a severely sick child, a Jesuit priest arrived and challenged the effectiveness of Black Elk's charms and ceremonies. Instead of being offended, Black Elk was impressed by the strength of the priest's faith. He began to study the Catholic faith and was baptized on December 6 (the feast of St. Nicholas) as "Nicholas." From that day on, Black Elk acted as a zealous catechist, spreading the gospel of Christ. His biographer quotes him as saying, "We have been told by those who are Christian that God sent to men his son, who would restore order and peace upon the earth; and we have been told that Jesus the Christ was crucified, but that he shall come again at the Last Judgment, the end of this world or cycle. This I understand and know it is true."

Black Elk studied the Bible and prepared Native Americans for Baptism. He also led prayer meetings throughout the Pine Ridge Indian Reservation, organized Catholic social activities, and served as a missionary to other Indian reservations.

Before his departure from Pine Ridge reservation in 1916, Father Henry Westropp, SJ, wrote about his experience of Black Elk: "Ever since his conversion he has been a fervent apostle, and he has gone around like a second St. Paul, trying to convert his tribesmen to Catholicity. He has made many converts. At any time of day or night he has proved himself ready to get up and go with the missionary. On any occasion he can arise and deliver a flood of oratory. Though half blind, he has by some hook or crook learned how to read, and he knows his religion thoroughly."

When Black Elk preached, he used a "Two Roads Map" to explain the importance of faith. The map showed two roads. "The Red Road" was the way of good. Along this road was the way of Christ and the holy gospel. It led to heaven, eternal salvation, and unending happiness. The second road, "The Black Road," was the way of evil. It led to hell, eternal damnation, and everlasting unhappiness. Black Elk told the people that the Red Road consisted of right conduct, human harmony, peace, and friendship. He taught them how to be good Christians on their way to heaven.

Celebrating Faith

Opening Song:	"Heaven Will Sing"
Leader:	As we come together in prayer one last time, let us thank God for all the blessings he has given us in this course of study. And let us pray that he will always help us walk with faithfulness on the path that leads to eternal life.

Side 1:	Praise the LORD!
	    Praise the LORD, O my soul!
	I will praise the LORD as long as I live;
	    I will sing praises to my God all my life long.

Side 2:	Do not put your trust in princes,
	    in mortals, in whom there is no help.
	When their breath departs, they return to the earth;
	    on that very day their plans perish.

Side 1:	Happy are those whose help is the God of Jacob,
	    whose hope is in the LORD their God,
	who made heaven and earth,
	    the seas, and all that is in them;
	who keeps faith forever;
	    who executes justice for the oppressed;
	who gives food to the hungry.

Side 2:	The LORD sets the prisoners free;
	    the LORD opens the eyes of the blind.
	The LORD lifts up those who are bowed down;
	    the LORD loves the righteous.

Side 1:	The LORD watches over the strangers;
	    he upholds the orphan and the widow,
	    but the way of the wicked he brings to ruin.

Side 2:	The LORD will reign forever, your God, O Zion, for all generations. Praise the LORD!

Psalm 146

Leader:	Let us pray . . .
All:	**God of loving kindness,** **listen favorably to our prayers:** **strengthen our belief that your Son has risen from the dead** **and our hope that the faithful departed will also rise again.** **We ask this through our Lord Jesus Christ, your Son,** **who lives and reigns with you and the Holy Spirit,** **one God, for ever and ever. Amen**

Morning Prayer, Office of the Dead

Review

1. What happens physically at death? What happens to the soul and the body at death?

2. What are three reasons Christians have for believing in life after death?

3. What is eschatology?

4. What are heaven, hell, and purgatory?

5. What will happen at the general judgment? What are other names for this day?

6. What will happen to the human body at the second coming of Christ? Why do they believe this?

7. How has the Church's belief in resurrection affected its stance toward cremation? How does the Church view cremation today?

8. What will be the signs that precede the arrival of God's kingdom in its fullness?

9. What are the Corporal Works of Mercy? What are the Spiritual Works of Mercy? What motive do Christians have for doing these good actions?

10. How are the symbols of Baptism incorporated into the Church's funeral liturgy?

11. Why do Christians pray for the dead? Give five examples of times when Christians pray for the dead.

12. What are seven steps that can be taken to live faithfully?

WORDS OF FAITH

death—the end of human life on earth; the permanent cessation of all vital bodily functions, and the separation of the soul from the body

eschatology—an area of theology that concentrates on the last or final condition of creation

eternal life—sharing in an everlasting union of life and love with God in heaven by those who have died in his friendship

heaven—the perfect sharing of life and love with the Trinity; an eternal relationship of oneness with God, of communion with him.

hell—eternal separation from God resulting from the choice to reject his love and grace even at the final moments of earthly existence

general judgment—Christ's judgment of both the living and the dead at the end of time

particular judgment—the reckoning that occurs for each person at the moment of death

immortal—a quality whereby the human soul will not die but will exist without end

parousia—another name for the second coming of Christ that will occur at the end of the world. The word *parousia* means "arrival, or coming."

Enrichment

Choose one of the following.

1. Imagine that you knew tomorrow would be the day of Christ's second coming. In a small group, describe how you would spend the rest of today. What things would you do that you have been putting off? What would seem important now and what would be not so important? Comprise a list from your discussion and share it with the class.

2. Make a collage of pictures of the moments of life on earth that come closest to the happiness of heaven.

3. Read parts of Dante's *The Divine Comedy*. Make a chart with three columns entitled *heaven, hell,* and *purgatory*. In each column place descriptions of heaven, hell, and purgatory as presented in Dante's work. What is your overall impression of Dante's work?

4. With a partner or small group, make a banner or poster that reflects the themes of hope and eternal life. Display the banner in the prayer corner or somewhere in your school where others will see it.

5. Investigate what Sacred Scripture says about the end times and what will happen.

purgatory—a state of purification between death and heaven that removes any remaining personal obstacles to eternal union with God. Purgatory frees the person from the temporal punishment (being deprived of the entrance into heaven for a time) due to sin.

resurrection of the body—at the end of time when Christ comes again in glory, the bodies of those who have died will be raised and reunited with their souls.

Catholic Source Book

SCRIPTURE

The Bible

The Catholic *canon,* or authorized version, of the Bible contains seventy-three books—forty-six in the Old Testament and twenty-seven in the New Testament. Catholic Bibles have seven Old Testament books or parts of books not included in other Christian Bibles. When these books are included in a Protestant Bible, they are usually found in a section called the *Apocrypha* or *Deutero-canonical Books.* The word *apocrypha* comes from a Greek word that means "hidden things."

The apocryphal books are not found in the present Hebrew Scriptures but were included in an early Jewish canon that included Greek writings, the *Septuagint.* Protestant Reformers of later centuries did not accept these books. Catholic translations of the Bible include

The New American Bible and *The New Jerusalem Bible.* Some translations, such as *The New Revised Standard Version,* which is used in this book and in the Catechism, are accepted by Catholics and Protestants.

Salvation History

The history of salvation begins with creation, reaches its highest point in Christ, and lasts until the end of time. It is the story told in the Bible—the story of God's saving actions for humans. Important events of salvation history in the Old Testament include God's promise to Abraham, the Exodus, the covenant given to Moses, the Israelites' entering the land of Canaan, and the establishment of the kingdom of Israel under David. In the New Testament, salvation history is seen as coming together in the life, death, and Resurrection of Jesus. It continues today in the life of the Church.

How to Better Understand Scripture

God is the author of Sacred Scripture. He inspired human authors to write the contents of the Bible. The Bible is a book of faith and not a factual eyewitness account of historical events. For this reason, the words are not to be taken literally, but more for their spiritual sense or meaning. We need to take into account the context in which the human authors were writing. They were writing for a particular time and place and for a particular group of people. The writers were also using particular literary forms. We can always rely on the guidance of the Holy Spirit and the Church to help us interpret the religious truths of Scripture.

Literary Forms in the Bible

The term *literary form* refers to the kind or type of writing an author uses. The following are some of the types of literature found in the Bible.

- **Apocalyptic** writing reveals or unveils and usually uses very symbolic language. This form of writing is found in the Book of Daniel and the Book of Revelation.
- **Historical accounts** were written to reveal God's activity in the world. The Book of Joshua is an example of a historical account.
- **Letters,** or epistles, were written by the Apostles and other early Church leaders and addressed to early Christians. Some letters were addressed to groups, others to individuals.
- **Legends** are imaginative stories from the past that are thought of as historical but have not been proven to be true.
- **Myths** are traditional stories about historical events that help explain why people see things a certain way.
- **Oracles** are messages from God spoken by prophets. They are often introduced by the words "Thus says the Lord."
- **Parables** are short stories told to make a point; Jesus' stories are the most well-known examples.
- **Psalms and canticles** are poems and prayers that were once sung.
- **Sagas** are long detailed accounts about people and events.
- **Proverbs** are prose or poetic statements or maxims for instruction.
- **Elegies** are poems or songs for the dead.

Gospel Formation

The Gospels announce the good news of Jesus. These books were formed in three stages.

1. **The life and teaching of Jesus**—Jesus' whole life and teaching proclaimed the good news.

2. **Oral tradition**—After the Resurrection, the Apostles preached the good news. Then the early Christians passed on what Jesus preached. They told and retold the teachings of Jesus and the story of his life, death, and Resurrection.

3. **The written Gospels**—The stories, teachings, and sayings of Jesus were collected and written in the Gospels according to Matthew, Mark, Luke, and John.

The Teaching of Jesus

The Beatitudes

The Beatitudes are the promises of blessing made by Jesus to those who faithfully follow his example. They give direction to the human heart for finding the happiness that can be found in God alone.

> *Blessed are the poor in spirit, for theirs in the kingdom of heaven.*
>
> *Blessed are those who mourn, for they will be comforted.*
>
> *Blessed are the meek, for they will inherit the earth.*
>
> *Blessed are those who hunger and thirst for righteousness, for they will be filled.*
>
> *Blessed are the merciful, for they will receive mercy.*
>
> *Blessed are the pure in heart, for they will see God.*
>
> *Blessed are the peacemakers, for they will be called children of God.*
>
> *Blessed are those who are persecuted for righteousness' sake, for theirs is the kingdom of heaven.*
>
> MATTHEW 5:3–10

The Parables of Jesus

Parable	Matthew	Mark	Luke
New patches on an old cloak	9:16	2:21	5:36
New wine in old wineskins	9:17	2:22	5:37–38
The sower and the seeds	13:3–23	4:2–20	8:4–15
The mustard seed	13:31–32	4:30–32	13:18–19
The wicked tenants	21:33–45	12:1–12	20:9–19
The budding fig tree	24:32–33	13:28–29	21:29–31
The two houses on rock and on sand	7:24–27		6:47–49
The yeast	13:33		13:20–21
The lost sheep	18:12–14		15:3–7
The two servants	24:45–51		12:42–48
The weeds among the wheat	13:24–30		
The buried treasure	13:44		
The fine pearl	13:45–46		
The net thrown into the sea	13:47–50		
The unforgiving servant	18:23–35		
The workers in the vineyard	20:1–16		
The two sons	21:28–32		
The wedding feast	22:1–14		
The ten virgins	25:1–13		
The talents	25:14–30		
The sheep and goats	25:31–46		
The seed that sprouts		4:26–29	
The watchful servant		13:34–37	
The good Samaritan			10:25–37
The friend at midnight			11:5–10
The rich fool			12:16–21
The faithful servants			12:35–38
The barren fig tree			13:6–9
The great feast			14:16–24
The lost coin			15:8–10
The prodigal son			15:11–32
The dishonest steward			16:1–9
The rich man and Lazarus			16:19–31
The master and the servant			17:7–10
The persistent widow			18:1–8
The Pharisee and the tax collector			18:9–14
The ten gold coins			19:11–27

The Miracles of Jesus

Healing miracles	Matthew	Mark	Luke	John
Cleansing of a leper	8:1–4	1:40–45	5:12–16	
A centurion's servant	8:5–13		7:1–10	
Peter's mother-in-law and others	8:14–17	1:29–34	4:38–41	
The paralytic	9:2–8	2:1–12	5:17–26	
Woman with a hemorrhage	9:20–22	5:25–34	8:43–48	
Two blind men	9:27–31			
Man with a withered hand	12:9–14	3:1–6	6:6–11	
The Canaanite woman	15:21–28	7:24–30		
The deaf man	15:29–31	7:31–37		
The blind men at Jericho	20:29–34	10:46–52	18:35–43	
The blind man at Bethesda		8:22–26		
The crippled woman			13:10–17	
The man with dropsy			14:1–6	
Ten lepers			17:12–19	
The high priest's servant			22:49–51	
The royal officer's son				4:46–53
The cripple of 38 years				5:1–9
The man born blind				9:1–7
Exorcism miracles				
Two demoniacs in Gadarene	8:28–34	5:1–20	8:26–39	
The mute demoniac	9:32–34		11:14–15	
The blind/mute demoniac	12:22–32		11:14–15	
The boy with a demon	17:14–21	9:14–29	9:37–43a	
The demoniac in Capernaum		1:21–28	4:31–37	
Resuscitation miracles				
The daughter of Jairus	9:18–19, 23–26	5:21–24, 35–43	8:40–42, 49–56	
The widow's son at Nain			7:11–17	
Lazarus				11:1–44
Nature miracles				
The storm at sea	8:23–27	4:35–41	8:22–25	
Feeding of the five thousand	14:13–21	6:30–44	9:10–17	6:1–14
Walking on water	14:22–23	6:45–52		6:15–21
Feeding of the four thousand	15:32–39	8:1–10		
Coin in the fish's mouth	17:24–27			
Cursing of the fig tree	21:18–22	11:12–14, 20–25		
Miraculous catch of fish			5:1–11	21:1–11
Water to wine				2:1–11

CREED

The Church's Creeds

Both the Apostles' Creed and the Nicene Creed are Trinitarian in structure and flow from the baptismal formula: Father, Son, and Holy Spirit.

The Apostles' Creed

The Apostles' Creed received its name because it is a summary of the Apostles' faith. However, the earliest reference to this creed appears in fourth-century writings, and the earliest text dates from the eighth century.

> I believe in God, the Father Almighty.
>   creator of heaven and earth.
> I believe in Jesus Christ, his only Son, our Lord.
> He was conceived by the power of the Holy Spirit
>   and born of the Virgin Mary.
> He suffered under Pontius Pilate,
>   was crucified, died, and was buried.
> He descended to the dead (*into hell*).
> On the third day, he rose again.
> He ascended into heaven,
>   and is seated at the right hand of God the Father.
> He will come again to judge the living and the dead.
> I believe in the Holy Spirit,
>   the holy catholic Church,
>   the communion of saints,
>   the forgiveness of sins,
>   the resurrection of the body,
>   and life everlasting. Amen.

The Nicene Creed

The Nicene Creed appeared after the Council of Nicaea in 325 and the Council of Constantinople in 381. These councils discussed the divine nature of Christ. The creed became part of the liturgy of the Church in Rome in 1014 and remains part of the liturgy today.

> We believe in one God,
>   the Father, the Almighty,
>   maker of heaven and earth,
>   of all that is, seen and unseen.
> We believe in one Lord, Jesus Christ,
>   the only Son of God,
>   eternally begotten of the Father,
>   God from God, Light from Light,
>   true God from true God,
>   begotten, not made, one in Being with the Father.
>   Through him all things were made.
> For us men and for our salvation
>   he came down from heaven:
>   by the power of the Holy Spirit
>   he was born of the Virgin Mary, and became man.
> For our sake he was crucified under Pontius Pilate;
>   he suffered, died, and was buried.
>   On the third day he rose again
>   in fulfillment of the Scriptures;
>   he ascended into heaven
>   and is seated at the right hand of the Father.
> He will come again in glory to judge the living
>   and the dead,
>   and his kingdom will have no end.
> We believe in the Holy Spirit, the Lord, the giver of life,
>   who proceeds from the Father and the Son.
>   With the Father and the Son he is worshiped
>   and glorified.
>   He has spoken through the Prophets.
>   We believe in one holy catholic and apostolic
>   Church.
>   We acknowledge one baptism for the forgiveness
>   of sins.
>   We look for the resurrection of the dead,
>   and the life of the world to come. Amen.

Catholic Church Traditions

The Universal Church

Eastern Church	Antiochene Tradition — West Syrian	Syrian Catholic Church Maronite Catholic Church Malankarese Catholic Church
	— East Syrian	Chaldean Catholic Church Syro-Malabarese Catholic Church
	Byzantine Tradition	Melkite Catholic Church Albanian Catholic Church Bulgarian Catholic Church Byerlorussian Catholic Church Georgian Catholic Church Greek Catholic Church Italo-Albanian Catholic Church Hungarian Catholic Church Russian Catholic Church Ruthenian Catholic Church Romanian Catholic Church Ukrainian Catholic Church Yogoslav Catholic Church Slovak Catholic Church
	Alexandrian Tradition	Coptic Catholic Church Ethiopian Catholic Church
	Armenian Tradition	Armenian Catholic Church
Western Church	Roman (Latin) Tradition	Roman Catholic Church

The Liturgy and Sacraments

The Sacraments of the Catholic Church

Sacraments of Initiation: The Sacraments of Initiation celebrate people's relationship with Christ and their full membership in the Church.

Baptism, Confirmation, and Eucharist

Sacraments of Healing: In the Sacraments of Healing God's forgiveness of sins and healing are given to those suffering physical and spiritual sickness.

Reconciliation (Penance) and Anointing of the Sick

Sacraments of Service: The Sacraments at the Service of Communion celebrate people's commitment to serve God and the community.

Holy Orders annd Matrimony

Order of the Mass

The Mass follows a pattern, with some differences according to the feast or season of the liturgical year. The two great parts of the Mass are the Liturgy of the Word and the Liturgy of the Eucharist.

Introductory Rites
- Sign of the Cross and Greeting
- Rite of Blessing and Sprinkling Rite or Penitential Rite
- Glory to God (Gloria)
- Opening Prayer

Liturgy of the Word
- First Reading
- Responsorial Psalm
- Second Reading
- Gospel Acclamation
- Proclamation of the Gospel
- Homily
- Profession of Faith
- General Intercessions

Holy Days of Obligation in the United States

Catholics are required to attend Mass on Sunday unless a serious reason prevents them from doing so. Catholics also must participate in Mass on certain holy days. In the United States the holy days of obligation are the feasts of:

- Mary the Mother of God (January 1)
- Ascension of the Lord (forty days after Easter or the Sunday nearest the end of the forty-day period)
- Assumption of Mary (August 15)
- All Saints' Day (November 1)
- Immaculate Conception of Mary (December 8)
- Christmas (December 25)

Liturgy of the Eucharist
- Preparation of the Altar and the Gifts
- Eucharistic Prayer
  - Preface
  - Thanks and praise for the great works of God
  - Holy, Holy, Holy Lord (Sanctus)
  - Calling on the Holy Spirit
  - Consecration of bread and wine
  - Memorial Acclamation
  - Offering the Eucharistic sacrifice to God
  - Prayers for the living and the dead
  - Doxology and Great Amen
- Communion Rite
  - Lord's Prayer
  - Sign of Peace
  - Breaking of the Bread
  - Invitation to Communion
  - Communion and Communion Song
  - Period of Silence or Song of Praise
  - Prayer After Communion

Concluding Rite
- Greeting
- Blessing
- Dismissal

Sacramentals

Sacramentals are sacred signs that help us live faithful lives and respond to the gift of God's grace given in the sacraments. With sacramentals, spiritual meanings and realities are signified or spiritual blessings are given by God's grace through the prayers of the Church. Specific signs: the laying on of hands, the Sign of the Cross, sprinkling with holy water.

Sacramentals are used to sanctify certain Church ministries, certain states of life, a variety of circumstances of Christian life, and the use of many helpful things.

Sacramentals include blessings (blessing of animals and new homes, for example), gestures, (the Sign of the Cross, genuflection), ceremonies (religious profession, dedication of churches), individual and communal prayer services (the Rosary, Stations of the Cross, Benediction of the Blessed Sacrament), and objects (holy water, blessed ashes and palms, candles, incense, crucifixes, icons, relics, rosaries, statues, paintings of the saints, medals, scapulars, holy cards).

Fast, Abstinence, and Days of Penance

All Christians, by the nature of their lives, are obliged to live in a spirit of penance whereby their exterior act of prayer, self-denial, and charity bear witness to the inner values of their faith. All the Fridays of the year and the entire Season of Lent are days of penance. Works of penance include voluntary abstinence, fasting, prayer, works of charity, and other acts of self-denial. Proportionately grave circumstances—sickness, dietary needs, social obligations—excuse a person from the obligations to fast and abstain, but not from seeking out other forms of penance.

All Catholics in the United States, from their eighteenth birthday until their fifty-ninth birthday, are required to fast on Ash Wednesday and Good Friday unless a serious reason prevents them from doing so. Fasting means one full meal and two lighter meals in the course of a day, with no food in between meals.

Abstinence generally refers to not eating meat on certain days. Catholics are expected to abstain from eating meat on Ash Wednesday, Good Friday, and, in the United States, the Fridays in Lent. The obligation to abstain from meat binds Catholics from the age of fourteen throughout life.

The Eucharistic Fast

To help prepare spiritually for the Eucharist, Catholics fast for one hour before Communion. They take no food or drink except water and medicine. The fast for those who are elderly or sick is fifteen minutes.

MORALITY

The Ten Commandments

1. I am the Lord your God. You shall not have strange gods before me.

2. You shall not take the name of the Lord your God in vain.

3. Remember to keep holy the Lord's day.

4. Honor your father and your mother.

5. You shall not kill.

6. You shall not commit adultery.

7. You shall not steal.

8. You shall not bear false witness against your neighbor.

9. You shall not covet your neighbor's wife.

10. You shall not covet your neighbor's goods.

Works of Mercy

Spiritual Works of Mercy

Teach the ignorant.
Counsel the doubtful.
Comfort the sorrowful.
Bear wrongs patiently.
Forgive injuries.
Warn the sinner.
Pray for the living and the dead.

Corporal Works of Mercy

Feed the hungry.
Give drink to the thirsty.
Shelter the homeless.
Clothe the naked.
Visit the sick.
Visit the imprisoned.
Bury the dead.

PRAYER

The Lord's Prayer

Our Father, who art in heaven,
hallowed be thy name.
Thy kingdom come;
they will be done on earth as it is in heaven.
Give us this day our daily bread
and forgive us our trespasses
as we forgive those who trespass against us.
And lead us not into temptation,
but deliver us from evil. Amen.

Glory to God (Doxology)

Glory to the Father, and to the Son, and to the Holy
    Spirit:
as it was in the beginning, is now, and will be forever.
    Amen.

Gloria (Glory to God)

Glory to God in the highest,
and peace to his people on earth.
Lord God, heavenly King,
almighty God and Father,
    we worship you, we give you thanks,
    we praise you for your glory.
Lord Jesus Christ, only Son of the Father,
Lord God, Lamb of God,
you take away the sins of the world:
    have mercy on us;
you are seated at the right hand of the Father:
    receive our prayer.
For you alone are the Holy One,
    you alone are the Lord,
    you alone are the Most High,
        Jesus Christ,
        with the Holy Spirit,
        in the glory of God the Father. Amen.

Prayer to Holy Spirit

Come, Holy Spirit, fill the hearts of your faithful.
And kindle in them the fire of your love.
Send forth your Spirit and they shall be created.
And you will renew the face of the earth.
Lord, by the light of the Holy Spirit
you have taught the hearts of your faithful.
In the same Spirit
help us choose what is right
and always rejoice in your consolation.
We ask this through Christ our Lord. Amen.

Serenity Prayer

God, grant me the serenity
to accept the things I cannot change,
the courage to change the things I can,
and the wisdom to know the difference.

Prayer of Saint Francis

Lord, make me an instrument of your peace.
Where there is hatred, let me sow love;
where there is injury, pardon;
where there is doubt, faith;
where there is despair, hope;
where there is darkness, light;
where there is sadness, joy.
Lord, grant that I may not so much
seek to be consoled as to console;
to be understood as to understand;
to be loved as to love.
For it is in giving that we receive,
in pardoning that we are pardoned,
and in dying that we are born to eternal life.

Prayers of Sorrow
Confiteor

I confess to almighty God,
and to you, my brothers and sisters,
that I have sinned through my own fault
in my thoughts and in my words,
in what I have done,
and in what I have failed to do;
and I ask blessed Mary, ever virgin,
all the angels and saints,
and you, my brothers and sisters,
to pray for me to the Lord our God.

An Act of Contrition

My God,
I am sorry for my sins with all my heart.
In choosing to do wrong
    and failing to do good,
I have sinned against you
    whom I should love above all things.
    I firmly intend, with your help,
    to do penance,
    to sin no more,
    and to avoid whatever leads me to sin.
Our Savior Jesus Christ
    suffered and died for us.
In his name, my God, have mercy.

Mary and Prayer

The Magnificat (Mary's Canticle)

Mary is honored above all other saints. She is called the Mother of God because her Son was true God and true man. When the angel Gabriel told Mary that she would be the mother of Jesus, Mary believed and accepted God's plan. Her yes sets the example for all believers. The Magnificat is her response.

My soul magnifies the Lord,
*   my spirit rejoices in God my Savior,*
for he has looked with favor on the lowliness of
*   his servant.*
Surely, from now on all generations will call
*   me blessed;*
for the Mighty One has done great things for me,
*   and holy is his name.*
His mercy is for those who fear him
*   from generation to generation.*
He has shown strength with his arm;
*   he has scattered the proud in the thoughts of*
*   their hearts.*
He has brought down the powerful from their
*   thrones,*
*   and lifted up the lowly;*
he has filled the hungry with good things,
*   and sent the rich away empty.*
He has helped his servant Israel,
*   in remembrance of his mercy,*
according to the promise he made to our
*   ancestors,*
*   to Abraham and his descendants forever.*

Luke 1:46–55

Hail Mary

Hail, Mary, full of grace,
the Lord is with you.
Blessed are you among women,
and blessed is the fruit of your womb, Jesus.
Holy Mary, Mother of God,
pray for us sinners,
now and at the hour of our death. Amen.

Hail, Holy Queen

Hail, Holy Queen, Mother of mercy,
hail, our life, our sweetness, and our hope.
To you we cry, the children of Eve,
to you do we send up our sighs,
mourning and weeping in this land of exile.
Turn, then, most gracious advocate,
your eyes of mercy toward us;

lead us home at last,
and show us the blessed fruit of your womb, Jesus.
O clement, O loving, O sweet Virgin Mary.
Pray for us, O holy Mother of God,
that we may be made worthy of the promises of Christ.

The Memorare

Remember, most loving Virgin Mary,
    never was it heard
    that anyone who turned to you for help
    was left unaided.
Inspired by this confidence,
    though burdened by my sins,
I run to your protection
    for you are my mother.
Mother of the Word of God,
    do not despise my words of pleading
    but be merciful and hear my prayer.

SAINT BERNARD

The Angelus

V. The angel spoke God's message to Mary,
R. and she conceived of the Holy Spirit.
    Hail, Mary. . . .
V. "I am the lowly servant of the Lord:
R. let it be done to me according to your word."
    Hail, Mary. . . .
V. And the Word became flesh,
R. and lived among us.
    Hail, Mary. . . .
V. Pray for us, holy Mother of God,
R. that we may become worthy of the promises
    of Christ.
Let us pray.
    Lord, fill our hearts with your grace:
    once, through the message of an angel
    you revealed to us the incarnation of your Son;
    now, through his suffering and death
    lead us to the glory of his resurrection.
    We ask this through Christ our Lord.
R. Amen.

The Rosary

Mysteries of the Rosary

Early Christians used beads or knotted strings to keep count of prayers. As devotion to Mary increased, it became popular to create psalters or books dedicated to Jesus or Mary, using biblical scenes. The Rosary we know today developed from both of these practices over time. While praying each decade of beads, think of one mystery in the life of Jesus or Mary.

How to Pray the Rosary

1. Sign of the Cross and Apostles' Creed
2. Lord's Prayer
3. Three Hail Marys
4. Glory to the Father
5. Announce Mystery; Lord's Prayer
6. Ten Hail Marys
7. Glory to the Father

Joyful Mysteries (Mondays and Saturdays)

> The Annunciation
> The Visitation to Elizabeth
> The Nativity of Jesus
> The Presentation of Jesus in the Temple
> The Finding of Jesus in the Temple

Sorrowful Mysteries (Tuesdays and Fridays)

> Jesus' Agony in the Garden
> Jesus' Scourging at the Pillar
> The Crowning with Thorns
> Jesus Carries His Cross
> The Crucifixion and Death of Jesus

Glorious Mysteries (Sundays and Wednesdays)

> The Resurrection of Jesus
> The Ascension
> The Descent of the Holy Spirit on
>   Pentecost
> The Assumption of Mary into Heaven
> The Coronation of Mary as Queen of
>   Heaven and Mother of the Church

Mysteries of Light—the Luminous Mysteries (Thursdays)

> The Baptism of Christ in the Jordan
> Jesus' Self-manifestation at the Wedding
>   Feast of Cana
> The Announcement of the Kingdom
>   Along with the Call to Conversion
> The Transfiguration
> The Institution of the Eucharist as the
>   Sacramental Expression of the Paschal
>   Mystery

Stations of the Cross

1. Jesus is condemned to death.

2. Jesus carries his cross.

3. Jesus falls the first time.

4. Jesus meets his mother.

5. Simon of Cyrene helps Jesus carry his cross.

6. Veronica wipes the face of Jesus.

7. Jesus falls the second time.

8. Jesus speaks to the women of Jerusalem.

9. Jesus falls the third time.

10. Jesus is stripped of his garments.

11. Jesus is nailed to the cross.

12. Jesus dies on the cross.

13. Jesus' body is removed from the cross.

14. Jesus' body is laid in the tomb.

Acknowledgments

For permission to reprint copyrighted material, grateful acknowledgment is made to the following sources:

Campus Life Magazine: From "The Nightmare of September 11" (Retitled: "The Darkest Day") by Mark Moring in *Campus Life* Magazine, January-February 2002. Text copyright © 2002 by Mark Moring.

Costello Publishing Co.: From *Vatican Council II: The Conciliar and Post Conciliar Documents.* Text copyright © 1975 by Harry J. Costello and Reverend Austin Flannery, O.P.

John M. Eades, PhD: Adapted from "The Boy and the Beast" in "No Small Miracles" from *Miracle on Boswell Road: True Stories of Unexpected Acts of Love* by John M. Eades. Published by Promise Press, 2000.

Judson Press: From "Jesus—A Brief Life" (Retitled: "One Solitary Life") in *The Real Jesus and Other Sermons* by Dr. James Allen Francis. Published by Judson Press, 1926.

Loyola Press: From *The Gift of Peace: Personal Reflections* (Retitled: "Joseph Cardinal Bernardin") by Joseph Cardinal Bernardin. Text © 1997 by Catholic Bishop of Chicago, a Corporation Sole. From *Raising Faith-Filled Kids: Ordinary Opportunities to Nurture Spirituality at Home* (Retitled: "Passing on the Articles of Faith") by Tom McGrath. Text © 2000 by Tom McGrath.

Gary Morsch: From "What I Did for Mother Teresa" (Retitled: "Faith in Action") by Gary Morsch in *Christian Reader*, May/June 2001. Text copyright © 2001 by Gary Morsch. Originally published in *Holiness Today*, November 2000.

National Catholic Reporter: From "The Fruits of Chavez's Labor Had Deep Roots in Prayer Life" by Cardinal Roger M. Mahony in *National Catholic Reporter*, May 7, 1993. Text copyright 1993 by National Catholic Reporter. From "Minnesota grandmother wins top missionary honor" (Retitled: "Simple Faith") by Catholic News Service in *National Catholic Reporter*, September 19, 2003. Text copyright 2003 by National Catholic Reporter.

Paulist Press, Inc., New York/Mahwah, NJ, www.paulistpress.com: From *The Seven Secrets of Successful Catholics* by Paul Wilkes. Text copyright © 1998 by Paulist Press, Inc.

Rachel Schlabach: "No Reason to Worry" (Retitled: "A Teen's Experience of God") by Rachel Schlabach from *Campus Life* Magazine, July/August 2001. Text copyright © 2001 by Rachel Schlabach.

Jeff M. Sellers: From "A Child Shall Lead Them" (Retitled: "Children's Movement for Peace") by Jeff M. Sellers in *Christianity Today*, December 3, 2001. Text copyright © 2001 by Christianity Today.

U. S. Catholic: From "10 ways to improve your prayer life" by Father Terrance Wayne Klein in *U. S. Catholic*, March 1999. Text © 1999 by Claretian Publications.

Williams & Connolly, on behalf of William J. Bennett: From "The Blind Men and the Elephant" in *The Moral Compass: Stories for a Life's Journey*, edited by William J. Bennett. Text copyright © 1995 by William J. Bennett.

Photo Credits

AP/Wide World Photos: 29, 153, 163, 173, 193, 195, 196, 222b, 223; John Chadwick: 30; **Art Resource:** 39, 71, 91, 97, 101, 105, 108, 183, 184, 198, 216; Art Resource/ National Museum of American Art, Washington, DC: 67, 122; Erick Lessing: 94; Giraudon: 102; **Bridge Building Images, Inc.:** 100; Jesus of the People © 1999 Janet McKenzie: 60; Nicholas Markell: 140b; **Corbis:** 2, 8, 99, 104, 118, 123a, 124b, 131, 133, 164b, 178, 192a, 209, 213, 214; Bettman: 28; National Gallery Collection: by kind permission of the Trustees of the National Gallery, London: 79; David Lees: 158; **Chester Dale Collections:** © 2001 Board of Trustees, National Gallery of Art, Washington: 96; Nancy Dawe: 49, 222a; **Editorial Development Assoc.:** 47; **Getty Images:** 2, 26, 41, 44, 53, 86, 106b, 126, 146, 151, 208; Bruce Ayers: 45; Mary Kate Denny: 88; Arthur Tilley: 148; David Young-Wolff: 155; David Higgs: 199; Kevin Loubacker: 210; **Joel Gordon:** 138; Joel Gordon: 56; **Image Works:** B. Daemmrich: 18; L. Kolvoord: 154; **Richard Levine:** 161; **Nicholas Studios:** Nick Falzerano: 45, 139; **Photo Edit:** 159, 162, 169; Myrleen Ferguson: 21, 127b; Michael Newman: 48; Mark Richards: 51, 134; Bill Aron: 95; Jonathan Nourok: 181b; Tony Freeman: 221; **Gene Plaisted/The Croisers:** 10, 35, 43, 58a, 62, 65b, 66a, 66b, 68, 73, 76, 121, 123b, 128, 130, 136, 187, 192b, 212, 218, 226, 228; **Bob Roethig:** 200; **James L. Shaffer:** 12, 18, 19, 33, 65a, 103, 113, 135, 137, 140a, 168, 188, 189, 190, 222; **Skjold Photographers:** 172; **Superstock:** 10, 32, 40, 58b, 59, 69, 72, 75, 78, 92, 98, 125, 164a, 185, 215, 217, 219, 220; Dahlem Staatliche Gemaldegalerie, Berlin/Bridgeman Art Library, London: 14; Kurt Scholz: 70; Emily Martin: 211; **Jim Whitmer Photography:** 16, 36, 50, 127c, 201; **Bill Whittman:** 111; World Vision: 194

People of Faith illustrations: **Lois Wolley:** 22, 52, 81, 114, 142, 166, 174, 202, 230

absolution   the forgiveness of sin, by a bishop or a priest who acts in God's name in the Sacrament of Reconciliation, or Penance (page 188)

actual grace   the assistance God gives us in a particular need or to perform a particular good action or to avoid evil (page 138)

adoration   worship and honor given to God as Creator and Sustainer of all that is (page 49)

angels   created beings who are pure spirits with intelligence and free will, but without bodies, who act as God's messengers (page 41)

Annunciation   the announcement of the angel Gabriel that through the power of the Holy Spirit, Mary, though a virgin, was to be the mother of the Son of God, who would be called Jesus. The Church celebrates the feast of the Annunciation on March 25. (page 65)

Anointing of the Sick   the Sacrament of Healing and Forgiveness for people who are seriously ill, elderly, or in danger of dying. In the sacrament, the person's forehead and hands are anointed with the blessed oil of the sick. (page 189)

Ascension   the taking up of the Risen Christ to heaven (page 104)

Assumption   the Church teaching that, at the end of her life, Mary, body and soul, was "taken up" (assumed) into heaven. The Church celebrates the feast of the Assumption on August 15. (page 66)

atheism   the belief that there is no God (page 28)

Baptism   the sacrament of new life in God and of incorporation into the Church performed with water and the words, "I baptize you in the name of the Father, and of the Son, and of the Holy Spirit"; the first Sacrament of Initiation (page 46)

Beatitudes   Jesus' eight teachings about the meaning and path to true happiness which depict the attitudes and actions that followers of Christ should have and the way to live in God's kingdom today. They describe the way to attain the eternal holiness or blessedness to which God calls all people. (page 79)

Bible   God's written word, composed by human authors and inspired by the Holy Spirit (page 12)

bishops   Church leaders who are the successors of the Apostles. Bishops receive all three orders of the Sacrament of Holy Orders. (page 157)

blasphemy   the serious sin of showing contempt or lack of reverence for God and his name (page 97)

canonization   an official Church statement by which a person is declared to have lived a holy life of heroic virtue. In the last stage of the process of canonization, the person is named a saint. (page 155)

capital sins   grave offenses, sometimes called "deadly sins" because they turn people completely away from God; called "capital" because they are the sources of other sins (page 106)

Christ   the Anointed One, the Messiah, Jesus Christ. As Messiah, Jesus restored all people to communion and friendship with God through his life, death, and Resurrection. (page 61)

Church   the assembly of the faithful—those "whom God's word gathers together to form the People of God, and who themselves, nourished with the Body of Christ, become the Body of Christ" (Catechism, #777) Through Baptism, "we are incorporated into the Church and made sharers in her mission" (CCC, #1213). (page 128)

communion of saints   all faithful Church members on earth, in heaven, and in purgatory; communion in holy things (*sancta*) and among holy persons (*sancti*) (page 155)

Confirmation   a Sacrament of Initiation that strengthens the spiritual life received in Baptism, sealing (or confirming) the person as being in union with Christ, making them ready to actively participate in the work and worship of the Church. The Holy Spirit is the prime agent in Confirmation. Through the powers of the Holy Spirit, divine filiation is deepened and an indelible character is imprinted on the soul of the recipient. (page 136)

conscience   the internal voice that helps individuals know right from wrong (page 182)

contrition   sincere sorrow for the sins one has committed, coupled with the resolution to do better in the future (page 185)

conversion   a sincere change of mind, will, and heart—away from sin and toward God (page 183)

covenant   a solemn promise, or agreement, made between two parties; the word means testament (page 14)

creationism   the theory that the Genesis story in the Bible is literally true, that God created the universe and everything in it in six days and out of nothing (page 28)

creed   a summary of the true beliefs held by a group (page 15)

crucifixion   a form of capital punishment by which a person was tied or nailed to a cross; the death of Jesus on the cross (page 98)

death   the end of human life on earth; the permanent cessation of all vital bodily functions and the separation of the soul from the body (page 208)

dignity the respect owed to all humans because they are made in God's image (page 16)

Easter Vigil the opening liturgy of the Easter celebration, held after sundown on Holy Saturday, during which salvation history is recounted and adults are initiated into the Catholic Church (page 110)

ecumenical council a meeting of the world's bishops, gathered by the pope to exercise their "collegial authority over the universal Church" (CCC, Glossary). Their decisions must be ratified by the pope. (page 158)

ecumenism the effort to strive toward unity among all Christian peoples. This involves communication and cooperation with people of other Christian faiths. (page 163)

Epiphany a revealing or showing; after Jesus' birth, God revealed to people other than the Jews, represented by the magi, that Jesus was the long-promised Messiah. (page 68)

eschatology an area of theology that concentrates on the last or final condition of creation (page 213)

eternal life sharing in an everlasting union of life and love with God in heaven by those who have died in his friendship (page 210)

Eucharist the Sacrament of the Body and Blood of Christ. The Eucharist is both a sacrifice and a sacrament. During the Mass, the bread and wine are changed into the Body and Blood of Christ. (page 168)

evolution a process of continuous change from a simple form to a more complex form. As a theory of the development of life forms, evolution includes the idea, for example, that apes and humans have a common ancestor. (page 28)

faith a theological virtue, a gift from God; the habit of responding positively to God (page 8)

forgiveness pardon for one's actions; being reconciled with God and others. The act of forgiveness includes the effort to let go of feelings of resentment, hatred, and hurt. (page 181)

free will the human ability to make decisions without being forced to choose or act in one specific way (page 16)

fruit of the Holy Spirit the good effects that are a result of living in the Holy Spirit. The fruits of the Spirit are love, joy, peace, patience, kindness, generosity, faithfulness, gentleness, self-control, goodness, modesty, and chastity. (page 134)

general judgment Christ's judgment of both the living and the dead at the end of time (page 217)

gifts of the Holy Spirit spiritual gifts given by the Holy Spirit that help people live God's love: wisdom, knowledge, reverence, courage, understanding, right judgment, and wonder/awe (page 128)

God the one and only Supreme Being who always existed and who will always continue to exist; there are three persons in one God, the Father, the Son, and the Holy Spirit (page 8)

Good Friday the Friday before Easter; the day Jesus died on the cross for our redemption (page 110)

gospel the good news—the message of Christ, the kingdom of God, and salvation. In the New Testament of the Bible, there are four Gospels—Matthew, Mark, Luke, and John—four accounts of Jesus' life, teachings, death, and Resurrection. (page 60)

grace our sharing in the life of God. "Grace is *favor, the free and undeserved help* that God gives us to respond to his call to become children of God, adoptive sons, partakers of the divine nature and of eternal life" (CCC, #1996). (page 18)

heaven the perfect sharing of life and love with the Trinity; an eternal relationship of oneness with God, of communion with him. (page 215)

hell eternal separation from God resulting from the choice to reject his love and grace even at the final moments of earthly existence (page 216)

holiness a state of becoming more God-like, living in his presence, or with his love (page 64)

Holy Orders a Sacrament at Service of Communion in which men promise to devote their lives to the Church as deacons, priests, or bishops (page 129)

Holy Spirit the third Person of the Holy Trinity (page 121)

Holy Thursday the Thursday before Easter. On this night, the Church celebrates the institution of the Eucharist at the Last Supper of Jesus. (page 110)

idolatry worship of a false god (page 34)

Immaculate Conception The Church teaching that God favored Mary by preserving her from all stain of original sin from the first moment of her conception. (page 66)

immortal a quality whereby the human soul will not die but will exist without end (page 219)

Incarnation the Second Person of the Blessed Trinity, while remaining God, assumed a human nature and became man. The Son of God became true man while remaining true God. (page 64)

Jesus name that means "God saves"; Jesus of Nazareth is the Savior whom God sent to redeem people from sin and eternal death. (page 61)

kingdom of God God's reign of justice, love, and peace (page 73)

kingly office part of the saving mission of Christ, in which he inaugurates God's kingdom on earth and holds supreme authority over Church members. All baptized Church members share in the kingly office of Christ. (page 161)

laity baptized members of the Church, including women and men in consecrated life, who are not ordained (page 157)

liturgy the official public prayer of the Church through which Christ continues the work of redemption through the Church's celebration of the Paschal mystery (page 46)

magisterium "The living teaching office of the Church, whose task it is to give authentic interpretation of the word of God, whether in its written form (Sacred Scripture), or in the form of Tradition" (CCC, Glossary). It guarantees that the Church remains faithful to the teaching of the Apostles in matters of faith and morals. (page 157)

marks of the Church the four essential or distinguishing characteristics of the Church: one, holy, catholic, and apostolic (page 129)

Matrimony a Sacrament at the Service of Communion, the sacrament that celebrates the sacred covenant between a baptized man and woman who promise to be faithful to one another until death. Marriage is ordered to the mutual love of the spouses and to the procreation and education of children. (page 48)

Mary   the mother of Jesus, thus the Mother of God (page 65)

Messiah   a savior sent by God to redeem people from the power of sin and everlasting death and to restore them to God's friendship (page 14)

monotheism   the belief in one God only (page 31)

mortal sin   a very serious wrong that is contrary to God's law. The effect of mortal sin—if not repented—is eternal separation from God. (page 106)

original sin   the first decision by humans to disobey God. All people (except Jesus and Mary) are born with original sin, a wounded human nature that is tempted to choose wrong over right. (page 42)

parousia   another name for the second coming of Christ that will occur at the end of the world. The word *parousia* means "arrival, or coming." (page 217)

particular judgment   the reckoning that occurs for each person at the moment of death (page 208)

Paschal mystery   the events involved in our redemption: the passion, death, Resurrection, and Ascension of Jesus (page 92)

passion   intense suffering for another, out of love for that person. The passion of Christ refers to the suffering and death of Jesus Christ out of love for humanity. (page 92)

Pentecost   The day, "when the seven weeks of Easter had come to an end, Christ's Passover is fulfilled in the outpouring of the Holy Spirit, manifested, given, and communicated as a divine person: of his fullness, Christ, the Lord, pours out the spirit in abundance" (CCC, #731). It occurs fifty days after the Resurrection of Jesus. We celebrate this day as the birthday of the Church. (page 125)

polytheism   the belief in many gods (page 31)

pope   the bishop of Rome and leader of the entire Catholic Church. As the successor of Peter, the pope is the head of the college of bishops. (page 157)

priestly office   the mission of Christ as priest, who offered everything in his life as a sacrifice to God. All baptized Church members share in the priestly office of Christ. (page 160)

prophetic office   part of the saving mission of Christ, in which he proclaimed the kingdom of God. All baptized Church members share in the prophetic office of Christ. (page 161)

purgatory   a state of purification between death and heaven that removes any remaining personal obstacles to eternal union with God. Purgatory frees the person from the temporal punishment (being deprived of the entrance into heaven for a time) due to sin. (page 215)

reconcile   to restore to friendship. Jesus reconciled all people to God through his life, death, and Resurrection. (page 64)

Reconciliation   one of the Church's Sacraments of Healing and Forgiveness; the sacrament through which the sinner is reconciled with God and the Church (page 188)

Redemption   God's saving activity in Jesus in freeing humankind from the bonds of sin and eternal death; the word means buying back or ransoming. (page 94)

religious vows   simple or solemn promises of poverty, chastity, and obedience made by members of religious communities so that they may more completely devote themselves to God and to service of the Church (page 158)

resurrection of the body   at the end of time when Christ comes again in glory, the bodies of those who have died will be raised and reunited with the soul (page 219)

Resurrection   God's raising of Jesus from death to new life (page 92)

revelation   God's communication of himself and his plan of loving goodness throughout history; Scripture and Tradition together make up the one source of his revelation. (page 10)

sacrament   an effective sign, established by Jesus and given to his Church, by which God shares his life through the work of the Holy Spirit (page 46)

sacramental   a holy sign used by Catholics that helps us to pray and remember God's love for us (page 112)

salvation   God's action accomplished through Jesus of freeing people from sin and restoring them to friendship with God (page 42)

sanctifying grace   God's divine life within us which makes us his friends (page 138)

second coming   the return of Jesus Christ as King and Judge at the end of time (page 105)

sin   an offense against God that causes a rupture of communion with him, wounds our human nature, and injures solidarity with others (page 106)

soul   the spiritual principle of humans (page 9)

stewardship   the responsibility God gave humans to take care of the earth and everything in it (page 41)

suffering servant   according to Isaiah, the one who would unjustly, but willingly, suffer and die for others (page 90)

Ten Commandments   the ten fundamental moral laws given by God to his people and recorded in the Old Testament (page 43)

Tradition   the living and authentic transmission of the teachings of Jesus in the Church (page 12)

Transfiguration   the event in which Jesus reveals his divine glory to his Apostles. This event prefigures or points to the Resurrection of Jesus. (page 72)

Transubstantiation   ". . . The change of the whole substance of the Eucharist bread and wine into the whole substance of the Body and Blood of Christ our Lord" (CCC, #1376). (page 169)

Trinity   the mystery of one God in three Persons: Father, Son, and Holy Spirit (page 35)

venial sin   a less serious wrong that weakens, but does not destroy, our relationship with God and other people, or a serious wrong done without full knowledge or free will (page 106)

vocation   one's calling or destiny in life (page 9)

INDEX

(*boldfaced terms in the text)

A

absolution, *188
abstinence, 240
Act of Contrition, 243
adolescence, 148–149
adoration, prayers of, *48–49, 185
Advent, 77, 109
AIDS, 120
alcohol and teenagers, 120
All Saints' Day, 216, 240
All Souls' Day, 216, 227, 228
angels, *41
Angelus, 244
Annunciation, *65, 112
Anointing of the Sick, 46, *189, 240
anti-Semitism, 99
apostolic, 132
Apostles, 15, 39, 72, 75, 95, 96, 99, 101,
     102, 105, 124, 125, 129, 131, 132, 150, 152,
     157, 187, 198
Apostles' Creed, 15, 35, 64, 93, 100, 121, 128,
     150, 182, 212, 238
Ascension, 92, *104, 112, 240
Assumption of Mary, *66, 112, 219, 240
atheism, *28, 31
atonement, 91
attributes of God, 34

B

Baptism,
     of Jesus, 37, 70
     Sacrament of, *46–47, 70, 103, 111, 127,
          128, 132, 136, 187, 239
Beatitudes, *79, 80, 198, 235
belief, 7, 31, 40, 60, 103
beliefs, 6, 7
Bible, *12, 234
     and creation, 40–42
     and learning about God, 32, 234
     and science, 28
     as God's word, 12, 14, 126
     books of, 13
     literary forms of, 235
     parts of, 12, 234
bishops, *157
Black Elk, 230
blasphemy, *97, 98, 184
Blessed Sacrament, 110, 240
Body and Blood of Christ, 96, 111, 152, 189
Book of Life, 91
building community, 163, 164

C

canonized, *155
capital sins, *106
catechumens, 111
catholic, 130
Catholic Social Teaching, 165–166

Chávez, César, 52
chrism, 47, 136
Christ, *61 (see Jesus)
Christian funerals, 224–226
Christianity and ecumenism, 163–164
Christmas, 67, 77, 109, 238
Church, *128
     and capital punishment, 107
     and eternal life, 210–211, 213
     and forgiveness, 185–187
     and resurrection, 103, 210–212, 217
     and science, 28, 29
     and teenagers, 153
     and war, 199–200
     and the Holy Spirit, 39, 124, 125, 128,
          129–130, 132, 134–135
     and the kingdom of God, 73, 154, 161
     and the sacraments, 46–49
     and the teachings of Jesus, 14, 133
     and the Trinity, 35
     as "one, holy, catholic, apostolic,"
          129–130, 132
     as the Body of Christ, 46, 153, 162
     as the communion of saints, 155
     as the community of faith, 19, 129, 130, 132,
          140, 153, 154, 162
     importance of, 152–153
     marks of, 129–130, 132
     meaning of, 150–151
     mission of, 15, 132, 154, 162, 163, 164
     Traditions, 239
Church Unity Octave, 140, 163
Church year, 77, 109–111
circumcision, 67
clergy, 157
Columbus, Christopher, 28
common good, 242
communion of saints, *155
Communion rite, 170
confession of sins, *185–186, 188
Confirmation, 46, 127, *136, 240
Confiteor, 243
conformity, 148–149
conscience, 10, *180
contrition, 138, 181, *185, 188, 243
conversion, *183
Copernicus, Nicolaus, 28
Corporal Works of Mercy, 222, 242
Council, First Vatican, 158
Council of Constantinople, 15
Council of Nicaea, 15
Council, Second Vatican, 14, 158
covenant, *14, 48, 67, 96, 111, 121, 125, 132, 152
creed, *15
creeds of the Church, 15, 238
creation, 40–42
creationism, *28, 30
crucifixion of Jesus, *98–99

D

Darwin, Charles, 28
Day, Dorothy, 202
Days of Awe, 91
de Chardin, Pierre Teilhard, 29
deacons, 111, 157–158, 224
death, *208–219
Delille, Henriette, 172
dignity, human, *16–18, 52, 165, 179, 242
Drexel, Katharine, 82

E

Easter, 77, 109
Easter Vigil, *110–111
ecumenical councils, *158
ecumenism, *163
Epiphany, *68, 77
eschatology, *213
eternal life, *210–219
Eucharist, 46, *168, 239
     and forgiveness, 189
     and holiness, 130, 138
     and Jesus' Resurrection, 103
     and the Church, 167
     institution of, 96, 110
     Liturgy of the, 168–171, 240
     meaning of, 189
Eucharistic fast, 241
evil, 42
evolution, *28–31
examination of conscience, 182
existence of God, 31

F

faith, 7, *8
     and science, 28–31
     and suffering, 88–89
     as enlightenment, 7
     as God's gift, 5, 8, 21, 39
     as our response to God, 4, 8, 35, 71
     communal aspect of, 18, 152
     description of, 7–9
     living our, 75, 221–222, 229
     Mary as model of, 65
     purpose of, 16, 35
faithful, being, 229
family and faith, 18
fasting, 240
forgiveness, *181–196
     and conversion, 183
     and the Church, 187–189
     Jesus and, 181, 184, 185, 186, 188, 190, 196
     of sins, 181–189, 190
     of ourselves and others, 190, 191, 192, 201
     our call to, 190–196
Frassati, Pier (Peter) Giorgio, 141, 142
free will, *16, 41, 138
fruit of the Holy Spirit, *134–135
Funerals, the Order of Christian, 223–226

G

Galilei, Galileo, 28
gifts of the Holy Spirit, *128
Gloria, 243
Glory to God, 243
God,
    and evolution, 28–31
    and forgiveness of sins, 182, 185–188, 190
    and prayer, 19–20
    as Creator, 9, 28–31, 35, 36, 40–42, 48–50
    as Father, 8, 35, 36, 46
    as Holy Spirit, 8, 35, 38–39, 46
    as immanent/transcendent, 38
    as love, 7, 8, 9, 11, 12, 14–15, 36, 58–74, 121, 192
    as one and only Supreme Being, *8
    as one with us, 92–93, 122
    as personal, 38
    as Son, 8, 35, 37, 46
    as Trinity, 8, 35–39
    attributes of, 34
    belief in, 31
    existence of, 31
    finding, 9, 10–11, 28–31, 32
    in history, 10, 11, 14–15, 92, 101
    in human reason, 10, 28–31, 32
    in Jesus, 14–15, 35, 37, 46, 58–76, 92–101
    in nature, 10, 32
    in others, 11, 38
    in Scripture, 12, 14, 32
    in Tradition, 12
    kingdom of, 73, 154, 161, 218, 220, 221
    nature of, 7–8, 32, 34–39
    our duty toward, 43
    our relationship with, 4, 9, 10, 14–15, 50–51, 60, 61, 67, 98, 113, 121, 133
    trusting, 50
    within us, 38
God's grace, *18, 138, 182, 210, 215, 219
God's plan, 14–15, 64, 74, 94, 111, 154
God's revelation, 10–11, 14, 64, 76
Golgatha, 99
Good Friday, *110
gospel, 15, *60
Gospels, 14, 62–63, 67–70, 76–77, 94, 95, 99, 102, 235
grace, *18, 138 (see God's grace)
    actual, *138–139
    sanctifying, *138
Great Commandment, 74

H

Hail, Holy Queen, 244
Hail Mary, 244
heaven, *215
hell, *216
Herod, King, 99
history, God revealed in, 11, 14–15, 92
holiness, *64, 130, 162
Holocaust, 99
holy, 130
holy days of obligation, 240
Holy Family, 68, 78
Holy Orders, 46, 127, 129, 136, *137, 157–158, 187, 240

Holy Spirit, *121–130, 133, 134–139, 141
    and Baptism, 46–47
    and charisms, 242
    and Jesus, 39, 70, 122, 124, 125, 133, 134, 185
    and Mary, 39, 65, 122
    and prayer, 139–141
    and Scripture, 12, 13, 65, 126, 234
    and the Church, 15, 39, 124, 125, 128, 129–130, 132, 135, 140
    as God's life, 38, 123
    as third Person of the Trinity, 8, 16, 35, 38–39, 121
    at Pentecost, 121, 125
    fruit of the, *134–135
    gifts of the, 128
    in Christian life, 121, 133
    listening to, 141
    sending of, 92, 112, 121, 124, 185
    symbols for, 127
    titles for, 123
Holy Thursday, *110
Holy Week, 110
human life,
    and God's spirit, 121
    as community, 17
    destiny of, 9
    dignity of, 16–18, 31, 51, 165, 242
    nature of, 10
    purpose of, 9
    rights of, 165, 242
    suffering and, 88–89, 92–93

I

idolatry, *34, 44, 45
Immaculate Conception, *66, 240
immortal, *219
importance of Church, 152–153
importance of groups, 148–149
Incarnation, *64
independence, 148–149
intelligent design, 28
Israelites, 14, 15, 91, 121

J

Jesus, *61
    and forgiveness, 180, 184, 185, 190, 192, 198–199
    and love of others, 74, 75, 79, 133
    and prayer, 78
    and Scripture, 78–79
    and the Holy Spirit, 39, 70, 122, 124, 125, 133, 134, 185
    and the kingdom of God, 73, 75, 154, 161, 218
    and the Last Supper, 96, 110, 124
    and the sacraments, 46
    as advocate for the poor, 70, 73, 78
    as Christ, 61
    as Emmanuel, 122
    as fullest revelation of God, 14, 58–76, 92, 154
    as high priest, 94
    as King of Glory, 95
    as light of the world, 110
    as Lord, 61
    as Messiah, 14, 61, 63, 68–69, 72, 90, 94, 102, 212
    as Passover lamb, 94

    as Redeemer, 92, 94, 105
    as second Person of the Trinity, 8, 16, 35, 37, 58, 61
    as Son of David, 95
    as Son of God, 35, 37, 58. 60, 61–65, 69, 70, 72, 210
    as Son of Man, 72
    as suffering servant, 90, 92, 94–100
    as teacher, 70, 73, 74, 79, 182, 235
    as Word of God, 14, 64, 76
    Ascension of, *104
    baptism of, 37, 70
    believing in, 60–76
    betrayal of, 97
    birth and childhood of, 67–69
    burial of, 100
    crucifixion and death of, 98, 99
    in the temple, 69, 112
    meeting God in, 58–76, 122
    message of, 60, 73–74, 133, 154
    parables of, 73, 235, 236
    passion of, 92–104, 112, 113
    public life of, 70–74
    Resurrection of, 37, 60, 61, 72, *92, 101–102, 103, 111, 112, 209, 210
    saving actions (miracles) of, 60, 71
    second coming of, 105, 212, 215, 216, 218
    sinlessness of, 70
    Transfiguration of, 37, 72
    trial of, 97–98
Jesus Prayer, 183, 184
Jewish holy days, 91, 95, 125
John Paul II, 9, 106, 112, 153, 191
John the Baptizer, 37, 70
Joseph, 67, 68, 69
Joseph of Arimathea, 100
judgment,
    general, *215
    particular, *212
justice, 165–166, 242

K

kingdom of God, *73, 154, 161, 218, 220, 221
kingly office of Christ, *161

L

laity, *157, 159–161
Last Rites, 189
Last Supper, 96, 110, 124
Law of Moses, 98, 133
Lent, 77, 109, 110, 238
life,
    after death, 210–213, 217
    and the Holy Spirit, 121
    as God's gift, 5
    choices, 120
    fully living, 4
    mystery of, 88
liturgy, *46–49
Liturgy of the Eucharist, 76, 111, 168–171, 240
Liturgy of the Hours, 46, 228, 239
Liturgy of the Word, 76, 111, 168, 240
Lord's Prayer, 20, 112, 170, 190, 243
love,
    God as, 8, 9, 11, 12
    God's love in Jesus, 58–74
    God's love through the Church, 154, 155
    Jesus' commandment of, 74
    of others, 74, 75, 79, 133, 154, 222

M

magisterium, *157
Magnificat, 244
making choices, 120
marks of the Church, *129
Marriage, 48, (see Matrimony)
Mary, *65
    and prayers, 243–244
    and the Rosary, 112, 245
    Assumption of, 66, 240
    feasts of, 156
    honoring, 156
    Immaculate Conception of, 66, 240
    model of faithfulness, 66, 156
    Mother of God, 65, 66, 155, 238, 240
    mother of Jesus, 39, 65, 67, 68, 69, 99, 122
    Mother of the Church, 155, 165–166
Mass, 76, 95, 96, 103, 110, 168, 240
Matrimony, 46, *48, 239 (see Marriage)
Memorare, 244
Merton, Thomas, 22
Messiah, *14, 15, 68, 72, 90–91, 94, 102, 111, 122, 212
miracles of Jesus, 71, 237
monotheism, *31
moral law, 241
mortal sin, *106
Mount of Olives, 96
Mysteries of the Rosary, 245

N

Nativity, 67, 112
nature and God, 10, 32
New Testament, 12, 13, 14, 61
Nicene Creed, 15, 37, 64, 76, 93, 121, 132, 150, 182, 212, 238

O

Old Testament, 12, 13, 14, 76
"one, holy, catholic, apostolic," *129–130, *132
ordained ministers, 157–158
Ordinary Time, 77, 109
Ordo, 77
original sin, *42, 64

P

parables, *73, 235, 236
parousia, *217
Paschal mystery, *92–104, 105, 109–111, 112–113
passion of Christ, *92–100
Passion (Palm) Sunday, 95
Passover, 69, 79, 92, 94, 95, 96, 110
peace of Christ, 198
peer pressure, 149
penance, 188, 241
penitential psalms, 185, 186
penitential rite, 76, 185, 186
Pentecost, 121, *125
polytheism, *31
Pontius Pilate, 97, 99
poor people and Jesus, 70, 73, 78
pope, *157

prayer, 19–20
    and holiness, 130
    and Jesus, 78
    and learning about God, 32
    and Mary, 244–246
    and the Holy Spirit, 139–141
    as gift from God, 19
    forms of, 139
    nature of, 19
    types of, 19, 49–50
Prayer of Saint Francis, 243
Prayer to the Holy Spirit, 243
prayers and devotions, 112–113, 243–246
prayers for the dead, 225–226
prayers of adoration, 49
prayers of blessing, 170
prayers of sorrow, 244
praying with Scripture, 80
precepts of the Church, 168–169
priestly office of Christ, *159–160
prophetic office of Christ, *161
psalms, 49, 186, 235
purgatory, 155, *215–216

R

reconcile, *64
Reconciliation, 46, 137, 138, 183, *188, 239
Redemption, 35, *94, 100, 111
relationship with God, 4, 9, 10, 50, 51
religion, 7
    and science, 28–31
religions, 7
religious, humans as, 9
religious life, 157, 162
religious vows, 158, 162
respect for life, 31
responsibility, 41, 43, 50, 52
resurrection, 209, 210, 216, 219
resurrection of the body, *219
Resurrection of Jesus, 37, 60, 61, 72, *92, 101–102, 103, 111, 112, 210, 211, 219, 238
revelation of God, *10–11, 12
Rosary, 112, 241, 245
Rosh Hashanah, 91

S

sacrament, *46
sacramentals, *112, 241
Sacraments of Christian Initiation, 46, 240
    Baptism, 46–47, 70, 103, 111, 127, 128, 131, 132, 136, 137, 189
    Confirmation, 46, 127, 136, 137
    Eucharist, 96, 103, 110, 111, 130, 137, 138, 168–171, 187
Sacraments of Forgiveness and Healing, 187–189, 240
    Anointing of the Sick, 46, 189
    Reconciliation, 46, 138, 185, 187, 189
Sacraments of Service, 48, 240
    Holy Orders, 46, 127, 129, 136, *137, 157–158, 187
    Matrimony, 46, 48
sacrifice, 91, 94
saints, 155

salvation, 18, *42, 75, 92, 135, 154
salvation history, 14–15, 111, 234
sanctification, 35, 133, 135
science and faith, 28–31
Scripture, 12, 13, 14–15 (see Bible)
    and God's revelation, 76, 234
    and holiness, 130
    and prayer, 80
    and Tradition, 12
    at Mass, 76–77
seal of the Holy Spirit, 136
second coming of Christ, *105, 212, 217, 218, 219
Second Vatican Council, 14, 65, 135, 158
Serenity Prayer, 243
Seton, Elizabeth Ann, 114
seven secrets of successful Catholics, 173
sexually transmitted diseases, 120
Sign of the Cross, 35, 76, 240, 241
sin, 41–42, 92, 105, *106, 138, 243
    capital, *106
    forgiveness of, 180–187
    mortal, *106, 138, 243
    original, 42, 185, 243
    social, *106, 243
    venial, *106, 243
social gospel, 166, 242
soul, *9, 31, 219
Spiritual Works of Mercy, 222, 242
Stations of the Cross, 113, 240, 246
stewardship, *41, 50, 51, 242
suffering, 88–93, 187
"suffering servant," 90–91

T

Ten Commandments, *43, 69, 74, 75, 242
thanksgiving for life, 52
Tradition, Church, *12, 15
Traditions, Church, 239
Transfiguration, 37, *72, 77, 112
Transubstantiation, *169
Triduum, 109, 110
Trinity, 8, 35–39, 46–49, 121, 167
trusting God, 50, 51

V

Vatican I, 158
Vatican II, 14, 65, 135, 158
venial sin, *106, 243
virtue, 8
virtues, 108
vocation, *9

W

war and the Church, 199–200
    just war doctrine, 199–200
Works of Mercy, 222, 242
World Trade Center, 89
worship, 46–49

Y

Yom Kippur, 91